'Hannah McGlade is to be congra~~t......~~ ~~.. ...~ ~~..........~~, ~~....~~ researched confirmation that legal and child protection systems are failing (abysmally) to protect Aboriginal children from rape and sexual abuse and, in fact, add to their psychological abuse. This book should be compulsory reading for judges, lawyers and human service professionals whose work involves children.'

Professor Emerita Freda Briggs AO,
University of South Australia

'Violence and sexual assault against children is a shocking problem, and one that poses significant difficulties in terms of detection, criminal prosecution and conviction. These issues can be exacerbated in Aboriginal communities where there may be a higher prevalence of the problem and simultaneously less trust in the criminal justice system. In these circumstances fewer offences are reported and prosecutions are less likely. Hannah McGlade's book builds on the experience of previous Australian inquiries into Aboriginal child sexual assault particularly those in the NT, SA, WA and NSW. She analyses the failure of government responses, and in particular the failure to develop processes which would facilitate Aboriginal communities working in partnership with government to solve the problem of Aboriginal child sexual assault. For McGlade, effective interventions can be found in Aboriginal justice approaches which build on respect for Aboriginal children's human rights, and the principles of self-determination and participation.'

Professor Chris Cunneen,
James Cook University

'This is a powerful and persuasive analysis of Aboriginal child sexual assault. Professional understanding, combined with painful personal experience, make this a work of compelling advocacy for children's rights to protection.'

Professor Chris Goddard,
Child Abuse Prevention Research Australia

'Hannah McGlade can now count herself as one of the brave Aboriginal women she writes about who "bravely acknowledged the harm of child sexual abuse". Her investigation into the widespread sexual abuse and exploitation of Aboriginal women and children is awe-inspiring. In it she shreds preconceived notions about its prevalence, its victims, the damage it wreaks and the self-serving justification of "customary law". In deconstructing the social and legal notion that such abuse was somehow 'traditional' she references the voices of the victims, including her own, the legacy of colonisation, and the rights contained in the United Nations *Convention on the Rights of the Child*. She dissects court transcripts and details the heart-wrenching experiences of those who tried to use the criminal justice system.

Dr McGlade argues that the climate of secrecy, helped along by a willingness to individualise the perpetrators as pedophiles (a term she refuses to use), ignores the fact that Aboriginal child sexual abuse is a societal issue of power and control perpetrated mostly by men. It is, as she says, the "murder of innocence".

Dr McGlade concludes where she began, with a passionate reminder of a child's right to security of their person, their dignity and their right to grow and prosper in an environment that supports and fosters their chances. She offers examples of, and hope for, a re-constructing and the re-creation of a culture free from the hideous and illegal exploitation of children.'

Dr Ailsa M Watkinson,
University of Regina, Canada

Our Greatest Challenge

Aboriginal children and human rights

Hannah McGlade

Aboriginal Studies Press

First published in 2012
by Aboriginal Studies Press

Aboriginal Studies Press
is the publishing arm of the
Australian Institute of Aboriginal
and Torres Strait Islander Studies.
GPO Box 553, Canberra, ACT 2601
Phone: (61 2) 6246 1183
Fax: (61 2) 6261 4288
Email: asp@aiatsis.gov.au
Web: www.aiatsis.gov.au/asp/about.html

National Library of Australia
Cataloguing-In-Publication data:

Author: McGlade, Hannah.

Title: Our greatest challenge: Aboriginal children and human rights/Hannah McGlade.

ISBN: 9781922059109 (pbk.)

Subjects: Child sexual abuse—Australia. Children, Aboriginal Australian—Crimes against. Children's rights—Australia.

Dewey Number: 364.153

Front cover: *The Protector*, Jody Broun, acrylic on linen, © Jody Broun.

Set in 11.5/14 pt Bembo by Midland Typesetters, Australia
Printed in Australia by Opus Print Group

Foreword

When Hannah McGlade confronts us with her title, *Our greatest Challenge: Aboriginal children and human rights*, she names the last frontier, that which is hardest to address: the sexual violation of children. She challenges us because we are still not getting it right.

Aged thirteen, young Aboriginal girl Dolly was sent to Yarrabah Aboriginal Mission in 1903. She had been employed at Normanton for ten years though she had never received any wages, possessed only two articles of clothing and was seven months pregnant.[1] Clearly she was a young Aboriginal girl who had been abused. Yet in his reports to the Home Secretary's office of the Queensland Government, 1901–1908, Dr Walter Roth wrote that he could find no instance of what now would be called child abuse within any of the tribal groups he was responsible for at that time in colonial history.[2]

As Hannah McGlade reminds us, the abuse of Aboriginal peoples, including Aboriginal children, is a part of our colonial history, something which continues to have serious implications into the present.

During a community meeting in Cape York in 1987, near where Dolly had been removed, an Aboriginal female Elder took me aside to ask for help. A five-year-old child had been sexually assaulted the previous week. Nothing was being done, she said. Could I do something?

Our work on the Aboriginal Coordinating Council was to support the movement towards what was called 'self-management', where Deeds of Grant in Trust were to be granted to the old Queensland Aboriginal reserves. At no time during these meetings was there any discussion about the needs of children to be safe in their communities, for the female Elders to speak about their concerns.

The woman asking for help was outraged and distressed. As I understood it, no child under Aboriginal Law would be treated in such a way. I talked to law enforcement officials, seeking an answer as to why no charges had been laid. At worst, I found explicit, overt prejudice and racism, and at least ill-formed, uneducated, and ignorant attitudes and opinions by those who should have investigated and laid charges. In some cases I found frustration and a felt powerlessness in some public servants.

I found troubling statistics about violence against Aboriginal women and children that seemed to be considered irrelevant within the broader government policies of 'self-management' and the two separate commissions of enquiry that were in place: the Royal Commission into Aboriginal Deaths in Custody, and the National Inquiry into the Separation of Aboriginal and Torres Strait Islander Children From Their Families. In later years, each state commissioned inquiries into violence against women and children which are explored in the book.

The UN conventions and declarations that exist mean nothing unless they are taken seriously and can be acted on. While it is easy to talk about human rights, it is much harder to work on the ground where human rights violations have become part of behaviour within what I call the generational violence–trauma vortex.

Recently a senior male political figure admonished those in a meeting who wanted to discuss the issue: 'When you talk about child sexual assault you traumatise Aboriginal people,' he said. What should have been said was: 'Recently in your community a two-year-old child was removed because there was evidence she had been sexually penetrated, and she had a sexually transmitted infection. Would the child not be traumatised by what had happened to her? Who speaks for her?'

Hannah McGlade speaks for the child when she advocates for a more trauma-informed human rights response to their needs.

However, child sexual assault is not an issue of relevance only to Aboriginal Australians. Child Wise states that after the drug trade, child sex slavery or trafficking is the largest and fastest growing criminal industry in the world, affecting 1.8 million children globally, and that an estimated 20,000 child pornography images are posted on the internet every week.[3]

In 2009, the people of Kaugere, a settlement on the edge of Port Moresby Papua New Guinea with a reputation for extreme interpersonal violence, asked me to run an education package for them, with a focus on human rights in relationship to family, community and street violence. While they had few rights in their own country, they understood they had to become responsible for the change they needed in their own lives, the community worked to develop an action plan for their needs.

The awareness of child sexual assault came reluctantly. It came because people started to talk with each other. They disclosed childhood experiences. They began to listen to media reports about specific assaults.

In the beginning, child sexual assault was named as part of the continum of violence in families and society, and the men in particular became uncomfortable and angry. As they settled more fully into the workshop and began to listen to the stories they were sharing, they began to accept the need to include child sexual assault in the work they were doing on violence generally. They developed an action plan for Kaugere which recognised that child harm needs a specific trauma healing response.

The people in Kaugere, and elsewhere, also teach us that unless we have a skilled, committed justice system, and governments who are willing to invest in our children's future, we cannot heal from the harm of abuse.

They show us that people can do something for themselves, just as the many Aboriginal women and men in Australia who are working together on such issues. We need to focus on programs which recognise the need for justice as healing for victims of violence across generations. I wonder if Dolly's offspring, wherever they are today, receive a just response to their needs.

Hannah McGlade's book calls for genuine recognition of Aboriginal children's human rights and asks for systemic reforms that can protect children, more particularly from the damage of intentional harm.

The title is confronting, but the challenge is clear. Hannah McGlade reminds us that child sexual assault is a serious human rights dilemma; one that has been neglected by us for too long, perhaps because we lack the courage to truthfully face our past and do the hard work that will take us into the future. This is a courageous book, asking us to take courageous action. For the sake of our children.

Professor Emerita Judy Atkinson

Contents

Preface

This book presents a critical exploration of Aboriginal children's human rights. In particular, it examines child sexual assault, a severe human rights violation of the child, and the nature of the response of the criminal justice system. It argues that abuses of Aboriginal children's human rights are shaped and formed within the entrenched societal forces of racism, colonisation and patriarchy, and white and black men's oppression of women and children. The deeply disturbing topic of child sexual assault is little understood, treated as taboo, and difficult to discuss in an impartial or objective way, making child sexual assault 'our greatest challenge'.

In recent times child sexual assault has been highly politicised in the Australian public domain as an Aboriginal 'problem', with controversial government responses critiqued as racist and paternalistic. The Australian Government has yet to acknowledge the traumatic impacts of our history, whereby the sexual assault of Aboriginal children was part and parcel of the European process of 'civilisation'.

This book shows that the adversarial criminal justice system is also formed by race and gender. Notwithstanding substantive reforms to the law, the courtroom experience is based on re-victimisation and trauma. In the context of Aboriginal child sexual assault, the fundamental principle of equality before the law can be readily denied.

This book argues that although Aboriginal human rights have traditionally been framed from a male perspective, the protection of Aboriginal children's human rights is also paramount. Indigenous human rights concepts and international Indigenous responses to child sexual assault will inform and guide us. The United Nations General Assembly's Human Rights Council urges all States: 'To give priority attention to the prevention of all forms of sexual violence and abuse against children by addressing its underlying causes.'[1] This book demonstrates that Aboriginal people are envisioning Aboriginal justice approaches to address the problem and stem the harm to future generations.

About the author

I am a Noongar woman or *yorga*, a human rights lawyer and writer. My Noongar family came from the Albany and Esperance regions of Noongar country, and were once known as Kurin Noongar. I was born in Perth in 1969 and my Noongar name is Woyung, meaning the red-tailed black cockatoo. My education in the non-Aboriginal system was a misnomer because I was homeless before I turned 16 and consequently was a 'high school dropout', but Aboriginal opportunities in education meant that I could achieve my dream of a university education. I graduated from law school, was admitted to the Supreme Court as a barrister and solicitor, and then specialised in human rights law. After teaching law, I worked in Canberra at the heart of federal Aboriginal politics. Growing up I experienced family violence and sexual assault.

As an Aboriginal person my study of Aboriginal child sexual assault reflects a process of Indigenous self-discovery, awareness, healing and social justice. I represent myself as much as the topic. According to Gloria Anzaldúa:

> to write is to confront one's demons, look them in the face and live to write about them. Writing is dangerous because we are afraid of what the writing reveals: the fears, the anger the strength of a woman under triple or quadruple oppression. Yet, a woman who writes has power. And a woman with power is feared.[2]

About this book

Aboriginal child sexual assault is now part of the mainstream political debate and public consciousness in Australia, but it is often dealt with in a superficial or shallow way. This complex issue cannot be understood or properly addressed without a comprehensive under-standing of the evidence, the underlying causes, the current nature of the responses of the criminal justice system, and the inter-national Indigenous literature suggesting forward-looking models and approaches.

This book includes interviews with Aboriginal women who experienced the court process in response to child sexual assault. I critically analyse a wide array of documentary data — government inquiries and reports, news reports, court cases, criminological research and literature concerning child sexual assault — and employ a methodological principle of critical race theory, namely that stories and storytelling, especially 'counterstories', can work to challenge and displace entrenched narratives and beliefs that shape cultural influences.[3] I also examine academic research concerning child sexual assault, with particular focus on the legal system, and international research concerning child sexual assault, Indigenous victims of sexual assault and Indigenous justice responses.

Although many people have commented negatively on the role of the media in relation to Aboriginal child sexual assault, in some instances the media have actively supported Aboriginal victims of sexual assault and the importance of the principle of legal equality. The media influence was likely responsible for several case law developments, including law reforms.

Chapter 1 places child sexual assault within a universal human rights framework, and an Australian and Aboriginal context. I acknowledge the harm and trauma that result from child sexual assault, and I speak about my own experiences of childhood, including victimisation and the legal system. I also acknowledge the theoretical approaches that have shaped my way of viewing this subject. Aboriginal children's human right to live free from such abuse is highlighted as our greatest challenge, one that is linked to our history of colonisation, patriarchy, power, control and land.

Chapters 2 and 3 aim to understand how Australia is facing this crisis and challenge. Chapter 2 addresses the impacts of racism, colonisation and trauma, and Chapter 3 acknowledges the role of patriarchy and gender oppression.

Chapter 4 details information from a decade of government inquiries into Aboriginal child sexual assault across Australia. I directly engage with the key findings and make my own observations. This decade of evidence about Aboriginal child sexual assault can leave no doubt that it is a serious human rights problem, and one that has also been 'hidden' and neglected by governments.

Chapters 5 and 6 concern the responses of the criminal justice system to Aboriginal child sexual assault. Chapter 5 draws on a range of sources, including criminological research and government inquiries concerning children, sexual assault and the law. It includes detailed case studies that indicate Aboriginal child sexual assault has effectively been sanctioned by the justice system. Chapter 6 concerns my local Noongar community. I examine three cases studies to highlight the experiences of Aboriginal victims of child sexual assault in the legal system. In this chapter I draw extensively on interviews with an adult complainant of child sexual assault, and an Aboriginal woman who supported a young family member through court and advocated publicly for improved legal responses for Aboriginal victim survivors. The case studies include the important decision of *R v Bropho* [2004] WADC 182 and reflect a significant moment in Noongar history in which Noongar women bravely took a stand against child sexual assault through the courts. At the same time, the cases highlight the ambivalence of the legal response to child sexual assault, the difficulties that can specifically face Aboriginal victim survivors, and the problem of traumatic re-victimisation.

Chapter 7 explores the development of Aboriginal justice models to address child sexual assault, and considers two highly acclaimed international Indigenous models. I also explore lessons for Australia, in particular the proper protection of child victim interests within Aboriginal healing models.

Chapter 8 concludes the book with a forward-looking assessment of how we might know our greatest challenge, arguing the significance of a genuine recognition of Aboriginal children's human rights. There is a great deal we can do to improve responses to Aboriginal child sexual assault, and to increase the wellbeing of our children and protect their fundamental human rights. We should rise to this challenge.

Acknowledgments

This book originated from my 2010 thesis, titled 'Aboriginal Child Sexual Assault (CSA) and the Criminal Justice System: The Last Frontier', which would not have been possible without the Aboriginal women who have demanded justice for children. I am indebted to the women who spoke freely with me about their knowledge and experiences of child sexual assault and the courts.

In 2007 I was privileged to receive an award from the International Council of Canadian Studies allowing me to undertake international fieldwork in Canada to explore the concept of Aboriginal 'Justice as Healing'. This was complemented by the 2008 Women's Community Award of the Western Australian Department of Communities. This international fieldwork was critical to the research, increasing my understanding of the issues and enabling me to experience firsthand powerful Aboriginal cultural and healing practices.

Dedication

This book is dedicated to all the Aboriginal children who cried out in the night but who were not heard.

In special memory of Susan Ann Taylor (1984–1999).

With my family near Albany, 1975.

Chapter 1

Introduction — Facing the challenge

Violence against children is now firmly recognised internationally as a global problem and a serious issue of human rights. As child victimisation expert, David Finkelhor, has stated: 'Children are arguably the most criminally victimized people in society.'[1] Despite this, in Australia, child sexual assault and exploitation are only now being publicly discussed, while the sexual assault of Aboriginal children is seen as an 'Aboriginal problem'.

Aboriginal child sexual assault is deeply disturbing which brings up feelings and emotions including shock, disbelief, anger, disgust, sadness, hopelessness and guilt.[2] Sometimes people do not want to get involved and I have seen the discomfort this subject invokes in most people. I recall an Easter family lunch where an elderly grandmother expressed her concern about the welfare of a young child in her family. The room quickly emptied, leaving me alone with her to listen and support as best I could. I felt upset that people had so quickly abandoned this woman and her grandchild.

Many Aboriginal people regard sexual abuse of children as horrendous. Numerous historical accounts of Aboriginal people have described the loving and indulgent relations parents had with children. From the outset, it is important to state that in talking about child sexual assault and abuse, Aboriginal men should not be stigmatised. Aboriginal child sexual assault has become a very high profile matter in recent years, but in saying this, it must not be assumed that

1

all perpetrators are Aboriginal, or that most Aboriginal men abuse children. My own grandfather, Rod McGlade Snr, was a hard-working Noongar man who lived in the age of segregation but never abused women or children. He was proud of my achievements and he told me so. He loved and protected his children as best he could. So many Aboriginal fathers and grandfathers are good men who have never harmed children and who have done their utmost to protect their children.

Child sexual assault is a serious matter for Aboriginal children, families and entire communities. It is a crime and the responses of the criminal justice system are critically important to addressing the problem. By not adequately addressing child sexual assault, we risk ongoing harm to Aboriginal children throughout their lives, and, moreover, onwards to the lives of their own children.

Child sexual assault is a significant disadvantage in a child's life. It can impact later opportunities in a myriad of ways, including the tragedy of suicide and repeat victimisation. It may not be a nice or safe topic to speak about, but it is one that should never be underestimated.

Aboriginal people and feminists have long embraced the philosophy that 'the personal is the political'. As such, my personal reflections of growing up Noongar, being a victim survivor of child sexual assault and my experiences of the criminal justice system, are central to this book. It is now time to recognise that the lived experiences and voices of Aboriginal victim survivors are critical to addressing child sexual assault in our communities. Acknowledging victim survivors and talking openly about child sexual assault is vital, and I affirm the wisdom of African-American poet Audre Lorde, who said that sexual violence is a disease 'striking at the heart of Black nationhood' and silence will not make it disappear.[3]

My Story: Growing Up Noongar

Who I am is critical to this research. My own experiences growing up Noongar and as a child victim survivor have been influential in developing my understanding and analysis of child sexual assault.

The commonplace nature of child sexual assault is inconsistent with the tendency to characterise it as something that happens 'to other people'. A few years ago one of my friends said to me that she sometimes felt that among her Aboriginal women friends it seemed to be a case of who had *not* been raped or sexually abused as a child. My friend went on to say how she saw this had impacted her friends. She felt that those who had been sexually abused as children were more introverted or quiet, while she and others who had not been sexually assaulted and abused as children were outgoing and extroverted in their personalities.

In the early 1980s I recall being a young schoolgirl and hearing a media report that one in four Australian girls had been sexually abused as children. At the time I attended a Catholic girls' school and sexual assault was never discussed by our teachers or in the school environment. We were taught that sex was for marriage, and contraception such as 'the pill' was not approved. I was shocked when I heard that so many girls were being sexually abused and I told a small group of friends what I had heard. One friend, a non-Aboriginal Australian girl, later told me that her stepfather had been coming into her room at night and forcing sex on her — in other words, she was being raped in her own home. She told me that her mother had not stopped him and she seemed resigned to what was happening to her. Soon after, she moved interstate to live with her grandmother. I think that my friend was relieved to tell me, but I was shocked and I never told anyone at school. It seemed that this was a subject obviously terrifying but yet unspoken, even accepted.

I was born in 1969 and my experiences of growing up Aboriginal included racial stigma and prejudice. It seemed that the days of the White Australia policy and supposed superiority of white Australians was not a very distant past. My school environment was full of racial undertones as Aboriginal people were still considered 'Abos', 'boongs', 'niggers' or sometimes plain old 'burnt toast'. Our school taught children that 'Aborigines' (or 'natives') were primitive people here before the white ('heroic') settlers arrived. I remember when my mum and aunty came to school to show our culture in a positive way, how excited the other school kids were to actually meet and learn about Noongar people. My mum told us that we never had to stand up for the national anthem because it discredited us as Aboriginal people.

As a girl I learned that Australian society projected female beauty, happiness and success as white, blonde and blue eyed. All Aboriginal children's self-esteem must have been harmed by this. The young men from the 'respectable' Noongar families always had one such girl on their arms, as if this was a sign of great success. Aboriginal women's worth was denigrated, and I was also taught from a young age that white men saw Aboriginal women and girls as 'sex'. As a girl I was warned about these white *bunjeymen* who cruised the parks and streets looking to solicit sex from Aboriginal women and girls.

I had a loving and close relationship with my great-grandmother, Ethel Woyung McGlade, who was born in the Noongar country near Jerramungup close to the turn of the century. Granny experienced hardship. Being a Noongar girl she was 'indentured' into servitude at a young age to the wealthy south-west pastoralists. It is said that Jim McGlade (who was of European Irish descent) 'took' Granny as his wife when she was just a girl, but my mother thinks he was kind and their marriage seemed to be a good one. Marriages between Aboriginal and non-Aboriginal people were illegal under the *Aborigines Act 1905* (WA) and so they had to live isolated in the bush.[4] My great-grandfather made the trips to town for supplies, and Granny and the children waited for his return. When my great-grandfather died his family attended the funeral but Granny was never to see them again.

Granny learned full well the hardships of Aboriginality and was reluctant to talk about being Noongar. Sometimes I begged her to tell me Noongar words and occasionally she did. She gave me her Noongar name, Woyung, and most importantly I feel that she taught me her Noongar qualities: kindness, love, strength, honesty and gentleness of spirit. Often I would camp with her at night and I felt very safe. Granny died in 1979 and not too long after I was placed in Sister Kate's Children's Home. I was lucky to have my Granny's love because in my growing up I unfortunately experienced emotional, psychological, physical and sexual abuse. Overlaying all that abuse is, of course, the wound to the spirit.

When I was young, my mother, Mingli, attended teachers' college and was in the first class of Aboriginal students in Western Australia to graduate as teachers. This was the 1970s. She would take me with her to Aboriginal meetings and rallies for land rights. I was having my consciousness raised and my mother was one of the early Aboriginal activists or Noongar 'Freedom Fighters'. This was at a time when it was not popular to be Aboriginal and some people were ashamed of my mum standing up for Aboriginal people's rights. 'Shame', they would say. My mother was independent, but this did not mean that women were encouraged to be so. I recall community meetings where men openly chastised women for speaking, and it was clear that women had an unequal standing compared to men.

Mingli was very cultural, giving up her European name and encouraging us as children to call her by her Aboriginal name given to her by Granny. She took us with her to the Kimberley region of the state, where we lived in a number of Aboriginal communities, sometimes sleeping outdoors under the stars. Like many Aboriginal children, I also came from a broken home and it often seemed that my parents did not always accept their responsibilities to their children. I was very young when their unhappiness and fighting led to divorce, and at that time I was put into a children's home with my little brother. It was a frightening place. After my Granny died I was left at Sister Kate's Children's Home, but my mum did not know that children were abused at the home. Afterwards, my sister and I went to board at the Pallottine Hostel in Rossmoyne with many Aboriginal teenagers of the Kimberley. There was abuse at Pallottine as well.

My father was a stockman in the Kimberley but was driving buses in Sydney when he met my mother. He was a non-Aboriginal person and so they had cultural issues to contend with. The marriage did not last long and after a while (and a new family) my father grew distant. Perhaps as Aboriginal children we could be readily forgotten. While our past has been painful we have now put it to rest. I also acknowledge my non-Aboriginal stepfather, my second father, who told me many times that being Aboriginal meant I could not be as good as a white person: it meant I had to be 'twice as good'. After the relationship ended, he went to live with the Aboriginal people of New South Wales in an alcohol rehabilitation centre, formerly the notorious Kinchela Boys' Home. I was with him when he passed, and respected his wishes to have his remains scattered in the country he loved in northern New South Wales.

I was about 13 years old when my mother brought her new man home from prison, a man who had just served time for the offence of 'carnal knowledge'. He became predatory and eventually violent in our home. Sadly, my mother chose him over her own daughters. My sister and I had no choice but to run away from home. I did not see my mother again for a long time.

While growing up I was unable to finish my education. At 15 I became homeless, and it was clear that I needed to start finding my own way in life. I had no family in my life at this young age. Later on my mother returned to Perth and we lived as a family again. There were some happy times but it was not always easy.

In the late 1980s and in the 1990s, along with my mother, I supported an Aboriginal Elder, Robert Bropho, who campaigned throughout Perth for land rights and respect for Aboriginal heritage and culture. I learned about the Waugyl, the Noongar Serpent Spirit who created the waterways and who oversaw everything and everybody in Noongar country. I was shocked to hear the 'yarns' that Robert was a perpetrator and abuser of girls and children. He was a leader and Elder, but there also came a time when I had to accept he had terribly abused children and young people.[5] I felt very badly for those girls: how did it look, all of us supporting him, when he had done so much wrong to them? Robert was later charged with several offences against children and was serving a six-year prison sentence when he died in October 2011.[6]

Even though I could not finish my schooling, I was able to enrol in the Aboriginal Bridging Course at Curtin University in Perth and then as a journalism student. I moved to Canberra and learned about Aboriginal entry into the law course at the Australian National University in Canberra. It was an unforgettable year to be accepted into Law and I worked very hard to make the transition to law school. I completed my law degree at Murdoch University and in 1994 became the first Aboriginal woman to graduate from a Western Australian law school. After graduating I worked as a law teacher and undertook further studies in human rights. I was interested in race discrimination law, and initiated several test cases including *McGlade v Senator Lightfoot* [2002] FCA 752, which established a legal precedent case of race vilification against Aboriginal people.[7] Subsequently, I moved to Canberra to work at the heart of Aboriginal politics and in relation to the national campaign for a treaty.[8]

A serious human rights problem

In 2012 the United Nations 'characterized violence against indigenous women and girls as a pervasive form of human rights abuse'.[9] The Special Rapporteur on the Rights of Indigenous Peoples, James Anaya, explained that:

> The history of discrimination of indigenous peoples has … resulted in the deterioration of indigenous social structures and cultural traditions, as well as in the undermining or breakdown of indigenous governance and judicial systems, impairing in many cases the ability of indigenous peoples to effectively respond to problems of violence against women and children within their communities.[10]

A United Nations study on violence against children, which was 'based on the idea that children have the right to be protected from violence',[11] stated that 'Every government should make very clear that all forms of violence against children are never allowed … This includes forbidding … harmful traditional customs such as *early or forced marriages* … and sexual violence'.[12]

Child sexual abuse is a crime against the child. It is a universal problem defined by the international organisation Save the Children as 'the imposition of sexual acts, or acts with sexual overtones, by one or more persons on a child'.[13] It includes the immediate abusive acts against the child and the basis of the exploitation of the child, including indecent touching, penetration and sexual torture, indecent exposure, explicit sexual language towards a child and showing children pornographic material.[14] Some people who abuse children use their positions of trust and authority over children to commit sexual abuse. Also, abusers may have commercial or other exploitative interests. According to UNICEF, 'in the last thirty years, child pornography has become a thriving enterprise: In the United States alone, revenues of the child pornography market have been estimated to be between US \$2 to \$3 billion per year'.[15] Although many countries still have a low age of legal consent for children, the Convention on the Rights of the Child protects all children aged 18 and under from sexual abuse, assault and exploitation.[16]

Although there has been a great deal of publicity about *Aboriginal* child sexual assault, it is a serious problem for all children — Aboriginal and non-Aboriginal, Australian children and children in all countries of the world. Christiane Sanderson, an expert psychologist in the United Kingdom, dispels the myth that child sexual assault occurs only in certain communities, social classes or cultures: child sexual assault 'does not happen only to other people in other communities or other cultures: it can happen to any child'.[17] The extent and severity of the problem has been recognised for many years. In 1983 Roland Summit, a psychiatrist and leading child abuse expert in the United States, wrote that 'Sexual abuse of children is not a new phenomenon … Children have been subject to molestation, exploitation and intimidation by supposed caretakers throughout the history of time'.[18]

Australian research confirms child sexual abuse as a serious problem impacting on Australian children. In 1990 the World Health Organization (WHO) Collaborating Centre at St Vincent's Hospital, Sydney, prepared a report on the prevalence and impact of child sexual abuse on health status around the world.[19] The report found seven studies of child sexual abuse in Australia, and said that the estimated prevalence of abuse in males was 5.1% and in females 27.5%, corresponding with rates in comparable countries. The report found that the onset of abuse occurs at a mean age of 10 years, with most cases of sexual abuse starting before the child is age 12. The abuser is a family member in about 40% of cases, and is known to the child in 75% of cases. The abuser is usually male, with a mean age of 32 years.[20]

Despite all governments committing to 'Closing the gap' on Indigenous disadvantage, the 'gap' for Aboriginal children is dramatically increasing. In 2011 Aboriginal and Torres Strait Islander children were subject to substantiation rates 7 times that of non-Aboriginal children in relation to their care and protection. According to the Commonwealth's annual report on Aboriginal disadvantage, the social strain endured by many Indigenous families and communities, combined with alcohol and substance misuse and overcrowded living conditions are contributing factors. It was also acknowledged that these figures are indicative and dependant on willingness of adults to report child abuse, and the efficacy of government policies and practices. However, the increase is likely to reflect actual increase of child abuse 'given little improvement in the social and economic circumstances of Indigenous people'.[21]

The leading Aboriginal child advocacy body, the Secretariat of National Aboriginal and Islander Child Care (SNAICC), has also acknowledged the prevalence of child sexual assault for Aboriginal children and families. In a handbook, *Through Young Black Eyes*, SNAICC states that sexual abuse happens to one in four girls and to one in nine boys who are under 18 years of age.[22] Important facts about child sexual abuse are identified, including that children rarely lie about or imagine sexual abuse, that the overwhelming majority of child sex offenders have no criminal convictions for their crimes against children, and that child sexual abuse is 'difficult to detect because of the secrecy that surrounds the crime and the large number of cases that are not reported to the authorities'.[23] There is growing concern that high rates of suicide among young Aboriginal people are linked to child sexual abuse.[24]

A common perception in society is that only paedophiles sexually abuse children. However, in view of the prevalent nature of child sexual assault — very often perpetrated by people the child knows (particularly family members) — the use of this term has been questioned. It has been argued that the term *paedophile* inhibits critical recognition that abusers are 'ordinary males', and shifts attention from issues of power and control to medical notions of sexual deviance, obsession and addiction, thereby individualising a social issue.[25] These concerns are supported by international child rights agency, Save the Children: 'The perpetrators of child sexual abuse are often viewed as a small group of sexually deviant male strangers labelled paedophiles. The focus on sexual deviance may lead to an under-estimation of the high occurrence of child sexual abuse and of issues like power and control.'[26]

Likewise, SNAICC says that we must 'Forget the myth that offenders are "strange dirty old men"'.[27] There is no stereotypical offender in relation to child sexual assault, and SNAICC considers that perpetrators:

- come from all walks of life and socio-economic groups
- can be male, female, married, single, heterosexual, homosexual or bisexual
- usually start abusing during their teenage years
- fool themselves and others by maintaining a mask of respectability

- work hard to control other's knowledge about their offences
- rarely enter treatment voluntarily
- can be infrequent offenders
- are prone to rationalise and minimise their abusive behaviours.[28]

For the above reasons, I do not use the term *paedophile* in this book. Also, the literal meaning translates from Greek as 'child lover', the most inappropriate terminology for child sexual assault, which is the most abusive, damaging and criminal conduct towards a child.

Despite its prevalence, child sexual assault is not a matter openly discussed in either Aboriginal or non-Aboriginal communities. However, Aboriginal women (and some men) are increasingly acknowledging it as a serious problem in our communities. I have heard many Aboriginal women, including Judy Atkinson, Evelyn Scott, Cathy Freeman, Tania Major, Marcia Ella-Duncan and Kerrianne Cox, bravely acknowledge the harm of child sexual assault. In speaking publicly about child sexual assault, Aboriginal women are challenging what SNAICC identified as the 'climate of secrecy' and societal conditions that allow abuse to go unchecked.[29]

While some people are speaking out, others show little awareness or concern of child sexual assault. Professor Marcia Langton writes that a 'notion of a universal childhood' means that many people have failed to recognise and understand that childhood consists of widely varying experiences from society to society.[30] Langton believes that society has promoted fantasy about children's lives rather than reality, and that 'The fate of millions of children defies belief. Reluctance to believe that children are at risk, often in horrifying circumstances, is an obstacle to efforts to provide protection and welfare'.[31]

We can learn a great deal from the work of the United States child abuse 'pioneers' of the 1970s such as Summit, who 'dared to introduce the idea that sexual abuse of children was a major public health problem as well as a moral issue'.[32] Summit and his colleagues challenged the then conventional thinking about child sexual abuse — including thinking at the time that such abuse was rare, harmless or even invited by children — with the following propositions:

- child sexual abuse and incest are not rare, and the perpetrators are usually not strangers but known and trusted adults in the child's life
- child sexual assault damages children both medically and psychologically and the damages can be long lasting
- sexually abused children who appear to be consenting or participating are instead submitting to the superior power of adults
- children's silence about ongoing sexual abuse does not imply consent but, rather, accommodation
- when they are questioned, child witnesses are more trustworthy than previously believed
- child sexual abuse is wrong because children cannot consent.[33]

The serious harm of child sexual assault, and failure by societies to condemn such abuse of the child, has been acknowledged by Save the Children:

> The issue of child sexual abuse deserves to be taken seriously by the world community. It is an invasion of the child's most intimate zone, a violation of the child's physical and psychological integrity and a transgression of the moral norms of the child and the society. It creates fear in the boy or girl, who may be harmed for life physically and mentally. The stigma and shame surrounding child sexual abuse in all societies usually leaves the child to face the harm in solitude. Disclosure of abuse seldom results in conviction — rather it is the child who is blamed and judged.[34]

No more shame — child sexual assault is harmful and traumatic

A major hurdle impacting our ability to address child sexual assault is the issue of shame. Sexual violence and abuse of Aboriginal children and young people is not uncommon, but shame can mean that sexual assault is treated as a private matter to be kept hidden and unaddressed. Traditionally, non-Aboriginal society has regarded violence against women and children and sexual assault as a private matter and it may be that Aboriginal people have adopted this cultural viewpoint. Rejecting shame is critical to addressing sexual violence.

In Aboriginal Australia child sexual assault is typically considered within the model of family violence. The family violence concept is important, but child sexual assault needs to be acknowledged as a distinct form of abuse directed at children and young people. The family violence concept encompasses abuse within the immediate and extended family, but adult offenders may not be related, so child sexual assault is not always appropriately conceptualised within the family violence framework. Sometimes within family violence discussions it appears that child sexual assault can be left unsaid and unspoken. As SNAICC recognises, we have a big task ahead of us:

> One of the toughest and ever-present challenges of addressing family violence and child abuse in our communities is to break the silence surrounding these issues. Only recently have these matters been exposed and discussed openly by sections of our Aboriginal and Torres Strait Islander community. Likewise we have only begun to realise the deep impact violence, abuse and neglect can have on children … [35]

Child sexual assault affects many Aboriginal children. It should always be recognised and never underestimated. Children and young people are profoundly impacted and suffer from psychological, emotional and spiritual wounds as a result of sexual assault, abuse and exploitation. Experts increasingly view child sexual assault within a trauma framework and consider that the impacts can be understood within a post-traumatic stress disorder model of interpersonal abuse.[36] It is now recognised that child sexual assault can affect children at the most critical level of healthy brain and neurological development, and this trauma can 'create permanent damage to the neural structure and function of the developing brain', especially where the child is young and the brain is growing.[37]

A major psychological impact of child sexual assault has been described as 'the shattering of the self',[38] which can lead to serious psychological problems, including: a profound sense of alienation from the self and others; anxiety; a profound sense of loss of self; loss of sense of worth; anger and rage, which may be acted on as violence, shame, fearfulness, powerlessness, self-harm and suicide attempts; obsessive compulsive behaviours; boundary difficulties; hypervigilance; psychosomatic complaints; long-term high activation of stress responses that deplete the immune system; sexual problems; and sleeping disorders.[39] Research has indicated that high-risk psychiatric disorders are linked to child sexual assault, with some data indicating that 40% to 70% of psychiatric outpatients were sexually abused as children.[40] Amnesia and disassociation (dissociative identity disorder) have also been identified as common responses.[41]

SNAICC has also recognised the serious effects of child sexual assault, including initial effects such as:

- medical conditions — sexually transmitted infections, pregnancy and physical injury
- emotional problems — guilt, shame, anger, anxiety, fear, depression and low self-esteem
- behavioural problems — aggression, delinquency, nightmares, phobias (such as fear of men), eating and sleeping disorders
- learning difficulties — poor concentration at school and truancy.[42]

Possible long-term effects are repressed anger and hostility, sexual dysfunction, promiscuity, prostitution, blurred role boundaries and confusion in families, discomfort or difficulty in intimate relationships, isolation, relationship/marital problems, low self-esteem, depression, mental health problems, substance abuse, suicidal or self-mutilating behaviour, and eating disorders.[43]

All major studies have shown that child sexual assault can have enormous harmful impacts on children. This evidence exposes as myth the widely held notion that child sexual assault is not very harmful to the child and/or that survivors should simply put it into the past and get on with their lives.[44] In considering Aboriginal children we need to further recognise that the impacts of racism, poverty, discrimination, traumatic life events or stressors — even stigma and shame on the basis of Aboriginality — can compound Aboriginal children's traumatic experience of sexual assault and abuse.

No matter how hard I tried I could not escape sexual assault

During the course of my doctorate, which examined Aboriginal child sexual assault and the criminal justice system and which led to this book, a woman I knew from high school came looking for me at my sister's house. Her father had beaten her and she said she wanted to 'tell the truth' about her family. Did I remember 'the ghost that lived at her house'?

Her father and his friend were non-Aboriginal men who had the face of respectability and authority. In public they were friends of Aboriginal people, but privately they thought nothing of abuse, violation and terror towards Aboriginal children.

The assault happened when I was a young teenager. I was living with a family I hardly knew and at that stage my parents were not in contact with me. A friend from one of my former schools asked me to a sleepover and as I had few friends I was happy for the invitation. I had no idea I would be in danger at her house.

I did not report the assault at the time and there were many reasons why. While I wanted to get help, my friend was fearful and was protecting her father. I begged her to escape with me, out of the window, but she refused, saying that she believed a 'ghost' lived at her house and had been coming into her room all the time. The drugging was horrific and incomprehensible. I had no parents in my life. I wondered who would believe me against all of them?

The assault was violent and I was forced to look my own death in the face. I made my friend go to Church with me the next morning and I begged God to take 'it' away from me. This was the worst thing that had happened to me and I did not feel I could live with it.

Many people will wonder how something so terrible could ever be forgotten but I know that some things are so terrible that they must be 'forgotten'. I have since learned that traumatic amnesia is common in cases of child sexual assault, especially in cases involving a young child and/or where violence is used.

I banished all conscious memory, but trauma is not something that can be banished. When I remembered as an adult it was so overwhelmingly terrible. I was angry that I even had to remember and know the truth. It took me some time to realise that, as upsetting as it was, I had to know. A fellow survivor commented that 'the light had been flicked on' and she was right, because in not knowing I was in the dark about myself.

Deciding to report the assault years later was not an easy decision. On an intellectual level (and as a lawyer), I believed it was the 'right' thing to report adults who assaulted children. I was also fearful that these men might still be abusing children. I was angry at what was done to me and I wanted them held responsible. Ultimately, I spent two years 'waiting' in the criminal justice system, but there were never any charges laid on the basis that the complaint had 'insufficient evidence' to merit prosecution. There is no statute of limitations on sexual assault but in my experience historical (dated) cases are not treated with any sense of seriousness and police may even discourage reporting.

After I made my statement the police told me that the school friend was not emotionally able to make her statement. Because I had started talking about what had been done to me I was denigrated in the community and threatened with legal action. Almost two years after I lodged the complaint the police advised they could not lay charges. Citing 'legal reasons', the offenders simply refused to be interviewed by police. The lack of justice was very upsetting.

I do not see my own experience as unique. Lack of justice for Aboriginal victims of sexual assault is more the 'norm' than the exception, thereby negating the fundamental principle of equality before the law.

People who have not experienced sexual abuse and violence have no idea what can result when victims disclose. During the course of my doctorate I became aware of several cases of young Noongar girls who took their own lives after disclosing. There were individual and cluster cases brought to my attention. A grieving Noongar grandmother told me about three suicide attempts (with two deaths resulting) in the space of one month in Albany following disclosures by the girls. I was shocked to read a news report about the suicides in which Aboriginal male leaders called for healing camps for boys. In another suicide cluster case, one Noongar woman asked why it was that no one was discussing the well-known perpetrator who had offended against the deceased Aboriginal boys. It really seems that there is too little understanding of and concern for victims. In addition to the trauma of child sexual assault, enormous pressure is put on victims, including the insidious dynamics that can result in victims tragically ending their own lives.

While I was waiting for the police determination I contacted the Australian Crime Commission, which had established the National Indigenous Violence and Child Abuse Intelligence Task Force in 2006. Two non-Aboriginal male officers were sent to talk to me.

It seemed they knew little about Aboriginal child sexual abuse. A female officer later told me the Australian Crime Commission had reversed a decision of these officers not to include the information I had provided in their database, known as ACID (the Australian Criminal Intelligence Database), which was established to assist with enhanced understanding and intelligence about the nature of child sexual abuse in Aboriginal communities. 'What was going on here?' I wondered. Didn't anybody care that white men had so terribly abused Aboriginal children?

I understand the description of child sexual assault as 'the murder of innocence'. After the assault I felt that I no longer wanted to keep the birth name that my parents had given me, taking the name Hannah from the Bible instead. Hannah wanted children but could have none. Distraught, she begged God for children and her prayers were heard. It seems I understood Hannah's grief, as if there were no children that lived in me. So many years later those responsible showed no remorse and I wondered if they had committed the perfect crime. Child sexual assault seems to readily fit this description but I now believe it is a serious breach of Aboriginal law which has a spiritual foundation. This means that anyone who offends against children and young people will be called to account.

The Northern Territory Emergency Response

As I was regaining memories and struggling with the aftermath, Australia was collectively forced to confront Aboriginal child sexual abuse. A sense of shock reverberated across the nation when on 21 June 2007, the then Prime Minister John Howard announced that Aboriginal child abuse in the Northern Territory was a matter of 'national emergency' that his government intended to address.

The Northern Territory Emergency Response (NTER) followed the Northern Territory Government Inquiry into the Protection of Aboriginal Children from Sexual Abuse and the release in 2007 of the report *Little Children Are Sacred*, which described Aboriginal child sexual assault as 'common, widespread and grossly under-reported', recommending that 'Aboriginal child sexual abuse in the Northern Territory be designated as an issue of urgent national significance by both the Australian and Northern Territory Governments'.[45]

The Prime Minister's public announcement was broadcast nationwide on Australian television, and was astounding in that never before had an Australian Prime Minister declared Aboriginal children and their safety and wellbeing a matter of national importance and priority. Key Aboriginal bodies such as the Land Councils voiced their immediate and strong opposition to the Intervention, condemning it as a racist 'land grab', but some Aboriginal people felt that it was time to stop the abuse of children. As one Aboriginal woman powerfully declared, 'Our leader is listening to the cry of the mothers'.[46]

There were many differing responses to the announcement of the Intervention. For many people there was a sense of shock — shock that abuse of children was being spoken of so openly, and shock that the government would send the Australian army into remote Aboriginal communities to deal with this problem. Some of us felt relief and hope that the sexual abuse, violence and depravity of life that too many Aboriginal children live with would finally be addressed. The Commonwealth Intervention, the NTER, was and still is regarded as very controversial, with a great deal of public opposition, including a complaint to the United Nations.[47] It achieved bipartisan political support and support of some Northern Territory Aboriginal communities and key Aboriginal women's organisation such as the Ngaanyatjarra Pitjantjatjara Yankunytjatjara (NPY) Women's Council.[48]

Soon after the announcement, the Australian Government introduced the *Northern Territory National Emergency Response Act 2007*, extensive legislation dealing with matters ranging from the compulsory acquisition of leases over Aboriginal communities, alcohol restrictions, law enforcement, permits, welfare quarantining and income management, and Aboriginal customary law.

Although immediate Aboriginal opposition to the NTER was apparent, responses by communities have been mixed. As noted by the Northern Territory Children's Commissioner:

> The ultimate objective of the NTER was to protect Aboriginal children in 73 Aboriginal communities, community living areas and town camps. The measures related to law and order, the

support of families, welfare and employment reforms, child and family health, education, and housing and land reform. Some of these initiatives were and continue to be controversial, particularly those that were perceived to be discriminatory and racially-based and which required the suspension of the federal Racial Discrimination Act. Other initiatives, such as funding for a significantly increased police presence in communities, for new safe houses to provide protection for women and children, and for health-related measures, have received broad community support.[49]

Aboriginal opposition to the NTER has certainly not been universal. Professor Marcia Langton, in her compelling article 'The end of "big men" politics', publicly rebuked the opponents of the Intervention measures, arguing that the opposition was from people who have 'little firsthand experience' of communities, people 'who have rarely visited these communities, or lost sleep and health in the degrading environments where the grip of alcohol abuse has shortened lives and brutalised all who live there'.[50] In addition to Langton, senior Aboriginal women of various Northern Territory communities and the major women's organisation, the NPY Women's Council, backed aspects of the NTER as benefiting women, children and families.

By contrast, the male-dominated Land Councils have opposed the NTER in Australia and taken their complaints to the United Nations. Their position has been supported by the office of the Aboriginal and Torres Strait Islander Social Justice Commissioner, an office occupied exclusively by Aboriginal male appointees since its inception in 1992. Opposition to the NTER has at times entailed denial of the problem of violence against women and children and child sexual assault.

At a Parliament House meeting of Aboriginal people with the National Council to Reduce Violence Against Women on 30 June 2009 Bess Nungarrayi Price, who grew up in Central Australia in Yuendumu, argued:

Those opposed to the Intervention — they want to protect us from white racism and government. But our people are dying from ignorance and violence in our own communities. The right to be safe from violence is a basic human right that is getting overlooked in the debate on human rights.[51]

Nungarrayi Price asked the Aboriginal men and women in Parliament House with her, 'How can we make a better future for our children, when our very own men in our community are saying women do not have any power in the eyes of the Aboriginal law?'[52] In supporting the NTER, Nungarrayi Price stated that she has been abused, slandered and treated as the enemy:

> I know plenty of Aboriginal women here who want the Intervention because they can feed their kids now. The protesters treat them like enemies as well. They never support the old women who come in from the bush to protest against the grog. They attacked the women at the women's centre at Yuendumu when they set up their own shop. They took the side of the violent men and the corrupt ones in our communities and refused to support the women worried about their kids or sick of being beaten up by drunks. They have never even tried to talk to us.[53]

Unfortunately, in the name of human rights, Aboriginal and non-Aboriginal men and women, in responses to and protests against the NTER, have effectively silenced Aboriginal women, instead supporting violent men and male-dominant community dynamics that work to sanction violence against women and children. I support the views of Aboriginal women such as Nungarrayi Price, Langton and the NPY Women's Council that the NTER was intended to support and address Aboriginal women and children's right to be safe from violence. I also support the findings of the NTER Review that recommended its continuance in a modified form and consistently with human rights standards.[54] The imperative of human rights standards was made clear by the United Nations Human Rights Committee in April 2009, when it noted that certain aspects of the NTER were inconsistent with human rights, and that 'The State party should redesign NTER measures in direct consultation with the indigenous peoples concerned, in order to ensure that they are consistent with the 1975 Racial Discrimination Act and the Covenant'.[55]

At the time of writing, the Stronger Futures legislation, which will replace the NTER and run for ten years, has passed the House of Representatives and is before the Senate.[56] However, many still view the proposed amendments as failing to accord to human rights standards.

Aboriginal and Torres Strait Islander Social Justice Commissioner Mick Gooda has called for the Australian Government's Stronger Futures legislation to meet international human rights standards.[57] All legislation must now be accompanied by a statement of compatibility with the United Nations human rights treaties to which Australia is a party, but the Stronger Futures legislation was introduced before this requirement took effect. Nevertheless, Gooda has said that 'it would be useful to subject the proposals to the process … [which] would "give people some more confidence" in the changes'.[58] He has also called:

> for more effort to lift the "cultural competency" of government workers, and to develop governance structures in Indigenous communities so the views of Aboriginal people are heard. 'I've been out to some of these communities, and people want fairly drastic measures to address the issues around … violence against women and children'.

According to Gooda, 'People want to be safe and secure. But they've got to own those solutions as well as owning the problems.'[59]

Although much criticism was voiced about the federal government's consultations of the NTER, there seemed little concern with the issue of violence against women and children.[60] There was also no acknowledgment (by either government or Intervention opponents) of Aboriginal children's human right to be consulted on matters that affect them, and the need for strategies to guarantee the principle of children's effective participation.[61]

Notwithstanding the NTER, Aboriginal children have been politically without voice and seemingly of little political significance, and the lack of interest in human rights extending to Aboriginal children has been noticeable. For example, there was no public comment or response to the Northern Territory Coroner's report in June 2009, concerning the 2006 death of a young Mutitjulu girl, Kunmanara Forbes.[62] The lack of supports for children and young people in Mutitjulu were publicly exposed in 2006 by ABC reporter Suzi Smith, who herself was subjected to formal complaints by some Aboriginal people from the community.[63] However, Smith's report was based on the knowledge of Aboriginal matriarchs such as Mantatjara Wilson (a founder of NPY Women's Council), who were prepared to speak openly about the abuse of children:

> The huge problem wasn't started by the children. The problem was started by the people who sell petrol to get children started on petrol sniffing and then to induce them to have sex with them for it. On our Lands, the police see this problem all around them, but they cannot catch the perpetrators. All Anangu people know what is going on, but everybody is too scared to speak out and report them to the police.[64]

The Coroner's inquest identified the 15-year-old deceased as being sexually abused by adult men at the community at a 'petrol sniffing house'.[65] Kunmanara had contracted three sexually transmitted infections from age 13, but by the time of her death the Mutitjulu Health Clinic had discouraged reporting to the Northern Territory Department of Family and Children's Services.[66] Kunmanara received no counselling, but prior to her death stated that her brother had beaten her as 'traditional punishment' for petrol sniffing.[67] The few attempts made at intervention were completely inappropriate; both the psychologist and Aboriginal community welfare worker sent to visit her prior to her death were males, possibly with no expertise in sexual abuse. Not surprisingly, Kunmanara was 'reluctant to engage' with either and refused to disclose sexual abuse.[68] As the investigating police officer explained, factors including community or cultural shame, lack of support systems, and adolescence all contributed to discourage disclosure.[69]

In his conclusion, the Coroner (who made no comment in relation to the impact that sexual abuse had upon this young girl's life) merely noted that the 'spotlight' of the NTER had done little to help Kunmanara:

> The death of this young girl was tragic. There is some irony in the fact that her physical and mental health continued to deteriorate despite the spotlight which was being shone upon

her by her community (and her) by the [Northern Territory] government agencies, the Australian government and the media. The sad lead up to her self-inflicted death is a reminder of the commonly difficult life circumstances for Aboriginal young people in Central Australia, and the continued responsibility of both the Aboriginal and wider community to maintain its efforts to improve these circumstances.[70]

Our greatest challenge — acknowledging and addressing child sexual assault

Speaking against child sexual assault and in support of victims is very difficult. From my direct experience, advocacy for child victims of sexual assault can result in personal and professional vulnerability, isolation and even abuse. Too often there is little support for children and victim survivors of child sexual assault, a phenomenon aptly explained by psychiatrist and trauma expert Dr Judith Herman: 'To speak publicly about one's knowledge of atrocities is to invite the stigma that attaches to victims.'[71]

In 1978 Suzanne Sgroi MD also described the reluctance and unwillingness of the medical profession in the United States to identify the true extent of the problem of sexual abuse of children as 'the last frontier' in child abuse.[72] Sgroi argued that:

> Sexual abuse of children is a crime that our society abhors in the abstract, but tolerates in reality … We tolerate sexual abuse of children because it is the last remaining component in the maltreatment syndrome in children that is yet to be faced head on … It seems to be 'too dirty', 'too Freudian' or 'too close to home'. Those who try to assist sexually abused children must be prepared to battle against incredulity, hostility, innuendo and outright harassment. Worst of all, the advocate for the sexually abused child runs the risk of being smothered by indifference and a conspiracy of silence. The pressures from one's peer group, as well as from the community, to ignore, minimize or cover up the situation, may be extreme.[73]

Aboriginal child sexual assault is a place where many are reluctant, fearful, unable or just plain unwilling to tread. I say this despite the 2007 NTER and note the concerns voiced by the Northern

Territory Children's Commissioner.[74] In his 2008–09 annual report, Commissioner Bath warned that the protection needs of vulnerable Aboriginal children in the Northern Territory are 'in some danger of being subsumed into broader policy initiatives aimed at addressing Indigenous disadvantage'.[75] Of concern, the focus on child protection and specifically child sexual assault is being lost within the NTER and the new policy frameworks, which focus on creating infrastructure and economic development. Additionally, the Australian and Northern Territory governments have no intention of establishing a collaborative partnership and memorandum of understanding specifically addressing the protection of Aboriginal children from child sexual assault, a key recommendation of the inquiry that precipitated the NTER.[76]

As anticipated by the Children's Commissioner, the NTER has resulted in an increase in Aboriginal child sexual assault substantiations.[77] But has it also contributed to an entrenched culture of 'denial' of child sexual assault? For example, in a paper published by the Co-operative Research Centre for Aboriginal Health and authored by the Australian Indigenous Psychologists Association, the risk factors for Indigenous social and emotional wellbeing were comprehensively considered.[78] The discussion concerning violence recognised the very high rate of family violence experienced by Aboriginal women, including homicide, but failed to acknowledge child sexual assault and abuse.[79] One has to ask, has the very subject matter post-Intervention become 'too political' for Aboriginal people?

A leading United States critical race theorist, Professor Kimberle Williams Crenshaw, argues that African-Americans are conflicted in acknowledging 'intra-community problems', such as violence and sexual assault, and weighing their own interests in avoiding issues that might 'reinforce distorted public perceptions'.[80] Crenshaw argues that 'the cost of suppression is seldom recognised, in part because the failure to discuss the issue shapes perceptions of how serious the problem is in the first place'.[81] According to Crenshaw, suppression in the name of anti-racism imposes 'real costs', namely, where information about sexual violence is not available, sexual violence is unlikely to be addressed as a serious issue.[82]

It seems that Aboriginal child sexual assault is also being suppressed as anti-racism, as evident from the submission of the Australian

Indigenous Doctors' Association concerning the NTER. The detailed submission repeatedly stressed the social and emotional harms said to have resulted from the Intervention measures. But it made no acknowledgment of the grave harm of child sexual assault, and moreover appeared to minimise the extent of child sexual assault:

> It is important to note that one year after the NTER was announced only three people have been convicted of child abuse. While this may not be the full story, it does cast doubt on basing the Intervention, which we have already said has negative impacts on health and wellbeing, on the main platform 'to protect Aboriginal children'.[83]

Similarly, Mick Gooda, the Aboriginal and Torres Strait Islander Social Justice Commissioner, one day after his appointment in 2010, argued that there had been no dramatic rise in prosecutions in the Territory for child abuse in the year after the Intervention was launched, commenting, 'What have we got, one more arrest in the period?'[84] However, the government's monitoring data showed a significant increase in both the reporting and conviction rates of child sex offences; for example, there were twice as many convictions in the first 18 months of the Intervention.[85]

Aboriginal suppression of child sexual assault after the NTER may also be related to concerns surrounding the government's infringement of Aboriginal people's human rights to self-determination. Although I do not agree that suppression is helpful, the question must still be asked whether Aboriginal child sexual assault can be effectively addressed in a wider context in which Aboriginal self-determination in relation to children's welfare is undermined and negated. There has been little progress towards a human rights approach described by Terri Libesman as 'consistent with a community development approach to children's well-being, and support for greater Indigenous participation and control over their children's welfare and well-being'.[86] According to Libesman, a senior lecturer in law at the University of Technology Sydney, the government's approach in the NTER 'echoes the paternalism of the protectionist period, which has left a legacy of harm and loss and which paradoxically is associated with contemporary child protection issues'.[87] Aboriginal self-determination in the area of child welfare and protection is a critical but largely unaddressed issue.

The *Bringing Them Home* report of the National Inquiry into the Separation of Aboriginal and Torres Strait Islander Children from Their Families, recommended more than a decade ago that national legislation be enacted between Australian governments and key Indigenous organisations to allow for transfer of control and responsibility for Indigenous children's welfare to Indigenous organisations that had willingness and capacity.[88] No Australian states or territories have addressed this recommendation and the United Nations Committee on the Rights of the Child has called on Australian governments to fully implement this important principle of Aboriginal human rights.[89]

Aboriginal child sexual abuse, 'our greatest challenge', should be understood in the context of the wider factors of colonialism, patriarchy, power, control and land. These influences have shaped and authorised an unjust criminal justice response that includes the re-victimisation of Aboriginal victim survivors. Aboriginal self-determination is relevant to child protection and should extend to the development of models addressing child sexual assault that respect Aboriginal culture, empowers and affirms victim survivors and human rights, and, most importantly, facilitates healing and helps to break the cycle of abuse.

Theoretical perspectives

Research is a personal process that invokes place, culture, histories and futures. My approach is most consistent with the critical research paradigm, which abandons pretence at neutrality and is openly committed to social change and reform.[90]

Being a lawyer I am trained to identify facts and look for evidence, but as an Aboriginal woman I readily accept the foundation of critical legal studies that law is not a neutral process but is connected to existing political processes and institutions. Legal reasoning is essentially political and oppressed groups rely on the power of law even though oppressed by law.[91] This book takes a critical legal stance[92] — with a specific commitment to social, legal and political change recognising Aboriginal people's human rights, particularly the rights of women and children.

Many theoretical perspectives have shaped the ways in which I view the world and the topic of child sexual assault. First and foremost is my identity as a Noongar woman, raised with Noongar cultural values and understanding. I am also influenced by non-Aboriginal society and the ongoing imposition of assimilation and non-Aboriginal cultural views and practices. As a victim of child sexual assault or rape, I have my own direct understandings and experiences, including that of survival and healing. Other theoretical frameworks include victimology, radical feminist theory, critical race theory, critical race feminisms and critical race praxis.

The foundations of victimology concern the development of victim's participation and rights, and critical victimology looks at victimisation as a social process.[93] For some people the term *victim* connotes negative images; however, I use this term in the criminological sense and consistently with human rights law:

> 'Victims' means persons who, individually or collectively, have suffered harm, physical or mental injury, emotional suffering, economic loss or substantial impairment of their human rights, through acts or omissions that are in operation within Members States, including those laws proscribing criminal abuse of power.[94]

At times I adopt the term *victim survivor*, although I am aware that many people impacted by child sexual assault recognise themselves as survivors. In some contexts victimisation is the paramount experience and the legal and personal experience of victimisation is so pervasive it would be misleading to speak of 'survival'. In my use of terminology I also acknowledge that many children impacted by sexual assault have not in fact 'survived' — they have taken their own lives, or died young in tragic circumstances. At the same time, I know the resilience and strength that many victim survivors hold.

A central proposition of the different strands of feminism is that 'society is organized by men in a way which privileges men, and operates to disadvantage women'.[95] Radical feminist theorist Professor Catharine MacKinnon has been a leading force in the development of equality jurisprudence in the United States, aimed at institutionalising 'social equality, rather than inequality, through legal equality initiatives'.[96] The goal of equality theory as described by MacKinnon is 'to close the gap between legal promise and social reality in the equality area'.[97] This new equality theory begins by articulating the 'systematic, pervasive and cumulative absence of equality in society' and by moving to put legal redress into the hands of affected groups through law.[98] Existing legal equality fails to capture the ways in which the legal system organises its participation in the subordination of women. Law actively engages in sex inequality, according to MacKinnon, by apparently prohibiting abuses it largely permits, such as rape. Legal concepts are designed from the point of view of the accused rapists and absent from the point of view of the assaulted women.[99]

The contemporary women's movement in the United States for civil equality is described as 'creating a new political practice and form of theory with major implications for the law'.[100] MacKinnon's theory of legal equality premises as fundamental the 'systematically excluded accounts, the pervasively silenced voices … the voices of certain people: the unequal'.[101] According to MacKinnon, this distinctive theory in being forged is a form of action through words:

> It is deeply of this world: raw with women's blood, ragged with women's pain, shrill with women's screams. It does not elaborate yet more arcane abstractions of ideas building upon ideas. It participates in reality: the reality of a fist in the face, not the concept of a fist in the face. It does not exist to mediate women's reality for male consumption. It exists to bear witness, to create consciousness, to make change. It is not, in a word, academic.[102]

The reality of the violence of sexual assault and women and children's pain is evident in this book. I agree with MacKinnon that we need to bear witness to the reality of women and children's lived experiences and that this is critical to creating the consciousness needed for social, cultural and legal change.

Aboriginal Australian women's critique of feminism has often been reluctant to engage with the issue of Aboriginal women's experiences of sexism and oppression by Aboriginal men. In contrast, in the United States proponents of black feminist thought have explored the issue of race and gender-based forms of oppression for black women.[103] Black feminist thought also identifies the lack of recognition of African-American women's knowledge and intellectual traditions as a reflection of the social systems of inequality to maintain black women's oppressed positioning in society, and includes the concept of 'standpoint' and the recognition that factors of class, sexuality, urbanisation, age and a host of other experiences shape diversity and experiences among African-American women.[104] Accordingly, no one has a neutral standpoint — rather, we are all 'embedded' in the world.[105] Black feminism is a 'journey towards self-identification', seeing and understanding how our lives have been shaped by the interlocking systems of race, gender and class oppression. This process has political significance, necessitating challenge and resistance to systems of oppression.[106]

Critical race theory is a theoretical framework developed in the 1970s in the United States as lawyers, activists and legal scholars became concerned that the advances of the civil rights movement had stalled, and that new theories were needed to help address the more subtle forms of racism.[107] The basic tenets have been described as follows:

- racism is ordinary, not aberrational, and is the usual way society does business and the common experience of people of colour
- racism serves an important purpose, both psychic and material
- race is a product of social thought and realities, categories that society invents, manipulates or retires when convenient
- intersectionality refers to the examination of race, sex, class, national origin and sexual orientation
- people affected by racism have a unique voice and competence to speak about race and racism.[108]

Critical race theory draws from critical legal studies to assert that cultural influences are at least determinative of legal outcomes as formal laws, and that these cultural influences are the background against which formal laws are interpreted and applied.[109] It is a rejection of liberal legalism and conventional forms of legal theory that have 'presented law as neutral, operating on everyone equally and without distinction'.[110] While liberal legalism claims law is a body of 'neutral, abstract principles unaffected by politics, society and personal viewpoints', critical legal theory holds that the liberal legal subject reflects the characteristics of the people who have made laws and disguised assumptions 'behind a veil of neutrality'.[111] Fundamental to critical race theory is the view that the law's substantive doctrines of formal equality and neutral procedures are structured to maintain white privilege and race oppression.

Critical race theory rejects three mainstream and entrenched beliefs about racism — that 'blindness' to racism will eliminate it; that racism is not just a matter of individuals but of systems and everyday operation within societal structures; and that one can fight racism without paying attention to other forms of oppression and injustice.[112]

Tribal critical race theory, an offshoot of critical race theory, argues that while critical race theory serves as a framework in and of itself, it does not address the experiences of Native American people in the United States, particularly colonisation.[113] While very much linked to colonisation of Native American, the overall and general understanding of tribal critical race theory is relevant to Indigenous peoples who have been colonised worldwide.

The relationships between race and other forms of oppression have led to critical race feminism, which is a feminist intervention in critical race theory and a race intervention in feminist theory. It develops and contributes to key analytical concepts of 'anti-essentialism' (described as a 'primary intellectual stance and dominant cultural norm'[114]) and 'intersectionality'.[115] The important critical race feminism contribution of 'essentialism' reflects the experiences of African-American women of being absorbed, made invisible and marginalised within predominantly white middle-class progressive movements, such as feminism. The work of Professor Angela Harris is associated with the critique of feminist theory as 'essentialist'. Harris criticises MacKinnon's works and theory of male dominance as responsible for promoting the idea that there can be an essential woman 'beneath the realities of difference between women', namely race and class.[116]

In the context of sexual violence, Harris argues that MacKinnon's analysis of rape as the subordination of women to men failed to reflect the experiences of black women. For African-American women, 'rape is a far more complex experience, and an experience as deeply rooted in color as in gender'.[117] Black women's experience of rape includes not only a vulnerability to rape, but also a lack of legal protection radically different to that experienced by white women.[118]

Professor Kimberle Williams Crenshaw expounds Harris's observations concerning African-American women's experience of sexual violence.[119] Crenshaw observes that identity politics frequently conflates or ignores intra-group differences, and moreover that ignoring differences between groups creates further tensions. Women of colour have an intersectional identity as both women and of colour, but this is rarely recognised within either feminist or anti-racism movements.

Crenshaw writes that while racism as experienced by men tends to determine the parameters of anti-racist strategies, sexism as experienced by white women similarly grounds the women's movement.[120] A troubling political consequence of the failure of anti-racist and feminist discourses to identify and address the intersections of race and gender, can mean that racism and patriarchy are effectively promoted within both discourses:

> The failure of feminism to interrogate race means that feminism's resistance strategies will often replicate and reinforce the subordination of people of color, likewise, the failure of antracism to interrogate patriarchy means that antiracism will frequently reproduce the subordination of women.[121]

Women of colour can be 'erased by the strategic silences of antiracism and feminism' — explaining why neither the anti-rape or anti-racism political agenda has focused on the black rape victim.[122] Crenshaw argues that multiple identities do not mean that we should give up on organising as communities of colour; rather, intersectionality provides a basis for reconceptualising race as a coalition between men and women. Adopting an intersectional approach requires that we 'abandon the general argument that the interests of the community require the suppression of any confrontation around intra-racial rape'.[123]

Critical race theory and critical race feminism (like black feminist thought) both embrace an activist dimension and support the philosophy that 'There is no true word that is not at the same time praxis'.[124] Theorists have expressed the concern that theory is not always as grounded in the political as it should be — accordingly, critical race theorists 'must strive to become more accountable … to the people, goals and ideals of the movement'[125] — and that anti-subordination theory and anti-subordination practice need to have a close and critical relation, especially in view of the 'continuing and accelerating degeneration of equality jurisprudence'.[126]

Despite the necessity of theory linked with praxis, there has been a noticeable absence of critical race theory within lawyering practices, which 'reveals a disjunctive between progressive race theory and frontline, political lawyering practice'.[127] Critical race praxis aims to combine critical, pragmatic, socio-legal analysis with political lawyering and community organising to practice justice for and by racialised communities.[128]

Critical race praxis has been described as the 'practical turn' of critical race theory,[129] and has the urgent imperative to acknowledge that 'Communities in crisis cannot await elegant legal theories. Immediate action and practical solutions addressed to real life exploitation and suffering, however imperfect, are crucial'.[130]

MacKinnon writes that legal theory should analyse legal issues in terms of the real issues, and strive to move law so that the real issues are the legal issues.[131] Relatively little attention has been given to critical race praxis and this may be related to MacKinnon's complaint that works that confront reality rather than abstractions are not considered legal theory. Critical race praxis is therefore likely to be 'looked down upon'. Established legal theory has distanced itself from the reality and practices of law and legal outcomes: 'Reality gets one dirty and involved, and talking about it requires knowing something about the world, which is harder than knowing something about the law of that aspect of the world. Theory is formal; substance is finger pointing, politics.'[132]

MacKinnon also points out that while 'neutral legal principles' are substantive, in actuality, judges and legal commentators typically believe they can apply their minds neutrally to legal issues. However, this has the effect of concealing bias (even from their own selves) and permits subconscious commitments on substance 'which tend to favor the status quo and established interests, to control'.[133]

Native American Professor Robert Williams observes that critical race theory ultimately clashes with the cultural values his elders taught him as a child, 'to think independently, and to act for others'.[134] The demands of critical race theory and 'legal theory' effectively meant that Williams could not meet his own cultural obligations, to give back something to community, rather than take, take, take: 'What these Arizona Indians wanted me to do was to get off my critical race theory ass and do some Critical Race Practice.'[135] According to Williams, critical race practice is 'mostly about learning to listen to other people's stories and then finding ways to make those stories matter in the legal system'.[136]

Chapter 2

Understanding colonisation and trauma

This chapter is concerned with understanding child sexual assault within an Aboriginal context, particularly within the impacts of colonisation and trauma. There is a great deal of non-Indigenous research about child sexual assault, but little concerning Aboriginal child sexual assault. Researchers have noted that 'The current framework for understanding child abuse and neglect is located within the white western world, where the vast majority of research has taken place'.[1] The dominant non-Indigenous model locates child abuse within a 'personal dysfunction model', but Aboriginal people locate child sexual assault within the wider definition of family violence, framing violence less as personal dysfunction than as a consequence of the impacts of colonisation, specifically historical and inter-generational trauma.[2]

Child rights agencies have identified the lack of rights held by children in all societies as a key underlying and causal factor of child sexual assault, and that 'A root cause that predisposes children everywhere to sexual exploitation and other forms of abuse and violence is the low status accorded to them by society'.[3]

This chapter focuses on the impacts of colonisation and trauma, including theories of trauma, the history of sexual abuse of Aboriginal women and children, the Stolen Generations, inter-generational trauma and the 'cycle of abuse'. I also consider the controversial argument that Aboriginal family violence has cultural foundations.

The impact of colonisation

Violence in Indigenous Communities, a 2001 report of the Commonwealth Attorney-General's Department, supports the widely held view that Indigenous violence, including family violence, is directly related to the history of colonisation and cannot be separated from the past nature of European and Indigenous relations.[4] The lead author, Queensland academic Professor Paul Memmott, was an early proponent of this theory of Indigenous violence, which was developed in the early 1990s during the course of the Royal Commission into Aboriginal Deaths in Custody (RCIADC). The RCIADC considered the impact of colonial expansion and aggression on Aborigines throughout Queensland up to 1898, and in the period from 1898 to post-1967 when Aboriginal people were under the exclusive control of the various Queensland Aboriginal Protection Acts. According to the RCIADC, this history has led to a wide range of social problems in Aboriginal communities today, including interpersonal violence and child sexual offences.[5]

The 2001 report acknowledged that patterns of contemporary violence among Aboriginal people 'have their origins in the violent dispossession of land by Europeans in the early contact period'.[6] Ongoing cultural dispossession and its consequences, which have taken different forms for more than 200 years, have had such an impact on Indigenous people socially, economically, physically, psychologically and emotionally, that violence in some Indigenous communities had reached 'epidemic' proportions.[7]

This dispossession of Aboriginal people from lands included the rejection of Aboriginal systems of law and governance, considered too 'barbaric' to be recognised by a 'civilised' legal system — or that were simply unable to survive European contact.[8] Unlike most other colonised countries, the British sought no treaty to recognise the status and rights of the Indigenous peoples.[9] Aboriginal people were categorised as 'primitive' and 'savages', and their sovereignty was rejected through the legal fiction of terra nullius, which in effect denigrated the social and customary nature of Aboriginal societies.[10] According to Aboriginal legal theorist Dr Irene Watson, 'We were made invisible by the colonists as was our connection to law and place. They did not see us or their own creation — genocide.

They made their role as perpetrators of the genocide invisible also. Invisibility was made legal by the *muldarbi* terra nullius'.[11]

Watson describes the *muldarbi* (bad spirit) terra nullius and the erasure of Indigenous people as an ongoing process, not limited to history but remaining today and taking other forms in the post-Mabo era. The continued ability of the Crown to extinguish Native Title is just one example of this.[12] It is also recognised that ongoing systemic forms of discrimination within the criminal justice system have contributed to very high incarceration rates of Aboriginal men, women and youths.[13]

Aboriginal people have always resisted the violence of colonisation. Resistance was highlighted nationally and internationally during the 1988 bicentenary protests when thousands of Aboriginal people campaigned for recognition of the violence of frontier history and the injustices against Aboriginal people, especially the lack of a treaty. I was one of many who travelled across Australia to Sydney in 1988 to counter the lie that Australia had been peacefully settled. Collectively, thousands of Aboriginal people across the nation raised our version of Australian colonisation, genocide and human rights violations — 'White Australia has a Black History', 'We Have Survived' and 'Don't Celebrate '88, 200 Years of Genocide'.

The systematic violation of Aboriginal human rights has been a matter that Australian society and governments have done their utmost to sweep under the carpet. The 1992 'Redfern Park speech' by former Australian Prime Minister Paul Keating is one of the few exceptions. In the United Nations Year of the World's Indigenous Peoples, Keating urged non-Aboriginal Australians to recognise this country's history of violent colonisation:

> It begins ... with the act of recognition. Recognition that it was we who did the dispossessing. We took the traditional lands and smashed the traditional way of life. We brought the disasters. The alcohol. We committed the murders. We took the children from their mothers. We practiced discrimination and exclusion. It was our ignorance and our prejudice. And our failure to imagine these things being done to us.[14]

Keating's understandings were greatly assisted by the work of many Aboriginal people who had provided autobiographical accounts of their lives and family lives under the various segregation and assimilation regimes. Historians such as Henry Reynolds had also documented extensively the violent nature of colonisation in Australia. The colonial frontier practices, which included killings, massacres and sexual assault of women and children, were all carried out and excused under the guise of 'peaceful settlement'.[15]

Non-Aboriginal Australia has been reluctant to recognise that prior to the introduction of the Commonwealth *Discrimination Act 1975*, open discriminatory and apartheid-like practices against Aboriginal people were commonplace. Until the 1960s Aboriginal people were 'citizens without rights' as parliaments, governments and bureaucrats denied Aboriginal peoples proper citizenry rights through successive acts of legislation and administration.[16] In 1997 the extent of the practice of Aboriginal child removal was documented by the Human Rights and Equal Opportunity Commission (HREOC), which considered the practice as 'a crime against humanity' and a breach of the international human rights law prohibiting genocide.[17]

Theories of trauma

In his 2003 'Violence dysfunction Aboriginality' address to the National Press Club, Professor Mick Dodson spoke about the extent of violence in Aboriginal life and the impact of trauma flowing from this violence: 'Violence is undermining our life's very essence, it is destroying us, and there are very few Aboriginal families that are not struggling with the debilitating effects of trauma, despair and damage resulting from their experiences of trauma.'[18]

Dodson identified historical trauma, inter-generational trauma, alcohol and drug induced violence, and 'dysfunctional community syndrome'.[19] His powerful address was influenced by, and is expounded by, Aboriginal trauma expert Professor Judy Atkinson, who has argued that colonisation involved:

> multiple layers of both acute and overt acts of violence, and chronic and covert conditions of control … These separately are traumatic and oppressive. Collectively, and compounding over generations. The pain may become internalised into abusive and self-abusive behaviours, often within families and discrete

communities. The rage is not only turned inwards, but cascades down the generations, growing more complex over time.[20]

Colonisation also involved forms of systemic power and control of Aboriginal people, involving overt physical violence, covert structural violence and psycho-social domination.[21] The result is that Aboriginal peoples have suffered a collective trauma that still impacts today: 'Large-scale epidemics, massacres, removals of whole populations to detainment camps called reserves, removals of children, splitting apart of family groups, physical and cultural genocide — these formed layers of traumatic impacts down the generations.'[22]

Trauma and oppression have been compounded over generations and 'internalised into abusive and self-abusive practices' within families and discrete communities.[23] Atkinson argues that the traumatic effects of colonisation can be recognised as post-traumatic stress disorder,[24] and argues for the necessity of healing intervention to address the issue of 'inter-generational trauma' — original traumas that are compounded down the generations until there is healing to break the cycle of trauma.[25]

The Commonwealth Attorney-General's Department has acknowledged trauma and the underlying factors of Indigenous violence as the 'deep historical circumstances of Indigenous people, which makes them vulnerable, leading to their enacting, or becoming the victim, of violent behaviour'.[26] The *Violence in Indigenous Communities* report argued that violence is a consequence of trauma (and the underlying issue of historical trauma) and the need for healing is paramount:

> The impact of personal, family and community disintegration in many Aboriginal societies, enacted by missions, statutes and regulations, and State and Commonwealth policies, is still being realised today and should not be underestimated if genuine and workable solutions to prevent violence in Indigenous communities are to be developed. What is required is treatment and 'healing' on a massive scale, including the healing of individuals, families and whole communities.[27]

The report considered that Indigenous violence has multiple originating causes and, in addition to underlying causes, recognised the precipitating causes (namely, particular events that might trigger a violent episode by a perpetrator) and the situational factors (for example, alcohol abuse or other exacerbating circumstances).[28] In support of the argument concerning underlying issues, and the impacts of colonisation, it was noted that statistically the Indigenous Queensland communities that formerly operated as mission centres had the worst incidence of violent crime.[29]

The impact of historical trauma is considered in a 2008 report by the Australian Institute of Criminology (AIC). *Risk Factors in Indigenous Violent Victimisation* argues that although the underlying factors of Indigenous violence are recognised, there are fundamental difficulties in 'attempting to delineate risk factors associated with victimisation from this historical perspective'.[30] Trauma is 'inherently difficult to measure' and reactions to an event are specific to an individual, but some individuals and communities have succeeded in life notwithstanding past traumatic events.[31] Many scholars consider that Indigenous violence is a result of colonisation and the historical treatment of Indigenous people by mainstream society.[32] The report notes different approaches that have been adopted in explaining how the impact of colonisation leads to violence, including:

- anomie theory — colonisation has stripped away Indigenous peoples' sense of meaning, value and purpose, undermining the capacity of Indigenous people to control the anti-social behaviour of members
- social disorganisation theory — colonisation and dispossession have led to a breakdown of Indigenous social structures, resulting in a loss of informal social controls
- social deprivation theory — which attributes violence in Indigenous communities to the impacts of economic and social disadvantage
- lifestyle/routine activity theory — alcohol and drug abuse is largely responsible for Indigenous violence.[33]

According to the AIC report, the evidence concerning Indigenous violence is largely theoretical in nature, supported by asserted knowledge or case studies with little empirical evidence. The report cites one study that sought to draw on empirical data obtained from the 2002 National Aboriginal and Torres Strait Islander Social

Survey.[34] The study reportedly found little evidence to support the anomie theory, but some evidence for the social disorganisation and social deprivation theories. There was strong support for the lifestyle/ routine theory, with high-risk alcohol consumption being regarded as the single strongest risk factor for Indigenous violent victimisation.

The impact of alcohol

Aboriginal lawyer and author Noel Pearson has also made a strong case that alcohol is a primary risk factor for Indigenous violence (and over-representation in the criminal justice system).[35] Pearson questions the assumption of the Royal Commission into Aboriginal Deaths in Custody of the 1980s that the over-representation of Aboriginal people in the criminal justice system was the direct consequence of the underlying social, economic and cultural disadvantage suffered by Aboriginal people since colonisation, and that this needed to be overcome because it leads to breaches of the law. Although Pearson does not dispute the underlying factors identified by the RCIADC, his view is that it failed to properly consider the issue of alcohol in its own right, disputing the 'symptom theory' on the basis that addiction is also a condition in its own right and not just a symptom.[36] Pearson believes that the alcohol epidemic perpetuates itself: 'The truth is that alcohol directly causes, exacerbates or prevents the resolution of other underlying issues.'[37]

The role of alcohol abuse in relation to Aboriginal child sexual assault was also highlighted by the 2007 Inquiry into the Protection of Aboriginal Children from Sexual Abuse, which found that alcohol was having an extremely detrimental effect 'on almost every aspect of community life including the safety of children'.[38] In the 45 communities visited, the inquiry heard anecdotal evidence that:

- alcohol abuse increases the possibility of a person committing sexual assault offences against a child
- alcohol abuse by children increases their vulnerability to sexual assault
- intoxication by family places children at risk of sexual assault
- alcohol is leading to the loss of Aboriginal culture
- alcohol is being used to facilitate sexual assault of children

- alcohol leads to physical violence and dysfunction
- alcohol negatively impacts employment and educational prospects
- alcohol is a major cause of family and social breakdown.[39]

The inquiry supported the Northern Territory Alcohol Framework as a matter of urgency, and agreed with Pearson that addiction is not just a symptom but a significant problem in itself, and the first step is to stop or at least reduce consumption.[40] It should be recognised that the identification of alcohol consumption as a primary risk factor for violence does not in itself negate the relevance of historical trauma. Pearson himself believes that trauma and dispossession have made our communities susceptible to drug and alcohol epidemics, although he states that this does not automatically cause abusive behaviour.[41] The inquiry and Pearson take a common sense approach that the epidemic of alcohol abuse must be treated and responded to in its own right — and not solely as a symptom of colonisation and trauma.

AIC confirmed in a 2010 report, *Indigenous Perpetrators of Violence: Prevalence and risk factors for offending*, that 'alcohol is now widely regarded as one of the, if not the, main risk factor for Indigenous violence'.[42] Statistical evidence considered by AIC indicated much higher levels of alcohol use by Aboriginal people than non-Aboriginal people in contact with the criminal justice system.[43]

Although the focus on alcohol use and its relation to offending is important, alcohol should be viewed in a holistic manner. Atkinson, who recognises alcohol as being 'at the core of family and community dysfunction', also explains that 'Aboriginal people's use of alcohol and other drugs is, in many instances, connected to the traumatisation in violence that has occurred over generations …'[44] Alcohol is a form of self-medication, and a way to numb and cope with feelings and trauma.[45] Although I agree that alcohol should be responded to in its own right, alcohol is very much related to the ongoing traumatic impacts of colonisation that must equally be responded to, as posited by Atkinson. This includes the history in which Aboriginal women and children were subjected to widespread sexual abuse and rape.

The history of sexual abuse of Aboriginal women and children

Colonisation included severe levels of sexual violence against Aboriginal women and children, both girls and boys. According to historians Professor Heather Goodall and Dr Jackie Huggins:

The processes of colonisation across the continent began violently with invasion, massacre and rape, and continue to be violent since that time. Sexual abuse of Aboriginal women and children by white men was a well-known outcome of such invasion and indeed was often a weapon of war. Sexual exploitation of Aboriginal women by white men has continued, part of the complex spectrum of relationships Aboriginal women have had with their colonisers.[46]

Goodall and Huggins describe the colonial stereotypes of Aboriginal men as violent and Aboriginal women as both 'chattels and promiscuous' as 'useful ideological tools' that justified violent repression and sexual exploitation.[47] These statements are consistent with the position articulated in 1986 in *Women's Business: Report of the Aboriginal Women's Taskforce*, which named sexual violence against Aboriginal women as part of violent colonisation practices:

> Since colonisation many many Aboriginal women have suffered physical and sexual abuse at the hands of white men. They have used Aboriginal women and girls as slaves in their homes and camps. They have abused Aboriginal women verbally and physically. They have been responsible for 'gin sprees' or 'gin busting' excursions — the object being to rape, maim or kill as many black women as possible.[48]

The report noted that rape of Aboriginal women was not confined to the rough frontier life, but often happened in the homes of 'respectable' white people and behind closed doors.

Atkinson has also written about the history of widespread sexual abuse and exploitation of Aboriginal women and girls by white men.[49] Some cases she documents using historical sources are horrific, including children as young as five being kidnapped for the purpose of rape and discarded when venereal diseases resulted.[50] This history of sexual abuse is exemplified by the well-known derogatory terms 'gin' and 'black velvet'; moreover, white society viewed sexual violation of Aboriginal women and girls as a 'familiar male sporting event'. White women knew but often maintained a silence and denial about the violence against Aboriginal women and children.[51] Atkinson's argument that this history of endemic sexual violence is a taboo topic provoking great sensitivity or silence is compelling:

Australians have never been able to acknowledge sexual violence in their history. It is now alright to write of the guns and the poisoned flour, the killing of black women and children. It is still taboo to acknowledge the horrific level of sexual violence towards Aboriginal women and girls by white males.[52]

That the horrific level of sexual violence perpetrated against Aboriginal women and white girls has been a taboo matter is evident from recent history texts, such as Bain Attwood's *Telling the Truth about Aboriginal History*, which does not acknowledge sexual violence or rape at all.[53] Attwood challenges the revisionist writings of historian Keith Windschuttle, but his book fails to acknowledge the history in which Aboriginal women and children were systemically subjected to sexual abuse and rape as part of colonisation. Attwood does not refute Windschuttle's claim that Aboriginal women and girls were culturally promiscuous: 'Traditional Aboriginal society placed no constraints on the women's sexual behaviour with white men. Their husbands and fathers appeared to encourage their prostitution'.[54] Windschuttle also denies that Aboriginal children were removed from their parents for racist or genocidal reasons, stating that government officers and missionaries wanted to rescue them from environments that were riddled with violence and sexual abuse.[55] According to Windschuttle, the good white people, public servants, doctors, teachers and missionaries 'found' young Aboriginal children in New South Wales, Western Australia and the Northern Territory suffering from sexual abuse and venereal diseases. In addition, he alleges that Aboriginal parents in the Kimberley sold their children as prostitutes to Asian pearlers.[56]

Windschuttle's arguments are an attempt at revisionism that denies the history of colonial sexual violence and constructs white settlers and missionaries as innocent. Historians such as Attwood have not grappled with Windschuttle's offensive allegations of Aboriginal women and children's immorality and 'prostitution'. It seems that Windschuttle's revisionist accounts are made possible because the history of sexual abuse of Aboriginal women and children is, as Atkinson identifies, still a taboo topic unrecognised in Australian historical accounts.

Historian Henry Reynolds is one of the few historians who acknowledge the widespread sexual abuse that was perpetrated during frontier times:

> On many stations there was no attempt to hide the extent of sexual relations between white station workers and black women. A pastoralist from the edge of the Nullarbor Plains told a South Australian Royal Commission in 1889 that he had known stations 'where every hand on the place had a gin, even down to boys of 15 years of age'. Similar comments were made to a West Australian Royal Commission six years later on. On Vitriol River stations, a witness observed that on many stations 'there are no white women at all'. On these the Aboriginal women are usually at the mercy of anybody, from the proprietor or Manager, to the stockmen, cook, rouseabout and jackeroo.[57]
>
> …
>
> On pastoral stations Aboriginal women were preyed on by any and every white man whose whim it was to have a piece of 'black velvet' wherever and whenever they pleased.[58]

Academic Fiona Paisley's research on the work of West Australian white women activists in the 1920s and 1930s supports Reynolds' assessment of the predatory culture of white men towards Aboriginal women and children. Paisley notes that some white women activists were very concerned about endemic sexual exploitation and abuse resulting in an increase in mixed-descent children, and were 'convinced of white men's sexual brutality towards defenceless Aboriginal girls and women'.[59] In the 1930s prominent campaigner Mary Bennett emphasised to the press and government officials the extent of this sexual violence:

> We are apt to think … that only a bad white man could molest a native woman, but this is not so. Wherever there is a white man's camp there is a need for protection for these girls. It is the average ordinary white man who is to blame for this trouble.[60]

In 1934 Perth magistrate Henry Moseley headed a Royal Commission into the condition and treatment of Aborigines, hearing evidence from Mary Bennett that for Aboriginal women and girls, sexual abuse was inevitable: 'whether she struggles against degradation to which she is forced, or whether she loses heart and gives up, eventually in nine cases out of ten, despair and disease destroy soul and body'.[61] Moseley, however, refused to accept Bennett's testimony and instead implied that Aboriginal women and girls were promiscuous and lacking in morality: 'intercourse between the white man and the aboriginal woman [exists] to a degree which is as amazing as it is undesirable'.[62] According to the Royal Commission, white men's 'desire for sexual intercourse is uppermost' and this could not be modified by legislation.[63] Moseley and the white colonial government he represented sanctioned the sexual abuse of Aboriginal women and girls. The result was many children of European descent; according to Bennett, 'wealthy squatters, station-managers and others' were equally the fathers, but the attitude of the men responsible for fathering these children was described as one of 'callousness and indifference' whether their children 'live or die'.[64] These were the children targeted by governments under the policy of Aboriginal child removal, and many of them experienced rape, sexual abuse and exploitation just as their mothers had experienced before them.

Former Australian Prime Ministers Paul Keating (in his Redfern Park speech in 1992) and Kevin Rudd (in his Apology to Australia's Indigenous Peoples in 2008) both gave powerful speeches in which they acknowledged the harms of colonisation and the hurt and suffering of the history of the Stolen Generations.[65] However, these profoundly moving public acknowledgments did not refer to the history of sexual violence and abuse of Aboriginal women and children, thereby exemplifying the ongoing way in which this particular aspect of history remains taboo and unspoken.

The history of the Stolen Generations

Prior to the National Inquiry into the Separation of Aboriginal and Torres Strait Islander Children from Their Families in 1997 there had been little recognition by mainstream Australia of the level of abuse inflicted upon Aboriginal families by past government practices. The HREOC inquiry powerfully recognised that Indigenous children were forcibly removed from their families and communities from the very first days of European occupation of Australia, and that not one Indigenous family has escaped the effects of this history.[66] The inquiry concluded that between one in three and one in ten Indigenous children were forcibly removed from their families and communities between 1910 and 1970. The removal of Aboriginal children breached the international prohibition of genocide:[67]

> Indigenous families and communities have endured gross viola-
> tions of their human rights. These violations continue to affect
> Indigenous people's daily lives. They were an act of genocide aimed
> at wiping out Indigenous families, communities and cultures,
> vital to the precious and inalienable heritage of Australia.[68]

Legislation proclaimed to make 'provision for the better protection and care of the Aboriginal inhabitants of Western Australia', instead led to the development of unprecedented 'repressive and coercive state control'.[69] According to legislation the 'Chief Protector' became the legal guardian of all illegitimate children of Aboriginal descent to the age of 16, with the right to move needy or orphaned children from their homes to missions or institutions.[70] In *Renee Baker File #28/E.D.P.*, authors Rene Powell and Bernadette Kennedy show that government policy and legislation was blatantly disregarded, and children were often simply removed or stolen from their mothers and families on the basis of their Aboriginality (in the terms of those days, their 'caste' or colour).[71]

The National Inquiry into the Separation of Aboriginal and Torres Strait Islander Children from Their Families was led by Sir Ronald Wilson and Professor Mick Dodson. It traced the history of legislated Aboriginal child removal throughout Australia, and documented the experiences of the Aboriginal children removed and the overwhelming effects of that removal, even on subsequent gener-ations. The inquiry visited every state and territory of Australia and took evidence (a total of 177 submissions were made) in both public and private sittings from Indigenous people, government and church representatives, former mission staff and many others.[72] It made 54 recommendations directed to 'healing and reconciliation' and urged all Australians to make the journey of reconciliation with 'an open heart and mind'.[73] All parliaments were urged to acknowledge the laws, policies and practices of past removals and to negotiate with Aboriginal people for the purpose of an official government apology.[74]

The inquiry found that although Aboriginal child removal was officially in the best interest of Aboriginal children, the children's experiences of white 'care and protection' were overwhelmingly harsh and very often abusive. Aboriginal children were discouraged from family contact by being told that they were unwanted and rejected, or even that their parents were dead, when this was not true. They were taught to reject their Aboriginality and to feel contempt for Aboriginal people. The conditions they lived under were harsh and they were often not properly clothed, fed or sheltered. Education was only basic even though the promise of a good education was often made to parents as an inducement to relinquish their children. Instead, children were prepared for manual servitude to white people and although wages were often promised to children placed in work environments, many never received payment. Excessive physical punishment and brutality was common, especially for children placed in adopted or foster care.

Aboriginal children were subjected to widespread sexual abuse

The evidence to the HREOC inquiry into the removal of Aboriginal children showed that sexual assault and abuse of Aboriginal children, especially girls, was widespread during this era. The inquiry acknowledged that children in every placement, whether institutional, foster care, adoptive or work, were vulnerable to sexual abuse and exploitation.[75] A total of 17% of females and 7.7% of males reported this experience to HREOC. It was also noted that witnesses were not asked specifically if sexual abuse had occurred and there are many reasons (personal and procedural) why people may have decided not to volunteer this information. Almost one in ten boys and just over one in ten girls told the inquiry that they were sexually abused in children's institutions. For girls, in particular, the risk of sexual assault in foster placement was far greater, with 29.6% of girls in foster placement reporting sexual abuse.[76]

Few Aboriginal people have spoken publicly about the sexual abuse that occurred during this history of Aboriginal child removal. In the late 1980s, Noongar leader Rob Riley powerfully broke the silence that surrounds sexual assault in the Aboriginal community when he publicly named his own experiences at Sister Kate's Children's Home. I remember standing at Sister Kate's in the crowd when Riley spoke to us, and I remember the quiet that went through the crowd. Talking publicly about sexual assault at that time was taboo, especially for an Aboriginal man. Tragically, Riley took his own life later that year. He is still remembered as a Noongar leader, and people even today speak of his fighting spirit and our loss.

Riley was very brave to speak as he did, because I understand from my private discussions with Aboriginal men that sexual assault is especially difficult, if not impossible, for them to speak of. Although Aboriginal men may not be able to speak about the sexual abuse, we must not forget that they were vulnerable and have been impacted terribly. In his profoundly moving account of the Kinchela Boys' Home, Redfern Elder Bill Simon writes about the sexual violence perpetrated against many Aboriginal boys at this home.[77] Simon, who understood that boys later turned on other boys as perpetrators, spoke of the powerlessness of the young victims: 'No one during my time would have been able to discuss this even though it had happened. It would have been too shameful and we would have received a beating for talking about it. No one would have believed us anyway.'[78]

In addition to Riley, other brave former child residents of Sister Kate's have also spoken about the horrific history of sexual abuse and assaults perpetrated upon them as children. Some of their experiences were recorded by HREOC, including the account of Millicent, who was taken to Sister Kate's in 1949 at the age of four, even though she had a loving and happy family environment.[79] At the home, Millicent and her brother were separated. They were told Sunday was the visiting day but they weren't told their family was not allowed to visit. They were told their families did not care for them and they had to forget them. At the home, Millicent was told it was very degrading to be Aboriginal and she should be ashamed of being Aboriginal. The Christian environment was entwined with corporal punishment, including whippings, physical abuse and public humiliation. According to Millicent, 'hurt and humiliation was part of our everyday life and we had to live with it'.[80]

Like other children, Millicent worked hard, caring for the children in the nursery, chopping wood and doing other household chores. In her first year of high school Millicent was sent out to work on a farm as a domestic and was raped by the man of the house.[81] She reported the rape to the Matron, who did not seek help for her but instead washed her mouth out with soap and warned her not to tell the other children.[82] The home sent her back to this farm, where she was repeatedly raped by several perpetrators. The home did nothing about the abuse that it facilitated. Millicent was blamed for her own rapes and told she was a disgrace and 'if anyone knew it would bring shame to Sister Kate's Home'. The rapes led to a suicide attempt, pregnancy and adoption of her baby against her wishes.[83]

I was placed in Sister Kate's Children Home as a child in 1980, well outside the era of the Stolen Generations. I was not at the home very long before I learned that children were being sexually abused and that I had to be careful. During the course of my research, I initiated a meeting with several former residents who were members of the Stolen Generations and who were impacted by abuse at the home. I learned from them that Sister Kate's children (boys and girls) were sent out with single males on weekends, under the permission of the home, and were subjected to sexual abuse. They were sexually abused in the care of families who took them over the weekend for a 'family' experience. Children would make sure they were untidy and dirty when the strangers came visiting, hoping they wouldn't be chosen. This was the 'privilege' and 'training' many of the Aboriginal children received at Sister Kate's, primarily after 1946 and the passing of Sister Kate. As noted by historian Christine Choo, 'the overwhelming memory of children who lived at Sister Kate's Home during this period is of deprivation, drudgery, hard work, cruelty and psychological, physical and sexual abuse'.[84]

Although there had been some legal settlements reached in Australia in relation to abuse of non-Aboriginal children in institutional care, I could find no reported negotiated legal settlements in relation to Aboriginal children. I was shocked to comprehend that (in Western Australia at least) there appeared to have been no civil acknowledgment of the sexual abuse of Aboriginal children in state and religious care. In 2004 I decided to call a meeting with former home residents and it was agreed at this meeting to establish the Sister Kate's Home Kids. We felt that the Church needed to be called to account for the serious abuse that was perpetrated by staff at the

Home and so we began discussions with the Uniting Church, which now held land that was formerly the Sister Kate's Home (for 'Fair Skinned' or 'Nearly White') Aboriginal Children.

After meetings with the Church it was clear it had not implemented the recommendations of the *Bringing Them Home* report, namely Recommendation 41, that churches return lands that were acquired or granted for the purpose of accommodating Indigenous children forcibly removed from their families.[85] I began to work towards reparations for Home Kids, as we negotiated with the Church (and subsequently the Indigenous Land Corporation) for the return of land for the purpose of a healing centre at the former Sister Kate's Children's Home.[86]

The testimony of survivors to HREOC revealed that the sexual abuse of children and young people was common throughout the homes and missions set up to assimilate and 'civilise' the Aboriginal race. There was no relief for the children, as one of my mission-raised aunties told me: 'No one heard our cries in the night.' Many Aboriginal children and young people experienced sexual assault and abuse, an intrinsic part of these genocidal processes. This is not ancient forgotten history. It impacts people even of my generation. Although my own experience of sexual violence was outside the historical era of the Stolen Generations, it is still very much connected. It is simplistic to think that those responsible for abusing children during that era did not continue to abuse other children in institutional care. I am certain that for my generation of Aboriginal people, sexual assault was also a common institutional experience, and persons responsible may well have previously abused children in their care during the era of the Stolen Generations.

Inter-generational trauma and the 'cycle of abuse'

The *Bringing Them Home* report acknowledged the psychological effects of sexual abuse upon children, which identified as confusion about sexual identity and sexual norms, confusion of sex with love and aversion to sex or intimacy, guilt, shame, lowered self-esteem and a sense of being different to others.[87] It cited research describing the effects of child sexual assault as a variant on the recognised psychiatric category of post-traumatic stress disorder, with the reported effects being sleep disturbance, concentration problems, irritability, fear, anxiety, depression and guilt. Common psychological impacts have been manifested in isolation, drug or alcohol abuse, criminal involvement, self-mutilation and/or suicide.[88]

In considering the effects of child sexual assault, HREOC cited research suggesting that:

> approximately one third of child victims of abuse grow up to have significant difficulty parenting, or become abusive of their own children. One third do not have these outcomes but the other third remain vulnerable, and, in the face of social stress there was an increased likelihood of them becoming abusive.[89]

The 'inter-generational effects' identified by HREOC include parenting difficulties, behavioural problems for the next generation, male violence resulting from loss of identity stemming from intrusion into family life and lack of male role models, depression, mental illness and anxiety.[90]

Judy Atkinson has argued that inter-generational trauma and the cycle of trauma is also directly relevant to child sexual assault: 'Well over half of the perpetrators of child sexual assault have been sexually abused as young boys without healing intervention to break the cycle.'[91] She cites research indicating that girls who were sexually abused are at a much higher risk of entering relationships with an abusive partner, and that women who experienced intra-familial child sexual assault also witnessed as children their fathers beating their mothers and/or siblings.[92]

Child sexual assault was recognised as inter-generational by the New South Wales Aboriginal Child Sexual Assault Taskforce (ACSAT) in its 2006 report *Breaking the Silence: Creating the future*.[93] During community consultations ACSAT was told that perpetrators were people who had sexually abused successive generations of children, with participants recalling perpetrators who had abused three generations of children.[94] Participants also suggested child sexual assault was being passed down from generation to generation, with some men who had been abused as children later becoming perpetrators.[95] Further, some women who had been victims of child sexual assault were now grandmothers or mothers who were not protecting their own children, and who saw sexual assault as 'just something you had to go through'.[96] Unfortunately, the report did not consider the impacts of the child sexual abuse associated with the government's child removal practices.

The cycle of abuse theory

Dr Brandt F. Steele, a leading United States psychiatrist and child abuse pioneer, argued in his classic paper 'Psychodynamic factors in child abuse' that the essential ingredient for sexually abusive behaviour is a lack of empathic consideration by the adult for the child, and this lack of empathy is caused by the abusive parent's own childhood history of neglect and abuse.[97] Steele acknowledged there was a taboo in dealing with the common phenomenon of child sexual assault, which he considered was not an isolated phenomenon but, rather, an 'obvious expression of seriously disturbed family relationships, always preceded by emotional neglect or mistreatment'.[98]

Parents who sexually abused children were described as having very much the same characteristics of parents who physically abuse children, namely they suffered from a severe lack of self-esteem, a poorly integrated sense of identity, a tendency towards social isolation, and a history of emotional deprivation, physical abuse and often chaotic family life in their early years.[99] Very often there was an absence of parental figures in early years, particularly fathers, and the child (now parent) had been moved from foster placement to foster placement.[100] Caretakers were often punitive or uncaring, with exposure to 'atypical sexual activities'.[101] Steele argued that as in physical abuse, there is often a history of generational repetition of sexual abuse. He concluded that parents who abuse 'are following understandable and predictable patterns of parent child interaction which has been basically determined by the way they themselves were cared for in their infancy'.[102]

These finding were supported by another leading United States psychiatrist, Roland Summit, in his 1983 seminal paper 'The child sexual abuse accommodation syndrome', which explored the effects of child sexual abuse on victims.[103] Summit believed that rage was a common response for many victims, and for male victims the rage was more likely to turn outwards in aggressive and anti-social behaviour, with depression, violence, misogyny, child molestation and rape described as 'part of the legacy of rage endowed in the sexually abused boys'.[104]

Steele's work continues to be highly considered, but it should be noted that the cycle of abuse theory has been increasingly challenged. Australian child protection expert Professor Chris Goddard has explained that the topic of inter-generational transmission of child sexual abuse is a controversial one.[105] Goddard notes that what appears to be the cause of contention is not the basis of the theory — that people who were abused as children can themselves become perpetrators of abuse — but the rate at which the transmission of abuse may occur.[106] Some experts continue to argue that a history of abuse is a major risk factor for future abusive behaviour; others believe that the probability of inter-generational transmission is overstated.[107]

Australian researcher Cameron Boyd has examined criticisms of the cycle of abuse theory and explains that, notwithstanding the popularity of what is described as the 'victim to offender cycle', the reasons for the dispute are:

- the inconclusive nature of the research about the extent to which victims of sexual abuse go on to sexually abuse
- the broader social and political factors in sexual abuse (such as the role of gender and power) are minimised.[108]

As many commentators have also pointed out, the cycle of abuse theory defies the data in that the majority of victims of child sexual assault are girls, with the perpetrators being overwhelmingly male. Boyd notes an implicit (but often unrecognised) assumption within this theory that boys and not girls will go on to sexually abuse.

The gendered aspects of the cycle of abuse theory were recognised by international trauma expert Dr Judith Herman, who stressed that female survivors are at a greater risk of repeated victimisation later in life: 'The risk of rape, sexual harassment or battering, although high for all women, is approximately doubled for survivors of childhood sexual abuse.'[109] Herman points out that female survivors of child sexual assault are far more likely to be victimised or to harm themselves than to victimise other people.[110]

There is no doubt that the cycle of abuse theory can be readily misunderstood and cause undue and improper stigma and discrimination for child victim survivors, the vast majority of whom (especially women) will never sexually abuse children. The theory is so popular that I once corrected an Aboriginal man who thought that male Aboriginal victim survivors of child sexual assault should automatically be viewed as perpetrators. The implication of inevitability inherent in this theory might 'strike terror into the hearts of boys who have been abused' or become 'a self fulfilling prophecy'.[111]

The cycle of abuse theory is misleading also in that many Aboriginal mothers (and fathers), because of their own experiences of childhood victimisation, have been overprotective of children. One of my Sister Kate's friends recalled how her son, at his twenty-first birthday party, erupted at her because he felt she had 'imprisoned' him growing up with her overprotective ways. She did her best to explain to him that what happened to her could never happen again in her family. I am a mother myself and I know exactly what she means.

The cycle of abuse theory has also been criticised by United States child abuse expert Cathy Spatz Widom, who argues that intergenerational transmission of abuse applies only to a minority of cases, and that most adults who abuse were not abused as children.[112] Spatz Widom argues that the cultural context of violence and the high degree of acceptance of violence in society are also relevant causal explanations. In her view the methodology used in various studies was problematic and she believes that approximately only one-third of individuals who were abused or neglected will abuse their own children, while the majority will not. Furthermore, 'Being maltreated as a child puts one at risk for becoming abusive but the path between these two points is far from direct or inevitable'.[113]

Spatz Widom also provides an important caution that what is often forgotten in this theory is that an exclusive focus on violence can preclude an examination of more subtle forms of emotional damage, including withdrawal, anxiety, depression and suicide.[114] In her view there needs to be more research concerning the role of 'protective factors' to further knowledge of what it is that has worked to protect many children from the adverse effects of abuse and neglect.[115] Spatz Widom's argument clarifies that the cycle of abuse theory can overshadow the internalised consequence of child sexual assault on victims, which is in itself a factor relevant to intergenerational abuse.

According to co-authors Angela Brown and David Finkelhor, depression is the most commonly reported long-term effect on adults sexually abused as children.[116] One empirical study indicates that a significantly higher proportion of mothers abused as children were more likely to have children who were also sexually abused; it was suggested that mothers who had been subjected to sexual abuse and assault as children maintained an emotional and physical distance from their children, potentially 'setting the scene' for the abuse to occur.[117]

Although it has been recognised that there has been a tendency to 'blame' mothers for child sexual assault, Brown and Finkelhor's assessment helps explain the tendency of child sexual assault to be repeated in the next generation. Child sexual assault is a profound psychological, emotional, physical and spiritual harm that can well impact a mother's ability to protect and care for her children, rendering them vulnerable to sexual assault. As with many Aboriginal people, child sexual assault is inter-generational in my family, and I believe my mother's abandonment of her children was related to her own unresolved experience of childhood trauma, including sexual assault. My mother never had the help she needed and was often unable to be loving and protective, and her neglect and abandonment of me as a child certainly 'set the scene' for rape. Offenders often target vulnerable children, presumably because detection and repercussion is less likely in such circumstance.

Notwithstanding the controversy in relation to the cycle of abuse theory, I accept that prior childhood sexual abuse can be relevant to later offending. Boyd's summary of the relevant literature concluded that several psychological mechanisms have been suggested to explain why some victims (predominantly male) have later offended. These include:

- re-enactment of their own abuse
- social learning and modelling (learned from an abusive environment)
- attempts to achieve mastery over negative experiences (that is, a response to trauma — becoming the aggressor to achieve a sense of control and power)
- sexual arousal conditioned by fantasies of abuse.[118]

The psychological explanations are important, but they cannot be viewed in isolation. As emphasised by Steele, the problem is an extremely complex one and 'no simple etiology will explain any one case'.[119] Understanding child sexual assault requires a wider and 'multi-causal' analysis, as articulated by Save the Children: 'Child sexual abuse is related to patterns of thought and behaviour that are shaped by a multitude of forces within families, communities and international society.'[120]

Child sexual abuse reflects structural power imbalances between generations, sexes, classes and races.[121] Within the Aboriginal context, these forces and structural imbalances are very much related to colonisation and its traumatic manifestations.

Aboriginal culture does not sanction sexual violence

Although Aboriginal people have firmly rejected family violence and child sexual assault as caused or excused by traditional culture, several non-Aboriginal commentators have recently suggested this is the case. These commentators directly challenge the view of Aboriginal leaders such as Mick Dodson, who in his 2003 National Press Club address expressly rejected any suggestion that violence is a part of Aboriginal culture: 'We have no cultural traditions based on humiliation, degradation and violation … Most of the violence that Aboriginal communities are experiencing today are not part of Aboriginal tradition or culture.'[122]

Dodson acknowledged that physical punishment was 'not unknown' in traditional culture; however, it was 'highly regulated and governed'.[123] Judy Atkinson agrees, arguing that violence within traditional Indigenous society is better described as 'assertive aggression',[124] according to which there existed structured means by which individuals and groups could express self-restrained anger or distress and processes by which kin could mediate and ensure boundaries so that 'the aggression does not become violence'.[125]

Many non-Aboriginal people have long promoted Aboriginal violence, including child sexual abuse, as a matter of Aboriginal culture. Atkinson recounts her experience working in Queensland Aboriginal communities in the 1980s, where government and white experts dismissed child sexual abuse as 'traditional'. She recalls the standard response from police and senior government people at the time: 'It's cultural. What can we do about it?'[126] Atkinson strongly maintains that violence was not part of Aboriginal culture prior to colonisation, and that Aboriginal law 'ensured all people lived within a set of known precepts that provided clear standards for inter-connecting relationships within both the human and non-human world'.[127] Aboriginal law promoted egalitarianism, generosity and fair dealings; in the words of the famous Australian anthropologist W.E.H. Stanner, it worked to 'unite hearts and establish order'.[128]

The linking of Aboriginal culture to family violence and child sexual assault diminishes the grave harm inflicted on Aboriginal people through colonisation. It effectively undermines the Aboriginal family violence framework that recognises the way in which colonisation systemically deprived Aboriginal people of basic human rights. Violence as Aboriginal culture conveniently blames Aboriginal people for the state of current endemic violence and positions non-Aboriginal society as 'innocent' and (very usefully) without responsibility. In recent years non-Aboriginal academics and commentators, including Joan Kimm, Louis Nowra and Stephanie Jarrett, have argued that violence today is linked to and explained by Aboriginal culture.

Legal author Joan Kimm, in her 2004 book *A Fatal Conjunction: Two laws two cultures*, argues that Indigenous violence is caused by factors within, as well as outside of, Aboriginal culture.[129] In addition to studying numerous court cases, particularly from the Northern Territory, Kimm documents several (non-Indigenous) historical anthropological accounts, making the following observations: 'if traditional society is examined it is apparent that there is a heritage of permissive violence towards women',[130] 'the weight of evidence is that there was considerable violence to women in traditional society from men'[131] and 'The sexual use of young girls by older men, indeed much older men, was an intrinsic part of Aboriginal culture, a heritage that cannot be easily denied'.[132]

Kimm's book usefully records the many cases in which the Australian legal system has sanctioned violence against women and girls on the basis of Aboriginal customary law, but she appears to accept unquestioningly and at face value the evidence put to the courts. Although she acknowledges that Aboriginal women criticise the court's acceptance of customary law claims in relation to violence, she states that she is 'not convinced', and that police, defence lawyers and/or judges cannot 'simply fabricate evidence about customary law' but must rely on evidence presented by male Elders and or anthropologists.[133] Kimm recognises that traditional law has been damaged such that its true context may never be able to be re-established,[134] but she controversially describes Aboriginal women's rejection of the assertion of cultural norms to justify rape as reflective of a 'contemporary and revisionist viewpoint' that does not recognise, for example, the cultural practice of 'sacred rape' that she asserts.[135]

Atkinson's review of *A Fatal Conjunction* is critical of the way in which the book fails to acknowledge how the Western legal system 'has the capacity to re-define, re-construct and re-create culture'.[136] Atkinson argues that Kimm contributes negatively to a re-definition and recreation of what has been constructed as 'traditional customary practice'. The voices of Aboriginal women and men who address violence are discounted, and the book does not acknowledge the 'multiplex and complex layers of colonising impacts to which people … are continuing to be subjected and which contribute to the levels of violence being experienced today'.[137] Atkinson also criticises Kimm for ignoring the history of rape and sexual violence perpetrated by the Christian churches upon Aboriginal children, querying whether it would be at all appropriate to characterise such history as reflective of Christian European 'cultural practices'.[138]

Louis Nowra's 2007 book *Bad Dreaming* supports Kimm's argument in its central premise, that much of the violence and sexual abuse occurring today is linked to Aboriginal culture and that 'Aboriginal men are still using culture to literally get away with rape and murder'.[139] Nowra relates knowledge gained through press statements and his own personal encounters and relations with Aboriginal people during the course of his life in the field of arts. He also provides 'historical' European accounts of horrific rape and violence, some of which are quite sickening and suggest that the writers (for example, Walter Roth, the Chief Protector of Aborigines in Queensland from 1904 to 1906) had no qualms in observing (without intervention) apparent violent gang rapes of young Aboriginal girls.[140]

Nowra repeatedly emphasises European accounts of Aboriginal men's physical and sexual violence (including incest), presenting voyeuristic and arguably pornographic 'historical' accounts as factual.[141] He only briefly recognises the colonial history of violence against Aboriginal women and children: 'Aboriginal women were murdered and raped by white men and were rendered sterile by venereal infections.'[142] Overall, however, the book provides very little acknowledgment of this aspect of history, thereby maintaining the taboo identified by Atkinson. The underlying proposition made by Nowra, that violence and sexual abuse is based in Aboriginal culture, implicitly positions non-Aboriginal men as innocent and having no accountability.

Nowra writes that one of the leading causes of Aboriginal violence is that: 'Women have not only been at the mercy of men's violence, but also captive to the idea that they do not represent Aboriginal culture: that only men do.'[143] Nowra's presumptions here are open to challenge. In particular, he fails to acknowledge the fundamental role of white society in the oppression of Aboriginal women. The reality is that many Aboriginal women represent their culture and in no way consider men to be their cultural superiors; however, Aboriginal women occupy a subordinated position because this is what has been (and still is) imposed as part and parcel of colonisation. Feminist lawyer Jocelynne Scutt argued years ago that: 'Anglo–Australian cultural imperialism was a two-pronged operation. First it ignored traditional Australian culture; it pretended it did not exist. Secondly, simultaneously with that pretence, it sought to impose on Aboriginal culture a vision dictated by the patriarchal nature of anglo-Australian culture.'[144]

Aboriginal academic Dr Irene Watson also identifies the influence of patriarchy within colonial practice and her comments are a useful response to Nowra's claims. Watson writes that Aboriginal women had sovereign laws that were well known and recognised by the men, and the Grandmother's law had a sovereign position.[145] The violence we are witnessing is sourced in invasion and colonisation, which displaced the sovereignty of men and women's laws.[146] Watson considers that there has been an 'unbalanced representation'

of Aboriginal law that leads to the potential for its demonisation —
where individual violence has been represented as a cultural norm.
By contrast, 'the blow torch gaze of the dominant culture … is never
turned back on western civility and its laws, which fail to protect
women from male violence'.[147]

Nowra does not acknowledge Aboriginal women's subjugated
role in Australian society. He suggests that 'Men must be taught that
their behaviour is wrong, just as is happening in non-Indigenous
Australia'.[148] However, oppression of Aboriginal women is still maintained by non-Aboriginal society. The empowerment of Aboriginal
women is critical, and non-Aboriginal society and government have
significant influence in this respect. Nowra calls on Aboriginal men
to acknowledge women's human rights,[149] but Aboriginal women's
human rights are also commonly violated (especially in structural
societal forms) by non-Aboriginal society, so this call must be
made equally across the board. Nowra's ultimate warning — that
Aboriginal men will be responsible for the demise of their own
culture and that they 'continue on the nightmarish trend to cultural
oblivion'[150] — absolves non-Aboriginal society of its role and responsibility in relation to Aboriginal violence.

Nowra's work has understandably been criticised by experts in
Indigenous violence. Aboriginal academic Professor Boni Robertson
points out that Nowra does not seek the views of Aboriginal women,
and his claims about culture lack rigor.[151] She highlights the need for
research concerning family violence and customary law, including
how cultural practices can be strengthened to employ sanctions
against violence.[152] Leading criminologist Professor Chris Cunneen is
even more critical, describing Nowra's book as 'deeply reactionary'
and 'drawing on a range of old and new prejudices about Aboriginal
people in Australia'.[153] Cunneen argues that Nowra has promoted
a fundamental message that 'family violence is the direct effect of
Aboriginal barbarism', and that Aboriginal society is uncivilised
and barbaric and Aboriginal people must therefore modernise and
assimilate.[154]

The argument of violence as Aboriginal culture was continued
by Dr Stephanie Jarrett in her 2009 paper, 'Violence: An inseparable part of traditional Aboriginal culture', in which she states, for
example, that 'The presence of horrific violence both before and

since white contact points to the possibility that Aboriginal culture is the main cause of the seemingly intractable violence that harms many Aboriginal lives'.[155] She fleeting acknowledges the history of violence in the West but argues that the key difference is that Western society has developed (in relatively recent times) effective philosophies and associated political and legal systems that can reduce violence.[156] Jarrett acknowledges the many Aboriginal men and women who are working hard to end violent norms,[157] but she believes that the Aboriginal culture of violence is so strong that the only effective course is for Aboriginal people and communities to adopt mainstream culture 'with its much stronger culture of restraint against violence'.[158]

Jarrett argues that Aboriginal society has not fully denounced (and continues to normalise and accept) violence, and that 'To overcome the chronic violence in the community, we must overcome resistance to acknowledging that profound cultural change is needed'.[159] Jarrett is clearly referring here to Aboriginal cultural change and her comments remind me of the observations of Alice Springs Crown Prosecutor Nanette Rogers, who claimed that 'men's business' in remote Aboriginal communities was according young men such status that they felt they could freely break the law and commit appalling and violent crimes.[160] Rogers describes recent cases she prosecuted, including the horrific and tragic rapes of babies and young toddlers. In her experience as a prosecutor, witnesses were regularly intimidated and reports were not followed up for fear of further violence.[161]

Aboriginal academics, including Dr Dawn Bessarab and Gary Lee, have recognised the way in which Aboriginal culture has been used to justify sexual assault. However, unlike non-Aboriginal commentators, they view this as an abuse and distortion of culture. According to Bessarab, there are some Aboriginal members of the community, including the perpetrator, who will falsely maintain that sexual abuse is a cultural practice.[162] Gary Lee also found that older men had abused their positions of power against children and young people, and sexual assault had been perpetrated within a 'fake cultural context'.[163] Lee states he had counselled boys abused by community Elders for what he described as 'very strange pseudo cultural reason', with abuse described as almost having a 'cultural sanction'.[164]

It is clear that perpetrators (and some community members) have abused and distorted culture to justify sexual abuse of children. As SNAICC recognises, perpetrators of child sexual assault are prone to rationalise and minimise their behaviour, and also fool themselves and others by maintaining a mask of respectability and conformity with others.[165] Sometimes perpetrators are, indeed, Aboriginal men who hold status in Aboriginal law. My understanding, and that of many other Aboriginal people, is that our culture has been broken down and people abusing children are also abusing culture.

I unequivocally reject Jarrett's central proposition of assimilation, particularly on the basis that assimilation is one of the greatest problems facing Aboriginal people today. It is clear that profound cultural change is needed, but non-Aboriginal people need to recognise this must be a societal wide commitment that includes Aboriginal women and children's right to equality and human rights. Jarrett does not see what Irene Watson describes as the *muldarbi* of terra nullius, the ongoing and structured systems of colonisation in which Aboriginal people (in particular, women) have been oppressed, subordinated and deprived of cultural legitimacy and human rights.[166]

In promoting assimilation, Jarrett fails to consider the possible significance of the human right of self-determination for Aboriginal women, and how this is critical to Aboriginal women's ability to address violence and abuse. Jarrett's view that integration (that is, assimilation) is the best recourse supports the offensive notion of white superiority and is unconvincing to Aboriginal women, whose experiences of violence is directly linked to colonisation.

Violence and sexual abuse was not Aboriginal culture in my family

In Western Australia the infamous *Aborigines Act 1905* prohibited intimate relations and marriages between white men and native women, but not for the protection of Aboriginal women and girls. It legislated the practice of racial segregation and apartheid at the same time as it permitted sexual exploitation of Aboriginal women and girls. According to historian Anna Haebich the legal prohibition (based on advice from the then Crown solicitor) was aimed at long-term relationships and not white men's occasional 'visits' to the Aboriginal camps.[167] White men's sexual abuse and exploitation is not ancient history. I recall as a child being warned about the *bunjeymen* who would frequent Aboriginal organisations, such as the Aboriginal Advancement Council on Beaufort Street in Perth, looking for Aboriginal women and girls solely for sexual purposes.

In my own family my loved Granny Ethel Woyung McGlade and her Irish-descent Australian husband Jim McGlade were in a precarious predicament, as their inter-racial marriage was not lawful under the Act. Granny's daughter worked for a farmer who raped her. She became pregnant and left her home and family never to be re-united. I imagine this tore my family apart, especially as the Act meant that their very existence as a family depended on keeping away from the attention of the police and native welfare officers, and maintaining friendly relations with the white people they worked for. There was no complaint they could have made on behalf of their beloved daughter. My grandmother never met her grandson, who was adopted, although some years ago he came to meet my family wanting to know his Noongar ancestry.

In thinking about the arguments made by Kimm, Nowra and Jarrett, I decided to talk with my mother, Mingli Wanjurri McGlade, to understand how she saw these claims about Aboriginal culture. Mingli is a respected Noongar Elder and has also had a 30-year relationship with Aboriginal people of the East Kimberley, who continue to actively practice traditional law and culture. Mingli relayed to me a conversation she had in the 1980s with the late Elder Paddy Roe (who was kind enough to allow my family to live in his community in the early 1980s). She asked him about the belief of Nyigina men towards women. She still remembers his response as he cupped his hands and said to her: 'We have to look after our women. They look after us, they cook for us, they mind us when we're sick, they give us our children. They are *very* precious.'[168]

In her many years of close contact with Mirriwong people of the East Kimberley, Mingli was only ever told that a man beating a woman is very bad, wrong and against the (Aboriginal) law. Mingli also relayed to me the way in which the Catholic male Elders of Turkey Creek (where she had worked) commented to her in passing about 'their promise' (bride) — it was very clear that there had been no consummation or intent to consummate those traditional marriages with young girls. Mingli's experience on law grounds in Broome and Kununurra was that women talk about respect for men's law, and men talk about respect for women's law.

I also spoke with my mother about our own Noongar family ancestry (described by anthropologists as matrilineal) and how we have never considered violence against women or children to be sanctioned by Aboriginal culture. Although my mother was assaulted as a child, she has never seen that as Aboriginal culture, but rather as wrongdoing on the part of the adult responsible.

My Great-Grannie was born in Jerramungup in the late 1890s. She was a most gentle, kind lady and violence was certainly not her culture. There were no traditions of Aboriginal male violence against women and children recorded in the book *My Dusky Friends* by Ethel Hassell, and about my Granny's tribe, stories and practices.[169] My Granny experienced full well the violence of colonisation that denied her citizenship and equality, denigrated her Noongar culture and language, prescribed her loving marriage to a non-Aboriginal man illegal, and seemingly permitted the rape of her daughter by a local white farmer.

In Noongar culture women were always very strong, and sexual violence against children is unimaginable. Pat Baines, an anthropologist who has lived and worked extensively with Noongar women, believes that Noongar people have a powerful perception of womanhood, one that originates from traditional Noongar culture.[170] Baines asserts that contemporary Noongar women have significant female ancestral powers from whom to draw strength, and that womanhood within Noongar identity is not weak or empty, but closely linked to the land and spiritual dreaming. In the south-west of Western Australia, Baines documents what many Noongar people still know to be true, that society was matrilineal, with children following 'in the mother's line'.[171]

Among the Noongar people today the figure of the *moorditj yorga* is still regarded as a clever and strong woman who is especially known for her 'deeds of fierce assertiveness'.[172] Baines acknowledges that the *moorditj yorga* continues to occupy a pivotal role in Noongar society, and that 'The notion of strong and talented women is part of Nyungar cultural representations'.[173] Baines provides the example of *Moodeitj Yorgas (Solid Women)*, a 1988 film produced by Indigenous filmmaker Tracey Moffatt. The production was conceived by a small group of Perth-based Aboriginal women, including myself, who made the decision to actively promote Noongar women as *moorditj yorgas*, not because we are 'cultural revisionists'[174] but because it is what we know to be true from our own knowledge of our history and culture.

Noongar people will also say that we have no words to describe the sexual violence and abuse of children that is occurring today — it is not a part of our culture, but something that has happened as a result of colonisation and the breakdown of our Noongar ways.

The converging factors

Save the Children warns that child sexual assault may 'reach epidemic proportions in a society where a number of converging factors combine and lead to a high rate of violence'.[175] As the United Nations has also recognised, parents play a key role and 'poverty hits children the hardest'.[176] It has a negative impact on children's right to 'participation, to protection from violence, harm and exploitation'.[177] The evidence indicates that child sexual assault has reached epidemic proportions across many Aboriginal communities, and this can be understood by reference to converging factors leading to a high rate of interpersonal violence. This chapter identifies historical factors to increase understanding of sexual assault of Aboriginal children, a serious problem that must be faced.

The ability to improve understanding of Aboriginal child sexual assault is critical. Aboriginal child sexual assault must be located within a historical context that acknowledges the trauma and violence of colonisation, including widespread sexual mythology and sexual violence against women and children. The policies of the Stolen Generations and beyond concerning Aboriginal child removal entailed endemic sexual assault, abuse and exploitation of Aboriginal children and young people throughout Australia. This historical context helps us understand psychological explanations for offending. The cycle of abuse theory is complex, and both non-Aboriginal experts and Aboriginal people have identified the problem of inter-generational abuse, thus linking histories with psychological factors and levels of abuse today.

Traditional Aboriginal society was not utopian and free of violence, but the categorisation of gender-based violence as traditional culture is very problematic. Native American Professor Andrea Smith has also identified this as an Indigenous perception in the United States and describes how colonisation has resulted in internal 'self hatred'.[178] Colonisation has not only impacted Aboriginal law ways; it has also resulted in a form of 'internalised' abuse within Indigenous communities. Perhaps non-Aboriginals should try to imagine the result of a dominant culture perpetuating through successive generations the lie that women and children of your race are good for nothing but sex, and available to be sexually objectified, violated and abused.

Chapter 3

Patriarchy, and women and children's oppression

This chapter explores feminist understandings of child sexual abuse that primarily emphasise power differentials between men, women and children. Within the context of Aboriginal child sexual assault, feminist theories have barely been considered, but this does not mean that feminism is irrelevant to Aboriginal women and children. Feminism may be viewed as a Western concept but my sense is that it is very much akin to the Aboriginal understanding that Aboriginal women 'are bosses ourselves'.[1] At the same time, I acknowledge that Aboriginal women who choose to identify and oppose male dominance and violence in communities can be stigmatised, marginalised and even subjected to violence simply for challenging men's deeply entrenched positions of authority in communities. Aboriginal women are also aware that the feminist movement has been a social movement largely based on the interests of non-Aboriginal women, and typically not including Aboriginal women. Notwithstanding that Aboriginal women's perspectives on feminism are few and far between, I consider such perspectives highly relevant.

This chapter acknowledges feminist perspectives on child sexual assault and explores the resistance to feminist perspectives in analysis of family violence and child sexual assault. In considering this issue I use case studies of important political events, examining the way in which the politics of 'race' have effectively negated violence and oppression against women and children, thereby entrenching (and sanctioning) Aboriginal men's power over, and abuse of, women and children. The two case studies incorporated in this chapter concern the now-defunct Aboriginal and Torres Strait Islander Commission (ATSIC) and the controversy in relation to allegations of sexual violence made against the former Chairperson Geoff Clark, and the Western Australian Government's closure of the Swan Valley Nyungah Community on the basis of child safety concerns. Both case studies show that Aboriginal politics urgently requires intersectional and transformative approaches to oppression, in order to be able to respond properly to Aboriginal child sexual assault and fully protect and respect the human rights of Aboriginal children.

My approach reflects my theoretical positioning as an Aboriginal feminist. According to Aboriginal Canadian feminist Joyce Green, Aboriginal feminism utilises the critique of feminism along with anti-colonialism to show how Aboriginal people, in particular women, are affected by colonialism and patriarchy.[2] Aboriginal feminism takes account of both racism and sexism, and 'Aboriginal feminists are the clearest in linking sex and race oppression'.[3] Aboriginal feminists are therefore identified as political adversaries not only by colonial society, but also by Indigenous male elites whose power they challenge.[4]

A reflection of power inequality

Australian academic Jan Breckenridge has critiqued the theories traditionally developed to explain child sexual assault, and has argued that they failed to analyse the problem in the social context in which it exists.[5] Breckenridge has stated the basic premises of the feminist explanation of child sexual assault as follows:

- the extreme representation of power inequality between men and women, adults and children
- these power relationships are connected with the broader agenda of patriarchy
- the patriarchal social order perpetuates the imbalance of power between men and women and the conditions giving rise to exploitation by men

- child sexual abuse is viewed as an act of power, and as a gendered offence
- feminism's starting point is the experiences of the victims.[6]

In the United Kingdom researcher Catherine Itzin has described child sexual assault as:

> an abuse of adult male power, which has to be understood in the wider context of gendered power relations, of male dominance and female subordination, of sex discrimination and sexual inequality and men's violence against women in the form of 'domestic violence' and sexual violence such as sexual harassment, sexual assault and rape.[7]

Consistent with these approaches, United States Professor Catharine MacKinnon argues that 'Sexual assault is sex based violation' and that 'sexual abuse is systematically inflicted by and on people who are socially gendered unequal to one another'.[8] MacKinnon describes sexual assault as propelled and motivated by forces of hierarchy, not biology, which explains the fact of biological female aggressors, as well as biological male victims and victims of both sexes.[9] As MacKinnon points out, many men do not use sexual aggression, and race and class are often relevant to victimisation. Sexual assault is based on social and political inequality and made possible in unequal societies because of the 'hierarchy of relations' between the parties.[10] MacKinnon defines rape as 'a crime of sexualised dominance on the basis of sex (which often includes sex and age, sex and race, sex and class variously combined and pyramided) that is legally unrecognised as such'.[11]

MacKinnon's interpretation of sexual violence is, as she identifies, supported by international authorities including the General Assembly of the United Nations, the Committee on the Elimination of Discrimination against Women and the Beijing World Conference on Women, which have all defined and condemned sexual violence as a gender-based function of unequal social power between the sexes.[12]

Child sexual assault and the family violence framework

While feminism (and also international human rights law) has framed an understanding of child sexual assault as linked to men's power over women and children, Aboriginal understandings of child sexual assault fall within the framework of 'family violence', which tends not to emphasise issues of gender inequality. This is clear from the comments of criminologist Dr Harry Blagg, who describes the family violence paradigm as representing a significant paradigm shift — in both theory and practice — away from the domestic violence paradigm with its emphasis on patriarchal power and 'narrow focus on criminalisation as the main response'.[13] According to Blagg, the family violence paradigm stresses the 'collective Indigenous experience of powerlessness and, at the level of practice, leans towards finding pathways to family healing, rather than new routes into the criminal justice system'.[14]

My concern is that such understandings of family violence minimise the harm of child sexual assault and inhibit understanding of the dynamics of child sexual assault, particularly the very real power imbalances that exist between predominantly adult male perpetrators and the children they victimise. The family violence framework also emphasises a collective Aboriginal experience based on racial discrimination and oppression; however, child sexual assault, although widespread and an aspect of the collective experience, has not been experienced universally in the same way as racism. Perhaps this can help to explain why, within the wide field of family violence, there can sometimes appear (contradictorily) little knowledge or interest in relation to child sexual assault. Also, sexual assault, especially child sexual assault, is a taboo subject and one that can be readily overlooked or made 'invisible' within the generic family violence paradigm.[15] My own way of addressing this difficulty is to name explicitly 'family violence and child sexual assault'. This also resolves the associated problem that child sexual assault may not even fall within the definition of family violence because offenders can often be people who are unrelated.

In 1992 Breckenridge expressed her concern that the family violence concept obscures the gendered nature of sexual violence and implicates all members of the family in the violence.[16] In relation to child sexual assault, most perpetrators are men; however, this does seem to be overlooked within the concept of family violence. I do not negate the important recognition that violence within

Indigenous communities is often 'family' based, but men's use of violence against women is generally most serious (resulting in very high homicide rates for Aboriginal women), and men are also overwhelmingly responsible for child sexual assault.

In emphasising gender inequality, feminists have articulated a 'continuum of male violence', arguing that violence against women and children is directly linked. In Australia it is clear that Aboriginal women are experiencing high levels of domestic or 'family' violence, including homicide, and that children are also experiencing high levels of child sexual assault. The co-existence of these twin problems supports feminist theory that a continuum of male violence exists, and that violence against women and children (including child sexual assault) is not distinct and separate, but inherently linked.

While the family violence paradigm importantly stresses Aboriginal collective disempowerment, it is also essential to recognise the role of gender, gender oppression and inequality. The family violence discourse, however, does not acknowledge Aboriginal women and children's distinct experiences of inequality and oppression within both the Aboriginal and wider society. Only rarely is gender recognised. One notable exception is recognition by the former Aboriginal and Torres Strait Islander Social Justice Commissioner Tom Calma, that 'Family violence is fundamentally an issue of gender equality'.[17]

One reason why gender is ignored concerns the traditional and dominant formulation of race politics (based largely on male privilege and power), which has tended to negate the gendered implications of race for Aboriginal women. Therefore, we see popular 'gender blind' assessments of Aboriginal family violence being made. Consider the following, made by the Australian Domestic and Family Violence Clearinghouse, which comments on the federal government's response to issues of child sexual assault in communities:

> Problems of family violence and child sexual abuse have their foundation in chronic Indigenous disadvantage, past and present removal of children from families, racism and a lack of basic infrastructure and services. They are also closely linked to drug and alcohol abuse.[18]

Unfortunately, the harsh reality of violence experienced by Aboriginal women and children is also related to gender and gendered oppression, which is minimised and even rendered invisible within such family violence understanding. This presents a significant problem in addressing the violence, because the root causal factors are not adequately identified and understood.

Racism has been accorded primacy

While the role of gender is negated, there is an entrenched and longstanding perception that racism is the primary form of discrimination and human rights violation being experienced by Aboriginal people. This is aptly captured in the statement made some years ago by Jackie Huggins and other Aboriginal women, who declared that 'Sexism does not and will never prevail over racial domination in this country'.[19] Subsequently, Aboriginal legal academic Professor Larissa Behrendt argued that a theory of male dominance is 'essentialist' and for Aboriginal women the issues are predominantly centred on race because of the influence of racism: 'The fact that we can feel our Aboriginality more strongly than our gender is a reflection that the repercussion of racism in Australia are often greater than those of sexism.'[20]

Blagg has interpreted such perspectives as representative of a universal Aboriginal wisdom:

> Aboriginal men, Aboriginal women, Aboriginal children tend to view themselves as Aboriginal first — the core of their identities adheres within their Aboriginality with its demands, obligations and unique collective experiences. While acknowledging the impact other forms of disadvantage … [has] on their life paths and life chances, they tend to see the core issues revolving around their status as Aboriginal people and attempts by the state to (variously) eliminate, restructure and reconstitute this Aboriginal identity.[21]

In making such identity claims Blagg claims to speak on behalf of Aboriginal women — adopting the position of 'speaking for' Indigenous women. His articulation of Aboriginal identity is constructed largely as gender and age neutral, but my own perspective as an Aboriginal woman is that in practice male representation and male experiences are most commonly the measure and yardstick of 'Aboriginality'. Within this predominantly male- (and adult) -defined construct of Aboriginality, the state is the violator of Aboriginal human rights, and human rights are primarily defined as Aboriginal/state conflicts, such as black deaths in custody and land rights. Issues relating to gender-based oppression and violence, and the especially powerless position of children, are simply not acknowledged. Racism is posited as the key experience of discrimination and sexual violence is able to easily remain hidden within such constructions of Aboriginal identity.

Gender-based human rights violations of women and children, and in particular child sexual assault, are extremely 'difficult' for Aboriginal women because this often involves criticising the abuse of power by men who are not only members of one's own racially oppressed community, but by virtue of gender very often occupy structural positions of power over Aboriginal women. Aboriginal women are fully aware that key powerbrokers in Aboriginal communities are men, and sanctions are invoked against women who dare to criticise men and refuse to play by men's rules. It has been made clear to me many times that powerful Aboriginal men may be hostile to Aboriginal women who speak critically against men's oppression and violence.

Some years ago Aboriginal writer Melissa Lucashenko noted that, although many individual black women had struggled to highlight issues of rape, domestic violence and child abuse, black male leadership had not given priority to the views of black women, and there was 'widespread denial' among Aboriginal communities about these issues.[22] Some issues, such as land rights, police brutality and poverty, are 'palatable issues for debate' because they do not require any analysis of power relations within the black community itself. Aboriginal women speaking about men's violence (rather than the actual violence being perpetrated) is controversial and threatening. In my experience, Lucashenko's description of this dynamic is apt today:

> In the situation in which Black men are dispossessed, brutalised by police, and generally as poor and unhealthy as Black women,

it is seen as unproblematic in the Black community for Black women to 'talk up' about the injustices of the State. Talking about the bashings, rapes, murders and incest for which Black men are themselves responsible, however, is seen as threatening in the extreme.[23]

Within Aboriginal rights discourse, few women are prepared to speak about Aboriginal men's violence; however, it should not be presumed that silences mean that gender is not relevant — rather, the opposite. The results can be extreme for the individual woman. Sometimes women are threatened with violence. Aboriginal women prepared to speak against men's violence very often experience intimidation, marginalisation and isolation. This partly explains why relatively few Aboriginal women are active in the violence against women movement. Marcia Langton acknowledged 'the ability of men to use force, in the final analysis, to preserve male dominance in ideology, in structures and relationships. This was so in traditional times and remains so, but in vastly changed circumstances'.[24]

For Aboriginal women, especially those unprotected by factors such as social class, speaking against male violence can be very risky business. Consider Merrillee Mulligan, beaten to death in Derby with a rock by a man after she opposed and threatened to expose his sexual abuse of a girl.[25] Merrillee's death was not considered significant by the criminal justice system; just another Aboriginal case of 'manslaughter', with the defendant sentenced to a two-year jail term.[26] Or Susan Taylor, the 15-year-old found hanging in the Lockridge Aboriginal community only two weeks after filing a police complaint of violence and sexual abuse. Was it racism that killed them? Was their gender really so marginal? Gender-related crimes of violence are horrifyingly common in Aboriginal families and lived experiences, but politics largely dictates silences and the silencing of women and children in relation to such violence.

I have heard an Aboriginal male leader claim (apparently on behalf of women) that the state (presumably as opposed to Aboriginal men) is the greatest offender of Aboriginal women's human rights. Such claims also reflect the conceptualisation of Aboriginal human rights as influenced by the gendered nature of international human rights law. As Professors Hilary Charlesworth and Christine Chinkin have argued, the primacy traditionally given to civil and political rights (known as 'first generation rights') was 'directed towards protection for men within public life and their relationships with government'.[27] Violence against Aboriginal women and children is not properly recognised within the rights framework that reflects the traditional public/private dichotomy of international human rights law and accords primacy to state-based civil and political human rights violations.[28]

Charlesworth and Chinkin also argue that violence against women should be seen not as aberrant behaviour of individuals, but as 'part of a structure of the universal subordination of women'.[29] Moreover, according to MacKinnon, the law of sexual assault cannot be regarded as private action, because the lack of equal protection of the law for women means that the state is also a violator of women's human rights.[30] However, when Aboriginal men claim that the state is the greatest violator of Aboriginal women's human rights, they minimise gender-based violation rather than the necessity of its recognition as a matter of human rights.

Aboriginal lawyer Heather Sculthorpe recognised years ago that it was 'not fashionable' to demand that women's interests be given priority. She argued against the common view that Aboriginal men suffer just as much as their abused victims, urging caution lest such 'fallacy becomes another myth which we will start to believe against all evidence in the same way that we were previously led to believe it was only white men who mistreated Aboriginal women or that sexual abuse did not exist in Aboriginal communities'.[31] Sculthorpe's warning that gender is indeed relevant, has not been promoted within family violence frameworks or the wider body of Aboriginal human rights discourse. This situation is not confined to the domestic but is interlinked with the international Indigenous rights discourse. Although the *Declaration on the Rights of Indigenous Peoples* affirms the equality of rights for men and women, emphasis is still primarily centred on Indigenous/state conflicts, rather than the issue of gender-based human rights violations. This is evident from the 2009 United Nations report *State of the World's Indigenous People*, in which little attention is given to the issue of violence against women and in which violence against women is positioned as a matter of colonisation (unrelated to gender inequality) and environmental degradation:

One health problem that Indigenous women are disproportionately affected by is violence, ranging from domestic violence … to violence against women through their forced displacement from their ancestral lands. It is inextricably linked to violations of the collective rights of indigenous peoples and colonization, because Indigenous women play a central role as bearers of collective traditional knowledge and as stewards of the collective ancestral lands, waters and other natural resources. In this sense, Indigenous traditions and Indigenous women themselves identify women with the Earth and therefore perceive degradation of the Earth as a form of violence against women. This conviction is more than a metaphorical allusion to Mother Earth. It is rooted in indigenous cultural and economic practices in which women both embody and protect the health and well-being of the ecosystems in which they live.[32]

This brief mention of violence against Indigenous women in a 250-page report is consistent with the popular conceptions of Indigenous human rights, notwithstanding the important equality principle enshrined in the *Declaration on the Rights of Indigenous Peoples*.[33] Within Indigenous international human rights discourse issues are routinely not presented in a fair or representational matter reflecting the severity of the human rights violation at stake, but, rather, consistently with traditional, societal and ideological constructions that favour existing power relations very much defined by and in favour of Indigenous men — to the disadvantage of women and children.

Aboriginal men have been most impacted by colonisation?

Aboriginal lawyer Pat O'Shane once claimed that since colonisation Aboriginal women have occupied positions of dominance in the family and leadership in Aboriginal communities, whereas Aboriginal men have occupied a 'rock bottom' status, having 'lost both their status and self respect'.[34] O'Shane's view that Aboriginal men have been most impacted by colonisation has become widely accepted, although it has been challenged on several occasions. In 1991 Audrey Bolger rejected this claim:

There is no doubt that colonisation has been destructive to Aboriginal men. Aboriginal women recognise this and say they are sorry for their men and understand their frustrations and anger. But it has been equally destructive to Aboriginal women. To deny this is to ignore those who were raped and humiliated by white men or who had their children removed from their care by white bureaucrats.[35]

The myth that Aboriginal men have been most impacted by colonisation continues to be repeated, most recently by researchers Janet Stanley, Adam Tomison and Julian Pocock: 'cultural disintegration and accompanying role loss has particularly hurt Indigenous men. In contrast to Indigenous women's roles, male roles have changed significantly in the past 200 years, becoming marginalised, with an accompanying loss of place and status.'[36]

Most recently a report by Joy Wundersitz for the Australian Institute of Criminology (AIC) also discusses colonisation and its aftermath as causing the particular marginalisation of Indigenous males, and thus accounting for the high rates of offending for Indigenous men (as compared to Indigenous women).[37] According to the AIC report, Aboriginal men's use of violence (including sexual abuse of children) is linked to their particular disempowerment flowing from colonisation.[38] The report says Aboriginal women hold a 'more socially secure position within Indigenous communities' but recognises that Aboriginal women were 'not entirely risk free'.[39] This discussion by Wundersitz is understandable in view of the longstanding position that Aboriginal men have been most impacted by colonisation. However, the AIC is well aware that non-Indigenous males similarly have high offending rates in comparison to non-Indigenous females. As AIC acknowledges, Indigenous women have very high rates of violent offending, and quite shockingly the violence offence rate for Indigenous females is five times as high as that of non-Indigenous males.[40] Appropriately, AIC notes that 'There has been a tendency to focus responses and intervention on Indigenous males while paying less attention to the violent offending of Indigenous females. Yet these data suggest that the incidence and nature of violent behaviour by Indigenous females requires closer scrutiny'.[41]

The AIC report identifies the direct link between a female offender's experience of childhood sexual abuse and later violent offending, and that this occurs regardless of race, as all females impacted by child sexual assault are at higher risk of violent offending during adulthood.[42] Indigenous and non-Indigenous women who experienced child sexual assault were 1.6 times as likely to become violent adult offenders. For all offenders (men, women, Aboriginal and non-Aboriginal), more extreme exposure to child sexual assault is linked to higher levels of suicide and self-harm.[43]

The claim that men have been more impacted and marginalised by colonisation is problematic, in that it can be readily used in a detrimental 'excusatory' manner in relation to family violence and child sexual assault. Offensively, within the claim, Aboriginal women can also be regarded as responsible for marginalising Aboriginal men. For example, according to feminist commentator Germaine Greer, 'When hunter gatherer societies begin to break down, it is invariably the gatherers, the women, who combine to hold them together, but in doing so they further marginalise their menfolk, including their own sons'.[44]

Aboriginal women are the fastest growing prison population in Australia, and are 'incarcerated at a rate higher than any other group in Australia'.[45] Aboriginal women suffer extreme rates of violence, including violence resulting in homicide. They are also experiencing mental health issues that are reaching epidemic proportions. A 2008 report concerning hospital admissions for interpersonal violence, victimisation and mental illness in Western Australia from 1990 to 2004, shows an ever-increasing rate of hospitalisation for Indigenous females, one that is 'consistently higher than Indigenous males since 1998'.[46]

The grave harms suffered by Aboriginal women as part of the colonisation processes should not be underestimated. Colonisation was patriarchal and the implications, including violence, were gendered in nature: 'Patriarchal colonisation brought with it particular forms of violence that promoted, in turn, powerlessness in colonised groups. Patriarchal colonisation also restructured the gender relationships in colonised groups, to exemplify the structural relations of the colonisers.'[47]

The constant revival of the myth that Aboriginal men suffered most from colonisation arguably reflects existing power relations that seek to maintain and support the unequal position of Aboriginal women and children. The positioning of Aboriginal men as primarily impacted by colonisation lends support to justice claims for Aboriginal men, more so than Aboriginal women and children.

Case study: ATSIC and allegations of sexual abuse

In this case study concerning my experiences at ATSIC, I highlight the ways in which Aboriginal men's justice claims are routinely (almost 'naturally') prioritised at the expense of women and children's fundamental human rights. Within Aboriginal politics the parameters of 'race' are prioritised over Aboriginal women and children's experiences of violence, particularly sexual violence. Aboriginal men's experiences of racial oppression are privileged to the detriment of Aboriginal women and children. This was made very clear to me when I worked for ATSIC, and at the time of the controversy surrounding the then ATSIC Chairperson, who in 2001 was publicly named by media as a perpetrator of sexual assault.[48]

At ATSIC I encountered the dominant male culture of the organisation, notwithstanding that ATSIC was supposed to be an organisation based on the fundamental human rights principle of self-determination for all Aboriginal people — men, women, children and Elders. ATSIC was established by the federal government in 1990 and described as 'a radical shift towards self-determination'.[49] However, the extent of the right of self-determination was ambivalent. In reality ATSIC was overwhelmingly a male organisation and women and children were without independent voice. Issues such as family violence and child sexual assault appeared to be off limits — even in the 'Indigenous rights' section where I worked. This male-dominant culture of ATSIC prevailed, notwithstanding that a number of Aboriginal women held senior posts with ATSIC.

When ATSIC was established it had its own women's department — and women's interests were clearly a part of the organisation — but in 1997 and as a result of government budget cuts (based on antagonism to Aboriginal rights by the former Howard government), the ATSIC Board (overwhelmingly male) decided the appropriate course of action was to close the Office of Indigenous Women.[50] In 2001, at the time of my engagement with ATSIC, I was shocked that women's affairs had been relegated to the part-time job of one lower-level staff member. Women's 'rights' were virtually non-existent, while international human rights (in particular, international travel) and a treaty were given high priority. Under ATSIC, the peak decision makers of Aboriginal Australia were men. Very few Aboriginal women participated at a senior level and, as the Board's decision to close the Office of Indigenous Women demonstrated, women's interests were easily overridden.

ATSIC's organisational culture reflected wider gender relations in which Aboriginal women did not hold an equal status to men. As I took part in treaty consultations across Australia, Aboriginal men tended to dominate. Becoming unsettled by women's margina-lity in the discussions, I began talking more to Aboriginal women about what a treaty might mean for them. At a meeting in Broome quite a few women attended, but were fairly quiet on the issues that ATSIC's male leaders had defined as treaty topics (for example, land rights and constitutional reform). As I engaged them in the discussions, they expressed their very real concerns about family violence, women's oppression and displacement; as one senior lady said, 'Aboriginal woman must be restored to her rightful place'.

My own experiences were confirmed by an ATSIC review, in which the women's advisory committee considered the imbalance of women's representation at senior levels. The imbalance meant that less attention was given to issues related to families and women, particularly the issue of family violence and child abuse.[51]

On 14 June 2001, I was shocked to read the headline of a Melbourne *Age* article — 'Geoff Clark: power and rape' — that claimed the ATSIC Chairperson, with whom I had a close role in relation to the treaty project, had been a rapist, a serial perpetrator of sexual violence. The front-page article by Andrew Rule reported sworn allegations that the ATSIC Chairperson had led a series of sexual assaults against a number of women in the 1970s and 1980s. The assaults allegedly carried out by Clark upon four women, including one Aboriginal woman who was his cousin and a child at the time of the alleged assault, were reported in horrific detail.

I soon began to reconsider my position working for the treaty project, but it seemed that I was in the minority. When the *Age* story was published, Aboriginal women employees and highly paid independent 'rights' experts alike were among Clark's strongest supporters, and they made their views well known. The sworn testimony of the four women who had detailed violent sexual assault was rejected as 'bullshit' or considered with no interest, let alone sympathy. A few Aboriginal women felt differently but we understood it was best to keep our views to ourselves.

After the *Age* publication all staff members received an official email memorandum from the ATSIC Board in which clear support for the Chairperson was shown — with the implicit message that we were also expected to show support. The Board's formal response drew heavily from a statement issued by the Criminal Bar Association, an overly legalistic response that argued that 'the truth or otherwise of the allegations is not the point' and that the 'due process of the law' was the 'best guarantee of achieving dispassionate and balanced resolution of conflict'.[52]

Clark denied the allegations: 'My only crime is that I am an Aboriginal and I have had the audacity to question the legitimacy of this country, to question the treatment of Aboriginal people … and I have called for a treaty.'[53]

Clark also had the support of socialists, as indicated by the *Green Left Weekly* article, 'What's behind the media campaign against Geoff Clark?': 'Opponents of racism should defend Clark's right to remain as ATSIC chairperson against what is clearly a political campaign waged by the capitalist media to discredit him and to force him to resign as head of ATSIC.'[54]

Surprisingly, one of Clark's strongest supporters was the New South Wales Aboriginal magistrate Pat O'Shane, who publicly declared to journalists that on the basis of her judicial experience 'a lot of women manufacture a lot of stories against men'.[55] O'Shane implied that there was a conspiracy against Clark and agreed with his claim that the *Age* article was racially motivated.[56] O'Shane was criticised by Boni Robertson, who said that she had not only cast aspersions on the victims of violence but also raised real questions about the impartiality of the courts.[57]

The Aboriginal response was very sympathetic to Clark — prominent Aboriginal people, both male and female, supported and publicly defended Clark. The allegations were diminished as 'trial by media', with the ATSIC Deputy Chairperson Ray Robinson categorising the *Age* story as 'against human rights'.[58]

I am not aware that any Aboriginal men or women publicly called upon the Chairperson to stand down pending criminal investigation. Some Aboriginal people must have held serious concerns, but censorship, fear and intimidation can run strong in male-dominated Aboriginal political spheres. Clark's most public criticism came from non-Aboriginal newspaper columnist Margo Kingston, who, in a series of articles questioning ATSIC's oppressive gender and race dynamics, pointed out that sexual misconduct claims swirled around senior ATSIC male officials.[59] Kingston also argued that there was a culture of silence and inaction in relation to family violence and the organisation should be disbanded: 'It's time to stop messing around. ATSIC must be overhauled, the cover-up must end and a fresh, new Aboriginal body put in place to lead the fight for the safety of Aboriginal women and children.'[60]

I am sure that many Aboriginal women have shared similar sentiments, and I know first-hand the repercussions that Aboriginal women who have criticised Aboriginal men's domination and violence are likely to experience.

The Victorian police did not lay charges, stating that as the alleged rapes happened so many years ago there was insufficient evidence to support convictions.[61] In 2007 Clark was found guilty in civil court proceedings of raping Carol Stingel, who had contacted police after reading the *Age* and the disclosures by Clark's cousin Joanne McGuinness. Stingel and McGuinness were pictured leaving the court together, jubilant at the long-awaited outcome.[62]

Professor Kimberle Williams Crenshaw's analysis of the Mike Tyson rape trial in the United States noted similar themes at play; for example, the vilification of the black rape victim and the 'long standing practice of using anti-racist rhetoric to deflect the injury suffered by black women victimised by black men'.[63] Crenshaw noted that black leaders were not alone in their failure to empathise with or support the black rape victim, and that black women were among the staunchest supporters and critics of the victim. She surmised that women distanced themselves from the rape victim as a way to deny their own vulnerability to rape, and also as resistance to feminist analysis because it conflicts with longstanding narratives that have viewed black men as the primary victims of sexual racism (highlighted by the history of lynching).[64]

A commentary by Dr Maria Bargh from a Maori perspective also offers insights into the issues raised by this case. In her article 'Hypocrisies', she questions how male violence flourishes in the Tino Rangatiratanga movement that purports to struggle for self-determination, peace and justice.[65] Bargh asks, 'Why are the perpetrators of rape and violence allowed to continue, and achieve, including in leading positions in "the movement"?' She shares her close observation that we are undermining our own wellbeing and interests when we unquestionably accept male violence and abuse as part of the rights movement:

> For a long time I personally had come to the decision that there are so few of us who 'believe' in 'the movement' that we must surely stick together despite hypocrisy. It has been argued for so long that we have bigger 'enemies', like the Pakeha dominated government or Neoliberalism, or capitalism itself. These are perceived and openly criticised as being the main enemy of 'the movement'. Certain events have led me to a different conclusion, however: a conclusion where 'the movement' is actually irreversibly tainted by the acceptance of perpetrators of rape and violence, un-punished, un-seen to and un-named, an enemy within.[66]

Having worked for Aboriginal male leaders who I believe committed serious human rights violations against women and children, I also see the Aboriginal rights movement as too often tainted with hypocrisy. I agree with Bargh that within a context of anti-racism, gender-based human rights abuses and violations can go readily 'un-punished, un-seen and un-named'. The retort of the ATSIC Chairperson that the rape allegations were racially motivated was significant because within the context of this entrenched rights hierarchy, his 'trump card' of race was critical to silencing those concerned about women's and children's human rights.

Case study: the closure of the Swan Valley Nyungah Community

Since colonisation non-Aboriginal men and women have exercised power over Aboriginal people. In some instances non-Aboriginal society has supported decisive actions to protect Aboriginal children, and I consider the decision of the Western Australian Government in 2003 to close the Swan Valley Nyungah Community (SVNC) one such decision. However, the circumstances surrounding the closure also highlight the tension inherent in the government's decision to act in a protective manner towards Aboriginal children. From this case study it is evident that this decision resulted in considerable backlash on the part of non-Aboriginal men and women and political institutions. This case study clearly highlights the tensions at play in the wider non-Aboriginal society in relation to sexual violence and abuse of Aboriginal children and illustrates my argument that Aboriginal women and children's human rights interests are not accorded priority over rights that have been traditionally associated with the rubric of race.

The decision to close the SVNC followed abuse allegations and the deaths of several children and youths. The government's action in the interests of children and young people resulted in a Legislative Council political inquiry that paid little regard to Aboriginal children's experience of sexual assault and violence.

The decision followed the inquest into the death of a young Noongar girl, Susan Taylor, and advice by governmental representatives (including senior Aboriginal representative Mick Gooda, then state ATSIC manager) that there was an unacceptable risk of safety to women and children at the SVNC. This risk included allegations of sexual abuse to children, domestic violence, substance abuse and intimidation of residents to prevent the reporting of these incidents to the authorities.[67]

According to an ABC *Lateline* program, Gooda's 'first big test came as Head of ATSIC in [Western Australia], when he chose to confront one of the great taboo subjects of Aboriginal Australia … [and] took the huge step of agreeing with the then Premier … Geoff Gallop, that the Swan Valley Camp had to be closed down'.[68] Gooda noted that 'the sovereignty issue comes second, third or fourth, somewhere down the list' when it came to the issue of 'safety of women and children [which] are probably the most important thing'.[69]

In response to the closure, the Greens WA instigated a parliamentary inquiry that concluded that the government's decision to close the SVNC was politically motivated and linked to concerns about 'public perceptions' in relation to its commitment to the issue of Aboriginal child abuse raised by the Gordon Inquiry (Putting the Picture Together: Inquiry into Response by Government Agencies to Complaints of Family Violence and Child Abuse in Aboriginal Communities).[70] The inquiry was very much divided along political lines, with the Greens and Liberal parties aligned, and the Australian Labor Party (ALP) members in disagreement.

The conclusion of the Inquiry that the closure was 'politically motivated' was inconsistent with significant evidence of abuse, violence and risk to children and young people at the SVNC. The government bodies charged with child protection also seemed incapable of protecting children at this community, as the inquiry documented and as reported by Jane Brazier, a senior departmental child protection representative:

6.62 Ms Brazier told the Committee that a child who had witnessed the rape of the two and a half year old toddler at the camp in April 2000 had also alleged the same perpetrators had sexually abused him. He alleged that he had also been sexually abused by another camp resident. The child witness had identified 10 children whom he considered were also being either physically or sexually abused at the SVNC.

6.63 These matters had come to Ms Brazier's attention due to the failure by DCD [Department of Community Development] to follow up the initial police interview with the child that took place in August 2001. The purpose of this interview was to obtain a statement of evidence for the prosecution of the two perpetrators. The police statement included allegations of the child's abuse. Prior to this interview the child witness also identified the 10 children to a DCD caseworker who took notes of the allegations. After an eighteen-month delay in following up these issues, DCD attempted to re-interview the child witness in late February 2003 after removing him from his school. Although the child witness acknowledged that he had made the previous disclosures, he did not wish to discuss those matters further.

6.64   Ms Brazier advised the Committee that she commissioned an independent inquiry into her department's failure. The report found that the 'window of opportunity' for a useful second interview had passed as a result of DCD delayed response. A principal reason was that the child witness returned to live at the SVNC with a person who he had identified as one of his abusers and therefore was not in a safe and secure place, well removed from the situation in which the alleged abuse had occurred.[71]

These specific child protection concerns should be viewed in light of the evidence to the Gordon Inquiry that the government's child protection body (then DCD) did not respond in a timely fashion to reports concerning Aboriginal children.[72] Statistical evidence supported this complaint by showing a slower rate of completion of investigations concerning Aboriginal and Torres Strait Islander children.[73] An independent DCD inquiry (written by child protection expert Rosemary Cant) confirmed that the DCD had not given enough priority to the allegations made by the child: 'Given the number of children and perpetrators allegedly involved, a task-force type response should have been considered immediately after the first interview. Instead, it was treated as a normal child maltreatment investigation and after the first interview was not accorded a particularly high priority'.[74]

Poor or negligent responses significantly impede, if not make impossible, an appropriate response by the criminal justice system. The delay in the case meant that those responsible for criminally abusing children would never be held to account, nor would children be recognised as victims and provided with the necessary support.

One has to ask what role the children's Aboriginality played in the department's failure. In addition to the children's identity, it should also be acknowledged that Robert Bropho, the influential male leader of the community, exercised considerable control over access to the SVNC.[75] According to evidence provided by Ms Brazier, there was 'a difficult relationship' between the department and the SVNC that resulted in a lack of contact between the Department and the SVNC.[76]

The findings of the government's ALP members (in minority) are a far more sensitive response to Aboriginal child sexual assault. These members acknowledged the subtle (but significant) power relationships that exist between perpetrators and child victims. They identified the marginalisation of victims and the understanding that disclosure may have severe consequences. It was accepted that in an environment of abuse, intimidation and violence, disclosing was no simple feat. The practice adopted whereby police and child protection were required to first report to the SVNC office (and Robert Bropho and/or his supporters) might well be seen as 'gate keeping', an affirmation of power by perpetrators over victims, and as undermining the confidence of victims in seeking support from such persons.[77]

The inquiry failed to acknowledge the serious problem inherent in supporting senior male perpetrators' governance and authority over small communities. This problem was recognised by the inquiry's ALP minority members, who noted that Aboriginal women advocates ensured that 'significant evidence regarding the history of sexual abuse and violence' came before the committee for its consideration.[78] The Greens and Liberals did not acknowledge these Aboriginal women advocates, who told me that they had stood silently outside the Western Australian Parliament to support the closure of the SVNC on the grounds of safety to children. I have no doubt from my observations and experiences that these women knew the community well and the accusation that the closure of SVNC was 'politics' was inaccurate. In my view there was a great deal of 'politics' associated with the report of the inquiry.

At the time the report was handed down, Robert Bropho was charged — but not convicted — of child sexual assault offences. From the media release issued by Greens WA members Robin Chapple (who instigated the Senate inquiry), it was clear that the Greens were concerned that the decision to close the community was made on the basis of what they described as 'unsubstantiated' allegation of child sexual abuse.[79] At this particular point in Noongar history, the prosecution of Noongar male perpetrators of sexual assault was virtually unknown. This was not helped by the Greens' attitude of disbelief against Aboriginal child victims, which was inconsistent with the sympathy they were willing to extend to (some)

rape victims. According to Greens member Giz Watson, the government should help rape victims through their court ordeal:

> There needs to be a balance between the rights of the accused and
> the survivor but currently it appears that the survivor is fair game
> in a courtroom. This discourages women from reporting attacks
> and carrying through with prosecutions. This in turn leaves sexual
> predators on the street and puts others at risk.[80]

However, Greens WA in this instance were unwilling to show
concern for Aboriginal child victims of sexual assault, and the very
serious problems associated with an Aboriginal perpetrator being
empowered in a position of authority and control over a small
community.

In his closing remarks to the inquiry, the Committee Chairperson,
Peter Foss MLC, condemned the closure: 'They have also been
dispossessed of their land, and it is historically obvious that much
of the dysfunction in Aboriginal society has occurred through this
displacement and the dispatch of Aboriginal people to the margins
of society.'[81] Aboriginal dysfunction (including child sexual assault)
was therefore characterised as a matter of colonisation, even where
the community had actually regained land. These comments and the
inquiry affirmed race and alleged racial oppression while negating and
rendering minimal the serious human rights abuse perpetrated against
Aboriginal children and young people. The comments support the
prevalent belief that family violence and child sexual assault are
caused by colonisation and dispossession and not gender.

Since the inquiry several cases have proceeded through the
criminal justice system against Bropho and in relation to young
victims and abuse associated with the SVNC. In 2008 Judge Nisbett
of the Western Australian District Court sentenced Bropho to a
three-year term of imprisonment (later doubled to six years), describing him as a bully and a repeat liar who had sexually abused the
complainant from the ages of 11 to 22.[82] (See Chapter 6 for more
details about Bropho.)

Consistent with the denial and almost non-existent nature of
Aboriginal women and children's human rights, in 2009 the United
Nations Special Rapporteur on Racism agreed with the majority

inquiry findings that the closure of the SVNC was a matter of politics and race discrimination.[83]

Aboriginal male violence and the feminist intervention

The radical feminist position that child sexual assault is directly related to male power is difficult for Aboriginal women who know that Aboriginal people have suffered collectively. The relevance of radical feminist theory concerning sexual violence was the subject of a 1989 publication co-authored by a non-Aboriginal radical feminist, Diane Bell, and a traditional Aboriginal woman, Topsy Napurrula Nelson.[84] The debate that surrounded this ground-breaking article has arguably inhibited later research conversations concerning Aboriginal child sexual assault and sexual violence. Previously, there had been little published at all about the issue of intra-racial rape. As Bell and Nelson noted, 'The silence regarding intra-racial rape is profound'.[85]

Bell and Nelson acknowledged the tensions that surrounded public discussions of Aboriginal rape, especially the charge of giving sexism priority over racism, but they felt it imperative to ask, 'who speaks of the anguish, shame and risk for Aboriginal women victims'.[86] They stated that, traditionally, 'Woman's body is important because it's mother', but that had changed and women and young girls were being sexually abused: 'Now young girl just get touched by anyone; they broke all her body … No-one can take your body; that's her own thing.'[87]

Bell and Nelson's article documented the historical conflict between white women feminists and Aboriginal women, acknowledging the criticisms by activist Bobbi Sykes in the 1970s that the women's movement was a power struggle between white men and white women, with little prospect that changes would 'trickle down' to black women.[88] Australian Aboriginal women (unlike African-American women) were criticised for an apparent lack of participation in the theoretical debates surrounding rape, and this was explained by way of the influence of socialist feminism, with its emphasis on class as opposed to gender oppression.[89] Radical feminist strategies, which emphasised universal key experiences of women and the need for separate institutions, were promoted, as they were considered to offer 'Aboriginal women the most likely strategy for success'.[90]

A strong critique of the article was written by Queensland Aboriginal historian Jackie Huggins and a number of other Aboriginal women.[91] Huggins and the other signatories disputed the central proposition that rape is 'everyone's business', which they argued reflected 'white imperialism' of other people's cultures.[92] They felt that rape in Aboriginal communities was a matter for Aboriginal people only: 'It is our business how we deal with rape and have done so for the last 202 years quite well.'[93] They also rejected the emphasis on gender oppression and radical feminism: 'Our country was colonised on both a racially and sexually imperialistic base. In many cases our women considered white women worse than men in their treatment of Aboriginal women.'[94]

Aboriginal women could appropriately identify with socialist feminists because colonisation means that the Aboriginal fight is against the state and social injustices, especially racism.[95] Colonisation meant that Aboriginal men and women suffered together and Aboriginal women did not want to be 'jockeyed into the position of fighting and separating' from men; in their view, 'Sexism does not and will never prevail over racial domination in this country'.[96]

Bell responded by way of a letter to the editor (and a further article, 'Intraracial rape revisited'[97]) in which she emphasised the importance of a 'woman-centred analysis' at a personal, community and state level.[98] Bell argued that 'Rape is indigenous to women, not just the experience of indigenous women', and that confronting Aboriginal rape required theorising around issues of both gender and race.[99] In her view, Aboriginal women will be 'constrained in their analysis' if they continue to insist that 'the locus of violence' is race and not gender.[100] Bell believed that the issue of male power was being avoided, and that 'No Aboriginal male activists have declared safety of women a priority'.[101] In her view Aboriginal women have preferred to speak only of inter-racial rape and not intra-racial rape.[102]

'Stop the abuse — strong Aboriginal women are watching you'

Bell's criticism of Aboriginal women was not entirely correct. Aboriginal women have in some instances been very outspoken about Aboriginal men's violence against women and children. I was a young woman in 1988 when I took part in the campaign 'Stop the abuse — strong Aboriginal women are watching you'. The campaign was organised by Aboriginal women employed by the Western Australian Department of Indigenous Affairs, Marie Andrews and Denise Groves, to highlight the issue of sexual violence being experienced in the Aboriginal community by Aboriginal women and children.

At the time of the campaign I was working at an Aboriginal radio station as a broadcaster, and I interviewed Marie Andrews. I saw this campaign as ground-breaking. As a young Noongar woman, it was apparent to me that sexual assault was simply not talked about in our community. The live broadcast interview went well but the next day the manager of the radio station called me into his office. He said that complaints had been made — child sexual abuse was a topic that Noongar people believed was not something to be spoken of publicly. He said that if sexual abuse of children happened, Noongar people dealt with it 'privately'. I was shocked and did not agree — this was a serious matter that had to be spoken of publicly.

In 2005 I interviewed Marie Andrews and Denise Groves to gain their perspectives on the campaign they had organised in the 1980s. Andrews said that at the time of the campaign she considered that it was imperative to question the then accepted Aboriginal political agenda, asking, 'What was the use of land rights if so many of our people were injured and oppressing themselves?'[103] Andrews and Groves said that while awareness was beginning to be raised at that time about oppression by Aboriginal men, the Department of Indigenous Affairs (which was and still is dominated by senior non-Aboriginal employees) was opposed to Aboriginal women's issues actually being put on the agenda.[104] They felt that this was consistent with the national political movement in which issues such as deaths in custody overshadowed gender-based violence.[105] Despite growing awareness of this issue, Andrews and Groves stated that there were prominent Aboriginal men known as perpetrators who were regarded as 'untouchable', and many Aboriginal women feared confronting male family members known to be abusing children.[106]

The 'Stop the abuse' workshops were seen as critical in empowering participants to better understand abuse and the support available for victims. Speaking about abuse was seen to be a part of the healing process, even if it meant speaking out about perpetrators.[107] There was denial in the Aboriginal community that youth suicides were linked to sexual abuse. This was something people did not want to talk about and they reacted angrily if it was acknowledged.[108]

Andrews asked, 'What has happened to us as a society that we no longer care about the rights of children or women or anybody in our society … what has become of us, where have we allowed these people to get in power and abuse that power … '[109]

During our conversation, Andrews and Groves wanted to discuss the issues surrounding the 1989 publication by Bell and Nelson. They agreed with the paper that rape by Aboriginal men was a taboo topic and that was the politics of the time.[110] Andrews spoke about the importance of consciousness raising:

> I'll argue black and blue with those women who say, 'No, it's a private business.' It's everybody's business and if we can get it out into the community that it's everybody's business then we'll all be watching out, looking out for each other, trying to help and heal each other and … get information out to young people and really deliberately and consciously try to change our society. But it is a big problem, that denial aspect and people who are threatened. I'll keep talking about it. They can call me every name under the sun … they can do that but I'll talk about it until the day I die.[111]

The 'Stop the abuse' campaign showed that some Aboriginal women held views similar to radical feminist perspectives of child sexual assault, namely that it concerns men's use of violence against women and children and that the silence surrounding violence had to end. The campaign was akin to the radical feminist understanding that child sexual assault is at its core an issue of male violence: 'This is what men do because they want to, because they can get away with it.'[112] The 'Stop the abuse' campaign also reflected the radical feminist endeavour to 'stop abusers abusing'.[113]

Speaking positions are regarded as pivotal … sometimes

Aboriginal critical theorist Professor Aileen Moreton-Robinson argues that within feminist Australian literature 'whiteness' remains 'invisible, unmarked and uninterrogated', while Indigenous women's subjectivities tend to be 'objectified' within the text.[114] At the same time, Indigenous knowledge of whiteness has been dismissed and suppressed and this practice has been directly related to the main-tenance of racial dominance and privilege.[115] Feminist theory has been seen as divorced from the reality of Aboriginal women's lives; moreover, white feminists and Aboriginal women 'speak out of different cultures, epistemologies, experiences, histories, material conditions which separate our politics and our analysis'.[116] Moreton-Robinson also argues that 'If we enter feminism and its debates, it is not on our own terms, but on the terms of white feminists whose race confers dominance and privilege'.[117]

Moreton-Robinson has revisited the controversy surrounding Bell and Nelson's publication, and says Bell failed to recognise her own positioning as a white woman and consequently promoted whiteness and white dominance in her reasoning.[118] Bell's criticism, for example, of Indigenous women for not developing theory around rape, positioned Aboriginal women as inferior and lacking in theory. Moreton-Robinson argued that radical feminism failed to recognise the white privilege and dominance that Aboriginal women commonly encountered within white feminisms, including the radical feminist movement. She rejects Bell's attempt to justify a sisterhood between Aboriginal and non-Aboriginal women.

There may be no 'sisterhood' between Aboriginal and non-Aboriginal women, but it is also increasingly obvious that Aboriginal women do not speak from one voice or one social position. In recognising the inequality and divide that exists between Aboriginal and non-Aboriginal women, should we not also acknowledge the diversity among Aboriginal women?

In the context of sexual violence, many Aboriginal women have been directly impacted but this has not been the experience of all. Some Aboriginal women have understanding and empathy in relation to sexual violence, but this is not universal.

Although Moreton-Robinson criticised Bell for not giving voice to the victims of sexual violence, her analysis gave no real voice to Aboriginal victim survivors and made no real acknowledgment of the human rights violation of rape and child sexual assault. Her criticisms were concerned with representation and the history of racism on the part of the feminist movement in Australia.[119] Most recently post-modernist feminist Adrian Howe described the Bell Nelson article as 'a classic case of white settler women speaking for and appropriating the voice of a racialised minority'.[120] She berated Bell but also analysed recent non-Aboriginal feminist publications, acknowledging that white feminists have 'disengaged' and 'retreated' from the issue of Aboriginal men's violence against women and children.[121] One white feminist text was described as securing Indigenous sovereignty by disavowing Aboriginal child sexual assault.[122] Howe urges white feminists to re-engage; to not speak for the subaltern 'Other' but 'contribute to the profoundly important political work of ensuring that Aboriginal women and children's lives count as fully grievable lives'.[123] Accordingly, white feminists should 'put *inter*-sectionality back into intersectionality, reassemble the analytical framework that positions violence against children as inextricably connected to violence against women and name the main perpetrators as men, including Indigenous men'.[124]

Bell and Nelson positioned sexual violence against Aboriginal girls as inextricably connected to violence against women, and named Indigenous men as perpetrators. I find Howe's continuing attack unconvincing. She urges white feminists to 'recover the voices of Aboriginal women protesters'[125] but does not recognise that white feminists long ago responded to the voices of Aboriginal women protesters in their retreat from the topic. The response lacks an understanding of the significance of 'race' politics and the silencing of Aboriginal women's voices in relation to gender-based violence.

Acknowledging race and gender

Aboriginal women are increasingly recognising and asserting that race and gender are relevant and intersecting at all times, thereby rejecting the notion that race oppression has primacy and that gender-based forms of oppression are somehow 'less than' serious for Aboriginal women and children. This understanding is critical because of the direct association between gender-based oppression and child sexual assault.

Irene Watson claims that 'The emancipation of Aboriginal women will come once we have dismantled patriarchy, but also the colonial institutions patriarchy has assembled along the course of its own history'.[126] Aboriginal psychologist and academic, Dr Pat Dudgeon, says: 'We know that we were put on the bottom of the heap of humanity. We know that the most extreme poverty and disempowerment were our fate, and those of us who escaped this see it in the lives of our sisters. Those who did practise the more subtle arts of resistance were physically and spiritually pounded down, sometimes by whites, by the institutions, and sometimes by our own men'.[127] Mick Dodson, too, has accepted that Aboriginal men are too often the perpetrators of violence, and that men have to take a stand and acknowledge the problem: 'We simply have to stop excusing unacceptable behaviour, speak up, say something, don't let this violence strangle us and who we are or who we know we ought to be. We must destroy the abusive cycle before it destroys us.'[128]

I was present at the Indigenous Family Violence Forum in 2009 where Bess Price from Central Australia spoke about her own first-hand experience of violence, including the tragic loss of a granddaughter. She asked the forum, 'How can we make a better future for our children, when our very own men in our community are saying "women do not have any power in the eyes of Aboriginal law"?'

Gloria Anzaldúa argues that the time for male excuses for violence is over, and affirms the imperative of *mestiza* (women of mixed racial ancestry) in supporting each other to change the sexist oppression of Indigenous men:

> Though we 'understand' the root causes of male hatred and fear and the subsequent wounding of women, we do not excuse, we do not condone, and we will no longer put up with it.
>
> From the men in our race we demand the admission/acknowledgement/disclosure/testimony that they wound us, violate us, are afraid of us and our power. We need them to say that they will eliminate their hurtful put-down ways. But more than the words, we demand acts. We say to them: We will develop equal power with you and those who have shamed us … As long as the woman is put down, the Indian and the Black in all of us is put down. The struggle of the mestiza is above all a feminist one.[129]

In Australia there has been resistance to the acknowledgment that colonisation was and still is very much gendered. Within Aboriginal race politics, gender-based forms of oppression, violence and sexual abuse of women and children is still minimised, marginalised and made invisible. Powerful political discourse promotes the Aboriginal male experience of race and punishes Aboriginal women who are prepared to speak against men's violence, particularly in relation to child sexual assault.

There are changes on the horizon. More Aboriginal women are acknowledging the role of race and gender, and some Aboriginal men have begun to acknowledge men's oppression of women and their responsibility to help bring about change. However, the problem is that detrimental race politics are linked to and implicitly support-ive of existing power relations and the continuing oppression of Aboriginal women and children in Australian society. Colonisation and patriarchy are interlocked and interwoven systems of oppression that subordinate and abuse Aboriginal men, women and children alike, although in differing ways.

Chapter 4

A decade of government reports and inquiries

For more than a decade now, key government inquiries concerning Aboriginal child sexual assault have been established throughout Australia. These inquiries have led to a wealth of information, knowledge and data, and significantly increased awareness of the nature and extent of the problem.

This chapter documents and analyses inquires that have been central to the development of Aboriginal, government and wider public consciousness and responses to Aboriginal child sexual assault. It highlights the nature and extent of Aboriginal child sexual assault, and acknowledges the failings of institutional responses. Without this understanding one might simply think that there is no problem, and that we have adequately functioning responses in place.

Inquiries have signalled the way forward for governments and Aboriginal communities, but important recommendations have not been implemented and valuable understandings risk being lost. However, the significant evidence established is critical to improve responses and the development of Aboriginal responses to child sexual assault.

The following reports, detailed in this chapter, make up a considerable body of knowledge that is critical to informing awareness, understanding and future responses to Aboriginal child sexual assault:

- *Children on Anangu Pitjantjatjara Yankunytjatjara (APY) Lands Commission of Inquiry: A report into sexual abuse* (The Hon. E.P. Mullighan QC, 2008)

- *Ampe Akelyernemane Meke Mekarle 'Little Children Are Sacred'*, Report of the Northern Territory Board of Inquiry into the Protection of Aboriginal Children from Sexual Abuse (Northern Territory Government, 2007)
- *Breaking the Silence: Creating the future: Addressing child sexual assault in Aboriginal communities in NSW* (Aboriginal Child Sexual Assault Taskforce, 2006)
- *Putting the Picture Together: Inquiry into response by government agencies to complaints of family violence and child abuse in Aboriginal communities* (Sue Gordon, Kay Hallahan and Darrell Henry [the Gordon Inquiry], 2004)
- *The Aboriginal and Torres Strait Islander Women's Task Force on Violence Report* (Aboriginal and Torres Strait Islander Women's Task Force on Violence, 1999).

Children on Anangu Pitjantjatjara Yankunytjatjara (APY) Lands Commission of Inquiry: A report into sexual abuse

The Children on APY Lands Commission of Inquiry was established in June 2007 as part of a wider inquiry by the South Australian Government into the abuse of children in state care.[1] Commissioner Mullighan QC and two Assistant Commissioners, one a senior Aboriginal woman who chose to remain anonymous 'for personal reasons', conducted the inquiry.[2] Although it was not made clear why the Aboriginal Assistant Commissioner chose to remain anonymous, the threat of intimidation and violence was recognised by the inquiry as a serious issue:

> During the field trips the Inquiry became aware of some women being too frightened to provide information to the Inquiry and some workers having been intimidated by senior staff in some communities. The Inquiry accepted there is widespread violence and fear in the communities which prevents disclosures of sexual abuse.[3]

The Commission's report is extremely distressing to read. It focuses on detailed case file studies of sexually abused Anangu children, and differs from other inquiries whose evidence of children's abuse was often more anecdotal. As the APY report made clear, the inquiry was not prepared to act only on indirect or anecdotal evidence of the existence of sexual abuse of children, instead investigating 'allegations' to ascertain evidence.[4] Understandably, in view of the fear factor, there were no direct disclosures made during the inquiry;[5] however, it was determined that on assessment of the evidence (files from NPY Women's Council, Families SA, police and courts, Department of Education and Community Services) and on a standard of 'reasonable possibility', there had been 141 particular children who had been sexually abused on the Lands.[6] Other evidence included reports and studies and, importantly, general evidence from community and workers. The inquiry found that 'the incidence of sexual abuse of children on the Lands is widespread',[7] notwithstanding that sexual abuse of children was also found to be completely foreign to Anangu traditional culture and law.[8]

Despite the violence and fear in the community, which prevented disclosure, there was strong evidence of under-reporting of child sexual assault on APY Lands.[9] The evidence from Anangu people, including teachers, health professionals and social workers, revealed that children are living in dysfunctional communities marked by violence and fear, drug and alcohol abuse, overcrowded housing, unemployment, and physical and mental health issues. The inquiry also learned that many Aboriginal girls on the Lands simply accepted that they would be sexually abused.[10]

The case files examined are heartbreaking. File after file reports sexual abuse and rape of children, many of whom are very young. Despite mandatory reporting legislation, in many cases the relevant departments had simply failed to act to protect children in clear circumstances that required action. It appeared that regardless of statutory obligations, lack of government resources simply prevented investigation.[11] Very often it seemed there was a negligent attitude to the safety of Anangu children, even an attitude of 'blame the victim'. One record showed welfare notes that suggested an underage 14-year-old girl was in a 'consensual sexual relationship' with a much older man.[12] The police declared that there was no risk to the child even though no interview had occurred and there was no evidence to form that assessment.[13] The welfare notes recorded that the 14-year-old (who was uncared for by her mother) was 'belted' with a stick by a family member who decided that the girl (rather than the adult male) was responsible.[14]

Most damning, the inquiry confirmed that very serious criminal allegations of sexual assault on children were not properly investigated, if investigated at all, by the police.[15] Very few cases looked at by the inquiry resulted in offenders being charged and convicted. As one perpetrator reportedly stated, 'white man's law does not apply on the lands'.[16] In one case a girl aged five was diagnosed with gonorrhea and also had other physical symptoms consistent with sexual abuse. The abuse was disputed by the parent but concluded on medical grounds. This was reported to police, but 'no police incident report was located and no child abuse case management records were sighted'.[17]

The lack of due legal intervention had serious effects upon the child victims, and the consequence of sexual assault and abuse on children was obvious from the case files. Many of the children and young people who had been abused later attempted suicide, became victims of severe domestic violence, became pregnant with children they could not care for, and developed serious substance abuse problems. The evidence clearly shows how child sexual abuse leads to a shocking decline in children's mental and physical health and wellbeing. The lack of appropriate response to child sexual assault was also evident from each and every one of these cases. The following graphic case is provided as an example of the violation of Anangu children's human right to bodily integrity, the lack of appropriate responses by health and legal authorities, and the longer-term consequence for the children.

> A carer took a three-year-old girl to a health clinic. Records indicate the girl's labia were swollen and red. No cause of this problem was recorded.
>
> When the girl was aged nine years, concerns were reported to welfare that the girl was being neglected. It was suggested that the girl was always hungry and dirty and had become withdrawn. Records indicate the notifier fed the girl for about a fortnight. Welfare investigated the matter and found that child sexual abuse had occurred. There was a history of alcohol abuse by close relatives. The girl experienced two further situations of confirmed neglect in the years that followed.

Records show that at age 13 years, the girl went to a health clinic with two adult female relatives and sought birth control as she was having sex with her boyfriend, age 16. There was no suspicion of sexual abuse referred to welfare. Some months later, there was a suggestion that the girl had a sexual liaison with a boy in another community. Welfare sought to discuss these matters with her family but they were not located and the case was closed.

None of these matters were reported to the police.

Welfare records indicate that as a 14-year-old, during a school lesson, when class members were asked to write about how they felt about themselves, the girl wrote the word 'abused' although she did not disclose to anyone any actual abuse. Medical professionals considered that she was exhibiting psycho-somatic symptoms related to anxiety and possibly a 'first sexual encounter'.

Some months later, the girl was again brought to the attention of welfare after she expressed suicidal desires and asked for help. She had been smoking marijuana and drinking. She was sent away for medical treatment and counselling under the care of relatives off the Lands.[18]

Some sexual abuse of children on APY Lands was extremely predatory and involved abuse of vulnerable girls by older men engaging the practice of 'sex for petrol'.[19] Girls were plied with petrol until they were vulnerable, and the long-term effect upon children was significant physical and mental impairment. The inquiry reported that at one community there were several men, aged in their forties, whom many suspected were involved in supplying petrol in return for sexual favours. Disturbingly, it was noted that adult predators were even seen 'hanging out at the school yard'.[20] The girls who were targeted were regarded as not having fathers or older male figures to protect them. In one instance a suspect was stopped and questioned several times; however, despite the police and welfare attempts, no one was willing to give an incriminating statement.[21] The police report recognised fear of reprisal, culture, gender and age, and the lack of familiarity with police, as barriers preventing disclosures.[22]

The backdrop to this abuse of APY children included key but dysfunctional Aboriginal organisations dominated by influential families and men who had to be supported as 'powerbrokers'.[23] The inquiry was told that often offenders came from powerful families with access to resources and had good English speaking skills, jobs and 'contacts with whitefellas'.[24] They were regarded as having clout with the European whitefella system — and not with traditional Aboriginal law. Anangu men and boys were responsible largely for the abuse, although, as the inquiry noted, two non-Indigenous men who held positions of trust in the community were charged with offences against young boys.[25] Often the child victims were ostracised in the community, reflecting the clear influence of perpetrators and their families.[26] It was reported that young girls had been sent away and on return were unable to fit in and settle back in the community.[27]

Sexual abuse was normalised in the APY Lands, with adult men holding an attitude of 'she's big enough' towards young girls, and the view that 'if you've got the body you do the thing'.[28] Aboriginal girls came to accept that they would be sexually assaulted and abused, as the inquiry noted: 'it is expected of them. They simply believe their resistance is futile.'[29] The inquiry was told there had been a lack of sex education in schools, although when such education commenced in one community there was an immediate positive impact, with the girls confidently calling out to the boys at recess, 'We can say no'.[30]

Sexually abused and victimised children lacked treatment and therapy, and were typically placed outside of their communities to receive such services.[31] Families SA submitted that therapy had to be conducted in a safe place, and this meant it could often not occur in the family environment or in the community.[32] It was also conceded that the 'relative absence of such services' meant that no therapy was provided or that the child was placed outside the home and community to receive therapy.[33] The provision of therapy, in the few instances it did occur, being outside of the home and family, was recognised as providing an added layer of trauma to the child victim.[34] The inquiry's recommendation for additional funding for Families SA to provide the therapeutic service to abused children is important, but it did not recognise that Aboriginal communities must also become therapeutic communities better able to meet the needs of so many children who have been sexually abused.[35]

Ultimately, the inquiry reached the conclusion that only a 'very small number' of allegations of child sexual abuse on the Lands had been made to SA Police, notwithstanding that it was considered reasonably possible that a 'high incidence' of abuse existed on the Lands.[36] The lack of police presence in many communities, and the level of fear held by community members — including Aboriginal education workers who were fearful of the requirement for mandatory reporting of suspicion of abuse on the basis that 'people will get us'[37] — was a major factor in the under-reporting of abuse. The perceived lack of support and ostracising of victims,[38] the reluctance of officials to report where it was required, and the police failure to properly investigate and prosecute[39] are clearly relevant to why child sexual assault is not reported.

Although NPY Women's Council assisted victims and gave evidence, the lack of advocacy for the victims was clear from the inquiry's finding that there had never been a criminal injuries compensation claim for child sexual assault on behalf of a child from the Lands.[40] The inquiry recommended that the South Australian Guardian for Children and Young People be empowered to act as an advocate for Aboriginal children (not in state care) who disclose sexual abuse.[41] This is a systemic response to the overwhelming problems resulting from the heightened environment of abuse of Aboriginal children and the systemic neglect of such children. Such a measure is intended to ensure greater legal advocacy and equality for disadvantaged Aboriginal children, and in my view is worthy of national consideration.

The Commission of Inquiry demonstrated significant knowledge and awareness of the severity of child sexual assault and of the negligence of governments and Aboriginal communities. While the inquiry was methodologically sound, based on case files of children and the standard of reasonable possibility, the direct voices of the children being so terribly impacted by sexual abuse and violence was missing. We do not hear them directly — perhaps understandably in light of the fear and intimidation and lack of support that they face. The inquiry highlighted extremely well the disturbing nature of child sexual abuse, particularly of young girls, the power of perpetrators and the way in which abuse had been normalised contrary to the Anangu cultural traditions, and the lack of systemic responses on the part of authorities charged with protection of children.

Importantly, the inquiry recognised that aspects of current Aboriginal governance structures are 'quite detrimental to the disclosure of child sexual abuse'.[42] It recommended 'That any change to governance of communities on the Lands be implemented promptly so as to reduce the extent of dysfunction and possible corruption in the communities'.[43] And further, 'That the nature of any change should have regard to the empowerment of Anangu and enhancing confidence in disclosing child sexual abuse and implementing measures to prevent abuse and address its consequences'.[44]

The inquiry highlighted the absolute necessity of good governance in Aboriginal communities as a response to child sexual assault. This has been indirectly acknowledged by the Australian Crime Commission's National Indigenous Violence and Child Abuse Intelligence Task Force, whose preliminary findings confirm that the abuse of power by people in prominent positions may facilitate criminality, or silence through threats the reporting of child abuse or violence.[45] Governance is an issue that Aboriginal communities and governments must address in the near future.

Ampe Akelyernemane Meke Mekarle 'Little Children Are Sacred'

The 'Little Children Are Sacred' inquiry was instigated in 2007 by the Northern Territory Government and was acknowledged as a response to significant media attention on sexual assault of Aboriginal children in the Northern Territory.[46] In particular, the context acknowledged by the inquiry included the ABC *Lateline* program in May 2006 in which Crown Prosecutor Nanette Rogers highlighted horrific (even fatal) cases of sexual abuse of children, and the subsequent *Lateline* program in December 2006 concerning a suspected abuser trading petrol for sex with young girls in Mutitjulu.[47]

The inquiry adopted a different methodology to the report concerning the APY Lands, which focused on determining in a more legalistic manner the extent of Aboriginal child sexual assault and the nature of responses. The Northern Territory inquiry considered its key task to be prevention, and accepted on the basis of the findings of previous inquiries in New South Wales and Western Australia that 'sexual abuse of Aboriginal children is common, widespread and grossly under-reported'.[48] However, the inquiry also acknowledged statistical data, as prepared by the Australian Institute of Health and Welfare, which indicated that Northern Territory Indigenous children were consistently over-represented as subjects of sexual abuse notifications, and nationally represented an average of 53% of cases from 2002–03 to 2005–06.[49] It was also stated that since 2001–02 there had been a 72% rise in cases concerning Indigenous children, as compared to an increase of 4% concerning non-Indigenous children.[50] However, the investigations typically resulted in very low rates of substantiated cases, indicating in the inquiry's view that there was 'a failure of the child protection system to substantiate and adequately protect children'.[51]

The *Little Children Are Sacred* report recognised a common theme of discussion among many Aboriginal communities, namely that people felt disempowered, confused, overwhelmed and disillusioned, and that this situation has led to communities 'being weakened to the point that the likelihood of children being sexually abused is increased and the community ability to deal with it is decreased'.[52] It was considered vital that communities become empowered through a determined and co-ordinated effort to break the cycle and provide the strength, power and appropriate support and services to local communities.[53] Both the federal and territory governments were seen as having the responsibility to lead, and this was clear from the inquiry's first recommendation:

> That Aboriginal child sexual abuse in the Northern Territory be designated as an issue of urgent national significance by both the Australian and Northern Territory Governments, and both Governments immediately establish a collaborative partnership with a Memorandum of Understanding to specifically address the protection of Aboriginal children from sexual abuse. It is critical that both governments commit to genuine consultation with Aboriginal people in designing initiatives for Aboriginal communities.[54]

Journalist Paul Toohey, in examining the wider political context surrounding the inquiry, in particular the growing tensions between Northern Territory Chief Minister Clare Martin (ALP) and the federal Aboriginal Affairs Minister Mal Brough (Liberal), noted the minimal response from the Northern Territory Chief Minister that she would not be responding to the report for several weeks.[55] According to Toohey it took Brough only six days to override the inquiry report and to announce the Northern Territory intervention and the intention of the Australian Government to 'send in the army'.[56] While the federal emergency intervention treated child sexual assault as a matter of 'national significance', the manner in which this occurred was not envisaged or supported by the report.

The report was extensive and contained 97 recommendations aimed at various government departments to improve their responses to Aboriginal communities and children at risk. The report usefully dispelled myths surrounding Aboriginal child sexual assault, for example, that only Aboriginal men offend against Aboriginal children, or that Aboriginal law is an excuse to justify abuse.[57]

I do not agree with all statements made in the report, for example, the claim made based on literature (uncited) that 'emotionally neglected children are often vulnerable to sexual abuse because of a (very understandable) desire for affection and love'.[58] This statement emphasises children's 'desire' and is controversial for that reason. Many offenders readily blame children's supposed 'desire' for love and affection as justification, and children have long been held responsible for 'seducing' adult offenders. As the inquiry was told, many sexually abused children were 'neglected' by their own families or did not have a strong family network. Children's primary status as neglected renders them vulnerable to exploitative adults — and this is where the attention should lie, in addition to an acknowledgment of the predatory adult nature of child sexual assault.

The inquiry noted that within communities there was a failure or reluctance to report. As one senior woman stated, 'Everyone talks loud after the event but are silent and doing nothing beforehand'.[59] In some cases there was a lack of understanding and awareness of child sexual assault, and there were also 'multiple causes of fear that prevents reporting'.[60] The possibility of violence and intimidation by other community members, the child victim being ostracised by the community, past negative relations with police and welfare, perpetrators going to jail, victims' and families' feelings of shame and community ambivalence were all recognised as factors that prevent reporting.[61] The high level of violence and the normalisation of violence also contributed to under-reporting and to the gravity of this problem. As one submission outlined:

[There is an] enculturation of violence, where the violence is socially and culturally accepted and therefore minimised and justified. This is reflected and reinforced by the mainstream society through individuals and institutions with which Indigenous people interact. Victims are often held responsible or blamed for the violence and/or the abuse that they experience.[62]

The inquiry recognised the Council of Australian Governments' acknowledgment that 'Indigenous leaders and organisations play a vital role in addressing the problem of violence and abuse' and to that end, agreed to support networks of Indigenous men and women in local communities so that they can better help people who report incidents of violence and abuse.[63] The inquiry also noted that in response to this the Australian Government committed $23 million over four years to June 2010 for the Indigenous Community Leadership initiative, to be led by the Department of Family and Community Services and Indigenous Affairs.[64] Upon making general inquiries to the department about this significant commitment, I was informed by a public servant that the leadership initiative was not focused on community-specific issues, such as child sexual assault, but aimed generically at the development of individual capacity.[65] While the inquiry findings (and the Council of Australian Governments) identified Aboriginal leadership specifically in response to child sexual assault as critical, this was not responded to by the Commonwealth.

The lack of services for victims was recognised by the inquiry, which noted that it did not have access to culturally appropriate counselling services, as they were virtually non-existent.[66] The non-Indigenous government-run Sexual Assault Referral Centres (SARC) were described as playing a pivotal role in facilitating individual healing from the trauma of sexual assault. However, they did not have the capacity to cope with demand and provide an appropriate professional service.[67] The inquiry recommended urgent action be taken to expand and upgrade SARC services, and to develop and adopt protocols for the management of victims of child sexual assault to ensure an appropriate standard of care.[68]

While the report generally focused on government services and responses, recommendation 23[69] provided that victim and community support programs be developed in remote Aboriginal communities, as well as urban settings, to (a) reduce the risks of children 'acting out' sexually, (b) being re-victimised or (c) becoming the victimiser. While acting out and re-victimisation are certainly possible effects of child sexual assault, victim and community support programs should be premised on the basis of recovery and healing from sexual assault trauma, and, importantly, on wider community responsibility and prevention. Aboriginal stigmatisation of victims is common and highly detrimental and must be addressed as part of the healing process. Recommendation 45 proposed that the government begin dialogue with Aboriginal communities 'to come up with innovative ways to effect a widespread healing process aimed at inter-generational and present trauma'.[70] Based on the compelling (and damning) evidence, the inquiry should have recommended widespread healing processes, specifically concerning the present and inter-generational trauma of child sexual assault.

Aboriginal healing processes and programs must affirm the importance of prevention and the need for the community's active role in prevention. As the inquiry acknowledged, environments may encourage or permit sexual assault of children to occur.[71] This is referred to as 'situational crime prevention' — a relatively new criminological approach that shifts the focus from the supposed deficits of offenders to the situational environment. Aboriginal communities (with government) can reduce risk to children through strategies based on situational crime prevention.[72] For example, communities can make it harder for offenders to gain access to children; they can teach children personal safety, and teach adults to recognise the signs of grooming. Control can be exercised over the 'facilitators' of offending (by reducing access to pornography, alcohol and drugs) and in relation to 'prompts' (to ensure offenders are not put in situations where they may be 'prompted' to re-offend), and by ensuring available services for offenders to seek help.[73]

The inquiry noted that communities can be assisted to reduce 'permissibility' by challenging offenders' excuses or attempts to minimise their behaviour. This can be applied to the whole of community so that everyone knows the damage sexual abuse does to children, and can not only challenge offenders but correct inappropriate views of other community members. Also, it is essential to increase the risk of detection, and communities should monitor known offenders to ensure they do not have access to children. Most importantly, the proper supervision of children reduces the risk of harm towards them.[74]

This approach requires families and communities to be prepared to act to prevent abuse, and communities can develop an agreed position, or community plan, as to how they will respond to sexual abuse.[75] Aboriginal communities have often appeared unable or unwilling to take action. Therefore, community education and awareness should be responded to as a matter of high priority. As the inquiry recognised, Aboriginal Elders, respected people and 'champions' need to speak out against sexual abuse, set appropriate norms of behaviour, and participate in community education and awareness.[76]

The inquiry urged government to drive a 'fundamental shift in family and community attitudes and action of child sexual abuse' by ensuring that high profile Aboriginal men and women are supported to provide positive, proactive leadership on the prevention of sexual abuse.[77] It also recommended that government 'actively support Aboriginal men to engage in discussions about, and address, child sexual abuse and violence'.[78] This presupposes that Aboriginal women are adequately supported when there is no evidence to suggest that this is so. Men do need to show leadership and be supported in that, but Aboriginal women's leadership roles are constantly undermined — seemingly even in response to the abuse of children, the majority of whom are girls. As highlighted in Chapter 3 of this book, the subjugation of women is a causative factor of child sexual assault and responses must not perpetuate the diminishment of women.

Although the inquiry held the view that 'Aboriginal law is a key component in successfully preventing the sexual abuse of children',[79] the discussion of Aboriginal customary law made no statement of child sexual assault as a violation of Aboriginal law. There was, rather, a rejection of the 'notion that Aboriginal law is connected to causing, promoting or allowing family violence or child sexual abuse', and Recommendation 71 aimed to ensure governments facilitate dialogue between Aboriginal law men, women and the Northern Territory legal system. At the same time there was no acknowledgment of the ways in which Aboriginal law can contribute to the protection of children.

This raises the question — has Aboriginal law become so displaced that the protection of children and punishment of offenders is no longer positively identifiable as a matter of Aboriginal law? According to Aboriginal Elders, 'The traditional fences have broken down and we need to repair them' (Gunbalunya Elder), 'We need to breathe life back into the old ways' (Anindilyakwa Elder) and 'Australian law has knocked us out' (Western Arrente Elder).[80]

The inquiry gave detailed recommendations concerning the establishment of Community Justice Groups[81] and Aboriginal Courts,[82] seemingly based on the view that once such systems and structures are put in place, Aboriginal law can be readily resurrected to address the issue of child sexual assault. The involvement of Aboriginal people in the administration of the criminal justice system is a fundamental human right but the breakdown of traditional ways, and the problem of re-victimisation for children (and their supporting families) who disclose, indicates that caution must be exercised. The inquiry recognised the Koori Courts in New South Wales and the advantage that such courts have in reducing recidivism and gaining better outcomes for victims, families and communities.[83] The Koori Courts, however, have excluded child sexual assault cases from their jurisdiction.

Again, the important voices of children and young people impacted by child sexual assault were not apparent in the report. There was one interview with a 14-year-old girl (edited to protect the victim) who was assaulted by a much older man. As typically reported, both the victim and her mother who supported her were ostracised from their community. The interview reflects the way in which Aboriginal people and communities can marginalise victims and protect perpetrators, thereby continuing to abuse and cause harm and damage to victims who have suffered from child sexual assault.

> After reporting the matter, Sarah said it was better for her that she left the community because of the anger she would have faced from others ...

Prior to the offence Sarah had been at boarding school inter-state. Since the court, she and her mother have led a transient lifestyle, living in at least ten different locations around the Top End. Sarah has been unable to continue her schooling. She said they have moved everywhere since the report. There was a problem with his family threatening her because the offender went to jail. They had wanted her to drop the charges. She still gets 'that nervous thing' (anxiety). It appears that they settle in a location for a time and then hear of threats against them, or are threatened directly, people knowing where they are or seeing people from that community, and they move on. They heard at one stage that people wanted them to go back to the community for a meeting 'culture way' but they wouldn't go as they were fearful 'they will probably kill us'. Sarah's anxiety continues with fears about what will happen when the man is released, 'he will do something to us like black magic and curse us'.[84]

As a result of the inquiry the Northern Territory Government established a Children's Commissioner tasked with monitoring government responses. It was noted that the key recommendation, that both governments, territory and federal, 'immediately establish a collaborative partnership with a Memorandum of Understanding to specifically address the protection of Aboriginal children from sexual abuse', had not been responded to.[85] While the Commissioner recognised there had been important progress, it was also noted that only 12 of the 41 recommendations had been fully met. Most of the inquiry's recommendations were aimed at government agencies and many are described as 'met' or 'partially met' by the Children's Commissioner.

Problematically, the government had not responded to critical recommendations aimed at Aboriginal community empowerment and understanding of child sexual assault, and increasing support for children. According to the Children's Commissioner the recom-mendation calling for a public awareness campaign concerning child sexual assault, involving Aboriginal leaders and all members of the community and undertaken in language and in a culturally appropriate manner, had simply not been met. Although there have been some scattered educational initiatives, these fall well short of 'a widespread and sustained campaign' with the goal of shifting attitudes towards child sexual assault. The Commissioner stated that, given the importance of community education as an abuse prevention strategy, priority be given to the development and implementation of the 'widespread and sustained' campaign.[86]

Although the Northern Territory Government was supporting Aboriginal men to hold forums, the failure to develop important community awareness responses showed the unwillingness of government to work directly with Aboriginal communities to address child sexual assault and the wellbeing of Aboriginal children. In abandoning the first and key recommendation of a federal–state memorandum of understanding concerning child sexual assault, the Commonwealth is equally implicated. The considerable resources directed towards government and non-government non-Aboriginal agencies can be contrasted with the lack of support to Aboriginal communities to improve knowledge, understanding and responses to child sexual assault. Surely, though, it is unquestionable that a key response to Aboriginal child sexual assault must lie with the Aboriginal community — the community that is the child's immediate community, and whose typical responses often inhibit disclosure and lead to more abuse of children.

Breaking the Silence: Creating the future: Addressing child sexual assault in Aboriginal communities in NSW

The Aboriginal Child Sexual Assault Taskforce (ACSAT) of New South Wales was set up in 2006 as a result of state government roundtables to address sexual violence in Aboriginal communities, and in response to the findings of the Aboriginal Justice Advisory Council's report of 2002, *Speak Out, Speak Strong*, which reported that approximately 70% of Aboriginal women in New South Wales prisons had been sexually assaulted as children.[87]

ACSAT visited 29 Aboriginal communities in New South Wales and child sexual assault was described as 'a huge issue' in every one of those communities.[88] Aboriginal people told ACSAT that child sexual assault was 'massive', 'an epidemic' and 'a way of life'.[89] Aboriginal boys and girls were recognised as the victims of child sexual assault, and perpetrators were often described as grandfathers, fathers, stepfathers, uncles, cousins or brothers of the child. Some non-Aboriginal men in communities were also identified as perpetrators. Offenders were often considered to be 'important people' within the community.[90]

ACSAT gained first-hand knowledge from Aboriginal people, undoubtedly many of whom were victim survivors or had close family knowledge of child sexual assault. The community members who participated in the consultations identified many themes, and the information gained constitutes vital Aboriginal intelligence and knowledge about Aboriginal child sexual assault. The following themes were identified:

- child sexual abuse is inter-generational
- child sexual assault is not well understood in Aboriginal communities
- perpetrators often 'groom' the children they target
- child sexual assault is seldom reported.

Aboriginal communities saw child sexual assault as inter-generational, identifying perpetrators as people who had sexually assaulted generations of Aboriginal children.[91] Some perpetrators were known to have assaulted three generations of children. In some instances, Aboriginal male perpetrators were identified as people who had once been victims of child sexual assault. Some Aboriginal mothers and grandmothers who had been victims of child sexual assault were seen as not protecting their own children and in some instances considered sexual assault 'just something you had to go through'.[92]

Community members believed there was a lack of general awareness about the dynamics of child sexual assault — what it is, how it occurs, the impacts on individuals, families and communities, and that it is a crime and not a normal way of life.[93] ACSAT noted:

This lack of awareness contributed to a culture of silence and denial that … is one factor that enables the sexual abuse of children to continue unchecked. In this culture of silence and denial, child sexual assault becomes a taboo subject that no one feels able to break, not even if they want to. As no one in the community is talking about it, nor condemning it, perpetrators [sic] actions are not challenged in any way and children are unable to discover what is happening is wrong nor identify anyone they could talk to about it.[94]

Community members felt that it was this lack of understanding that explained why it was common for community members to side with the perpetrators where disclosures had occurred, and to blame children for lying and 'just saying it to make trouble'.[95] It was also felt that a lack of understanding of child sexual assault and its impacts might explain why some people were sympathetic to perpetrators.[96]

Aboriginal communities have close kinship networks and a culture based on principles of caring and sharing.[97] This atmosphere was exploited and manipulated by perpetrators who targeted children by 'grooming' them (for example, giving gifts and taking the children to special events or away on holidays). It was recognised that grooming could be difficult to detect because of the close kinship networks and Aboriginal culture of generosity. Also problematic was the recognition that the people who were 'grooming' children were often people who 'occupied respected community positions' and had the trust of the community.[98]

There were many reasons why child sexual assault was regarded as seldom reported. These included fear, shame and guilt, threats from the perpetrator, lack of understanding about what was happening, pressure from the family, fear of not being believed and disclosure not being acted on, having no one to tell and not knowing who to tell.[99] Some families supported children who disclosed, but the consultations indicated that children who disclosed were often not believed or listened to. Entire cultural networks were affected as disclosures commonly resulted in serious family rifts; presumably for this reason many people were pressured by extended family not to report.[100] Victims were pressured not to report for fear that the perpetrators 'will end up in jail', and that reporting will 'make trouble for the whole mob'.[101] Also, the fact that abuse had been inter-generational and unaddressed meant that people did not know how to address disclosures, as one participant reported:

> The young girls are telling the grandmothers, but the grandmothers are not listening, because it most probably happened to them and nobody listened to them and they're saying to these young little girls, they're saying 'Go away, you're making trouble for the family'. But they're not; they're actually trying to reach out to their grandmothers for help.[102]

Other factors that impacted on reporting included the geographic isolation of Aboriginal communities, which meant that some communities received very little information about child sexual assault and were perhaps unable to report even if they wanted to. It was noted that information flowing in and out of such communities could be monitored and controlled by community leaders, some of whom may be perpetrators.[103] In the few cases that child sexual assault had been reported, there had been a poor response from the service delivery providers, who were sometimes described as 'rude', 'ignorant' and 'hopeless'.[104]

ACSAT was told that the legal system was not adequately supporting child victims or their families in the instances where disclosures were made. Service responses on occasion were inappropriate (for example, parents assisting children in making disclosures to police were arrested on outstanding warrants). Children were also told their statements were not clear and they were made to repeat their stories over and over. Children were told there was not enough evidence. No one explained what the process entailed and there was no follow up once the police report was made. There were also long waiting times for investigation, with abuse sometimes continuing.[105]

Community participants who were victim survivors of child sexual assault spoke about the damage this had caused them and the long-term impacts upon their lives. Betrayal of trust and feelings of isolation were common, as was guilt, shame, anger, confusion and feeling responsible for the abuse. Despair, depression, self-harm and suicide attempts were also recognised as impacts.[106] Child sexual assault was also viewed as impacting whole communities, where families and communities became at 'war' after disclosures were made.[107] Children who are sexually abused may become involved in substance abuse and risk taking. The participants believed that, 'Kids are acting out, behaving badly and are seen as naughty. One of the reasons they are probably doing that is because of sexual abuse'.[108] Further, 'It's not just molestation. It opens up a circle of drugs, hate, no trust and self-loathing'.[109]

It was believed that many perpetrators had themselves been victims as children, either in their communities or in institutional care. According to ACSAT the research supported this concern, with one study reporting that more than half of the perpetrators

interviewed had been sexually abused as children.[110] Although the
link between victimisation and later offending is unquestionable,
ACSAT's comments need to be regarded cautiously as it is also
believed that the majority of male victims do not go on to re-offend,
and women (who are disproportionately the victims of child sexual
assault) represent only a small minority of perpetrators.[111] As ACSAT
observed, 'One of the greatest barriers to communities and government providing an effective response to child sexual assault in
Aboriginal communities is a lack of understanding of the issue and
the long-term impact it has on the individuals who experience it
and communities'.[112]

ACSAT recommended that a comprehensive education and
training strategy for governments, non-government organisations
and communities is a vital strategy in targeting what was recognised as a 'huge' issue throughout New South Wales Aboriginal
communities.[113]

ACSAT provided a thorough examination of government responses to Aboriginal child sexual assault, which are summarised here.
At the Commonwealth level, ACSAT noted that although there
was a policy statement on child abuse, child sexual assault was not
acknowledged within that statement. It recommended that the
Commonwealth develop a national statement addressing child sexual
assault in conjunction with states and territories.[114]

In relation to New South Wales, ACSAT found there was no
overarching policy that specifically addressed child sexual assault
in Aboriginal communities and that a state-wide evaluation policy
framework should be developed to ensure that the continuum of
New South Wales Government services delivers a more effective
and efficient service to Aboriginal children, young people, families
and communities.[115] ACSAT found that there was a lack of consist-
ency and co-ordinated response in relation to Aboriginal child sexual
assault and that a holistic response, informed by an overarching policy
framework, was required. This need was illustrated by the following
example cited in the report:

> A number of girls, who were around 15 years old, had disclosed
> to someone at their school that an uncle had sexually assaulted
> them. The girls were cousins and did not live with the uncle.

The school reported the assault to DoCS [Department of Community Services]. DoCS reviewed the case, considered the parents of the girls to be protective and decided there were no further care and protection issues. DoCS referred the matter to police for investigation. However, as far as the community could see, no investigation took place.

The young people wanted to access counselling; however NSW Health said they couldn't provide counselling until the police had interviewed the girls. Neither DoCS nor NSW Health spoke to the police about the investigation, so the case remained stagnant. The girls received no formal support and began using drugs and acting out at school.

A community member was then entrusted by the community to provide support and advocacy to the girls so that they could get the help that they needed. However, each service that they approached, including DoCS, Police, Health and even the school, said it was 'not their responsibility' and they could not talk about it with the community member anyway because she was not from an organisation involved with the girls, nor was she the girls' parent.[116]

This example shows how the lack of overarching policy framework led to disjointed service delivery and ultimately resulted in an inappropriate (almost non-existent) service response to the young victims. The lack of appropriate government service responses in all likelihood marginalised, stigmatised and re-traumatised the young girls who disclosed. ACSAT therefore recommended an Aboriginal Child Sexual Assault Coordination Unit be established to ensure the development of the state-wide policy evaluation framework, to liaise with government, communities and non-government organisations about Aboriginal child sexual assault policies and programs, and to ensure that programs address child sexual assault within a 'holistic' context accessible by the local community.[117] The dimensions of a holistic response were described as including:

- a focus on supporting participants' identities and healing
- input and co-ordination between communities, government and the non-government sector
- successful community ownership and sustained engagement in addressing community issues

- genuine partnerships with a strong commitment of time and resources.[118]

Surprisingly (or perhaps not so), ACSAT did not identify a holistic response as victim-centred. Although Aboriginal communities have an important role to play in addressing child sexual assault, it is possible that within the Aboriginal context the promotion of 'holistic' responses is not based on victim-centred practices. If this is so then we need to have an upfront dialogue about that. The fact that some male perpetrators were once victims is not a good reason to preference 'holistic' responses that do not place the victim at the centre. I can only speculate why ACSAT did not adopt the accepted terminology *victim*; however, this approach may not be helpful to Aboriginal victims who too often are not treated appropriately as victims. Within the legal arena the term *victim* is understood as inviting a standard of responses that should not be traded away for 'holistic' community responses.

As various New South Wales non-Aboriginal government department responses showed, the distinct needs of Aboriginal child victims were overwhelmingly not being met. Equality in the Australian context clearly did not translate into equitable government practices and procedures. This was very clear from ACSAT's inquiries into the New South Wales Commission for Children and Young People (CCYP) set up to promote the safety, wellbeing and welfare of children — but whose important mandate apparently did not extend in practice to Aboriginal children.

As ACSAT revealed, most Aboriginal people had little involvement with the CCYP or even knew what it did, there were no Aboriginal persons employed by the CCYP, and none of its children's programs were specifically aimed at promoting the health and wellbeing of Aboriginal children. ACSAT recommended the appointment of an Assistant Commissioner to provide leadership for CCYP's work with Aboriginal children, young people and communities, and the appointment of Aboriginal team members to promote the wellbeing of Aboriginal children and young people.[119] These important recommendations were not implemented by the CCYP.[120]

Other noteworthy recommendations were aimed at the lack of Aboriginal counsellors and the wait times for counselling;[121] the need for victims to be supported by advocates throughout the process;[122] the need for culturally appropriate police investigatory process;[123] the development of culturally appropriate court preparation materials;[124] the employment of Aboriginal Witness Assistance Support staff to assist people through the court process;[125] and the need for a protocol and support service in relation to Aboriginal prisoners who disclose while incarcerated.[126] ACSAT also considered communities' views that sentences were 'rare' and/or 'too lenient' and recommended that Aboriginal advisory panels be established to be consulted on sentencing.[127] It was also recognised that judges did not understand the dynamics of Aboriginal child sexual assault and that training of judges was needed.[128]

The New South Wales Government, in response to the report, adopted the *New South Wales Interagency Plan to Tackle Child Sexual Assault in Aboriginal Communities 2006–2011*.[129] The plan contains 88 measures within four strategic directions: law enforcement, child protection, early intervention and prevention, and community leadership and support. Some of ACSAT's key recommendations are not responded to in this plan; for example, the appointment of an Assistant Commissioner to assist with Aboriginal children and young people or the establishment of an Aboriginal Child Sexual Assault Coordination Unit. It is unclear whether there has been any development of the ACSAT final recommendation that acknowledged that the problem was such that governments needed to consult with Aboriginal communities to research, develop and implement a new model to address child sexual assault through the continuum of the legal process, from initial investigation to sentencing.[130]

Disappointingly, the lack of proper implementation appears linked to government fiscal concern. This has been criticised by the New South Wales Aboriginal Land Council, which has complained that the government provided no funding to implement the recommended responses.[131] The government's plan has been described as 'hobbled by bureaucratic inertia' and inadequate funding.[132] Unlike the Northern Territory inquiry, which has resulted in significant monitoring and funding, the New South Wales ACSAT inquiry appears to have been left 'on the shelf' and largely forgotten by government. In addition to fiscal concerns, one could ask whether the significant final recommendation that embraces Indigenous participation and self-determination was implicitly rejected by government unaccustomed to working in partnership with Aboriginal people. The New South Wales inquiry appears to be another sad example of the Aboriginal complaint of endless government inquiries into Aboriginal affairs that remain unheeded and without due response, notwithstanding the severity of the issue at stake.

Putting the Picture Together: Inquiry into response by government agencies to complaints of family violence and child abuse in Aboriginal communities

In Western Australia the Gordon Inquiry was triggered by a coronial inquest into the death of Susan Taylor, a young Noongar girl whose death at a Perth Aboriginal community in 1999 shocked many in the Noongar community. During the 1990s I visited the Swan Valley Noongar Community (SVNC) on several occasions. The SVNC was promoted as an urban land rights success and the shocking deaths of Susan and other young people were incomprehensible. Many of us quietly wondered, 'What was the cause?' According to the Coroner, the cause of death may have been suicide but ultimately this would never be known because there had been 'insufficient' police investigation into her death.[133] On the evidence presented, the Coroner reached the conclusion that Susan Taylor had been sexually abused and that this abuse had 'played a large part in the circumstances of her death'.[134] The inquest also made serious findings about the extent of Aboriginal child sexual assault in the state: 'It was apparent from the evidence received at the Inquest hearing that there is widespread rape and sexual abuse generally committed against young Aboriginal persons like Susan throughout Western Australia. It is also very clear that few of those cases are reported.'[135]

The then Premier Geoff Gallop announced an official government inquiry, which was established in January 2002 and resulted in a 642-page report.[136] Aboriginal Magistrate Sue Gordon was appointed Chairperson to examine the issues raised by the Coroner's inquiry into the death of Susan Taylor, and the way that government agencies dealt with the issues of violence and child sexual abuse at the SVNC and other Aboriginal communities in Western Australia.[137]

This unprecedented six-month inquiry, described as 'a watershed moment in this State's history',[138] made 197 findings and recommendations addressed to a number of government departments, including the Department of Justice, the Western Australia Police Service, and the Departments of Community Development, Health, Education, Housing and Indigenous Affairs. The government's response included significant funding investment into many initiatives over five years.[139] The response attempted to provide immediate services to protect Indigenous children, such as the creation of new staff positions for child protection workers, Aboriginal support workers, and specialist child protection and family violence officers.[140] It also expanded government programs such as the Strong Families Program, the Child Protection Unit and the Princess Margaret Hospital, the Sexual Assault Service, and the Victim Support and Child Witness Service.[141]

At the same time, the response aimed to break down systemic barriers to enable more effective service delivery, and this was said to involve 'a commitment to do things differently and a committed focus on working with Indigenous people to create change'.[142] Suggested systemic changes included the establishment and appointment of a Children's Commissioner, a Deputy Children's Commissioner with Aboriginal responsibility and a Child Death Review Committee, and the introduction of 'Legislative Impacts Statements in relation to Aboriginal people and their children' (Recommendations 144–147). The Western Australian Government accepted all of Magistrate Gordon's recommendations except, surprisingly, the establishment of a Children's Commission (Recommendation 144), stating that it did not feel such a body was necessary because it would be 'duplicative of existing child accountability and advocacy processes'.[143]

Importantly, the Premier acknowledged that it was not just Aboriginal communities that had failed to respond to Aboriginal child abuse, but past state governments as well: 'we are making up for eight years of inaction where people talked about the problem, but did nothing about it.'[144] The Gordon Inquiry revealed an extraordinary level of government inaction, including:

- the Department of Health's Office of Aboriginal Health had no specific policies, procedures or agendas to address family violence and child abuse in Aboriginal communities[145]

- the Department of Justice Victim Services, including the Victim Support Service and the Child Witness Services, did not employ Aboriginal staff, nor provide cultural awareness training to services, workers and volunteers who assisted the services; this was notwithstanding the statistical over-representation of Aboriginal victims and a 1988 review of victim legislation that raised concerns about the need for Indigenous issues to be given 'significant attention'[146]
- the Western Australia Police Service Child Abuse Unit did not employ Aboriginal police or Aboriginal police liaison officers[147]
- although the Department of Education had developed a Child Protection Policy, neither schools nor parents seemed aware of the policy[148]
- the Department of Indigenous Affairs, with the responsibility for Aboriginal community legislation, considered that 'child protection, family violence and other related issues are not issues of self-governance or community orders and that it would be inappropriate to deal with such issues' through the *Aboriginal Communities Act 1979* (WA).[149]

The Gordon Inquiry assessed the issue of mandatory reporting of child abuse, pointing out that Western Australia was the only state that had not introduced mandatory reporting.[150] As the inquiry noted, the lack of mandatory reporting meant that the state had a far lower rate of substantiated child abuse than other Australian states, and the second lowest rate of substantiated child abuse in Australia.[151] The inquiry acknowledged that mandatory reporting can result in system overload for some child protection services, and this in turn can lead to stricter 'gate-keeping', which may mean less cases are accepted for actual investigation and case management.[152] Although the inquiry was not mandated to consider a system of mandatory reporting of child abuse, its terms of reference did include the mandatory reporting of sexually transmitted infections in children.[153] This was consistent with the Coroner's recommendations and findings that many young Aboriginal children were suffering from sexually transmitted infections at rates 'grossly higher' than for Caucasian or Asian children.[154]

The Gordon Inquiry favoured mandatory reporting where children suffered from sexually transmitted infections and acknowledged the harm that could result from failure to report or take action, also stating that mandatory reporting could highlight the problem and increase funding for support and investigative services rather than merely sending them into crisis.[155] Magistrate Gordon also made public her support for mandatory reporting of all suspected child abuse. She stated that the sexual abuse of children was a criminal offence and that the message needed to be sent to the wider community that it would not be tolerated.[156] While there was local debate about mandatory reporting, I agree with Magistrate Gordon and Professor Freda Briggs of the University of South Australia, who argued, 'surely it is not appropriate in the twenty-first century that professionals responsible for the care of children should be given a choice as to whether they report abuse or collude with the perpetrator and allow it to continue'.[157]

Mandatory reporting for professionals has since resulted. The Gordon Inquiry also resulted in an increase in specialised Department of Community Development (DCD) officers, Child Protection Workers, Aboriginal Support Workers and Family Violence Officers. Notwithstanding the commitments and progress made, there are ongoing and serious deficiencies in the government departments' handling of Aboriginal child abuse matters. This was evident in 2005 when the Western Australian Parliament established a Legislative Council Select Committee Inquiry to investigate cases of children who were abused in foster care. Submissions from foster care groups and former DCD workers indicated that the needs of even the most vulnerable children were still not being met because of a lack of experienced child protection workers and big caseloads.[158] According to the Aboriginal residential care group Djooraminda, it reported ten critical incidents to the department from April 2004 to September 2005, but all critical incidents lacked a response from the respective caseworkers.[159] The Yorganop Aboriginal Childcare Corporation also reported that children had been left without a case manager several times in that past year, and that calls to the department were not responded to. Further vital decisions were delayed or deferred.[160] As far as these Aboriginal agencies were concerned, the child protection system was still not even responding to critical reports.

In 2005 the Western Australian Auditor General voiced his serious concerns about the Gordon Inquiry recommendations and the implementation of the report and associated action plan.[161] The Auditor General was reported as stating that no progress reports were written and there was no way to track what had been done or what changes had been made.[162] In 2009 the Western Australian Parliament Legislative Assembly Inquiry repeated the concerns, recommending that the Auditor General be asked to again review the implementation of the responses to the Gordon Inquiry.[163] This request has still not been responded to.

It is now very apparent that some key Gordon Inquiry recommendations were simply not implemented or given proper regard. One glaring example is the recommendation concerning the appointment of a Deputy Commissioner for Aboriginal Children. In 2007, with other Perth Aboriginal women, professional women working in justice, health and child protection, I publicly called upon the state government to implement the Gordon Inquiry recommendations in relation to the Children's Commission and Deputy Commissioner for Aboriginal Children. The government revisited its initial decision not to support the establishment of the Children's Commission; however, the recommendation that recognised the significance of Aboriginal children through the appointment of a Deputy Commissioner for Aboriginal Children continued unsupported by government. Then shadow children's minister Barbara Scott disagreed, arguing that 'The gravity and level of abuse in indigenous communities shows there must be an assistant children's commissioner appointed [to] deal solely … with cases of abuse of Aboriginal children'.[164]

I am aware from my own consultations that many Aboriginal people and key organisations continue to support the recommendation for a Deputy Commissioner for Aboriginal Children, and affirm the necessity of senior Aboriginal women's presence, knowledge and leadership in relation to Aboriginal children. The Gordon Inquiry supported the budding concept of Healing Centres[165] and recommended the establishment of the 'One Stop Shop', a holistic approach to deal with a wide range of factors and problems linked to family violence and child abuse, including drug abuse, gambling, early parenting, health and welfare.[166] The One Stop Shop would be supported by a specialist team and directed by Local Action Groups, established within communities to guide the work of the centres and government agencies.[167] It was recognised that a high proportion of

Aboriginal people did not access the mainstream government Sexual Assault Referral Centres (SARC), and government non-Indigenous models of service delivery were less likely to be accessed by Aboriginal people.[168] However, the community-based concepts of Healing Centres, One Stop Shops and the Local Action Groups have not resulted; the government has preferred to implement multi-function police stations based on the statutory child protection mandate.

The Gordon Inquiry spoke of a 'community development approach that works with leaders and members of community, and focuses on strengthening families and communities capacities'.[169] It recognised that a 'sea change' in government policies and practices was needed, and that power and decision making needed to be devolved to the community and that Aboriginal people should be assisted in devising solutions.[170] The importance of a partnership with communities, described as a principle 'regularly espoused, but hard to find real examples of', was acknowledged.[171] Similar to the APY inquiry, it was also acknowledged that Aboriginal governance and leadership had 'serious and fundamental problems'.[172]

Many millions of dollars were allocated to government departments in response to the Gordon Inquiry, but safe houses for Aboriginal children and young people impacted by sexual abuse are largely non-existent. None exist in the city of Perth, once home to Susan Taylor, whose death triggered the inquiry. There is very little in the way of Aboriginal community education and awareness about child sexual assault, nor specialised therapeutic responses for children. From my own experience I have observed that very few government personnel appear at all knowledgeable (or even concerned) about the issues facing Aboriginal victims of child sexual assault.

The Coroner's findings in the Susan Taylor case remain as relevant now as then. Aboriginal children in Western Australia are grossly over-represented as victims of child sexual assault, but no specific responses have been developed to address the enormity of the problem. In 2009, a decade after the death of Susan Taylor, I organised a commemoration in her name to coincide with 25 November, the United Nations Day for the Elimination of Violence against Women. Several key agencies, including SARC, Amnesty International, angelhands, Yorgum Counselling Service and Reclaiming Voices, supported and took part in the event, which was well attended by the community and government sector alike. The commemoration was a significant (and culturally appropriate) acknowledgment of Susan Taylor, child sexual assault and the impacts on Aboriginal children, but there is much work to be done.

Following the commemoration I informally engaged several Aboriginal stakeholders to identify further work needed. Objectives identified included the prevention of Aboriginal child sexual assault, support for victim recovery, raising Aboriginal understanding and awareness of child sexual assault (especially the harm caused to young victims), the development of Aboriginal therapeutic and healing interventions for victims, and the promotion and development of responsible Aboriginal leadership. Also, the legal responses need improvement in dialogue with Aboriginal communities that have a key responsibility to address child sexual assault.[173] Unfortunately, this work remains unsupported and is arguably not sustainable. Community-based initiatives are critical to addressing child sexual assault, but the 'sea change' urged by the Gordon Inquiry has not eventuated.

The Aboriginal and Torres Strait Islander Women's Task Force on Violence Report

The Queensland Aboriginal and Torres Strait Islander Women's Task Force on Violence, headed by Professor Boni Robertson, had wide-ranging terms of reference in advising government on policies and programs addressing family violence, recommending changes to the law (including whether customary law should be recognised), and consulting widely with agencies and Aboriginal groups and persons for its report.[174] It recognised violence in Indigenous communities as endemic, severe and requiring urgent attention: 'Violence is now overt; murders, bashings and rapes, including sexual violence against children, have reached epidemic proportions with both Indigenous and non-Indigenous peoples being perpetrators.'[175] The atmosphere in Aboriginal communities was described as one of 'continuing fear from which there is no escape'.[176]

Elders told the inquiry that they were concerned about the level of neglect of children.[177] The Task Force stated that, 'Although sexual abuse against children was discussed when the Task Force raised the subject, the reluctance to discuss it is a serious concern'.[178]

Aboriginal children, who made up nearly half of the children under child protection orders, were overwhelmingly recognised as victims of sexual abuse: 'Sexual abuse is an inadequate term for the incidence of horrific sexual offences committed against young girls and boys in a number of Community locations in Queensland over the last few years'.[179] The Task Force considered that this may have been related to 'negative male socialisation' associated with misuse of alcohol and drugs and the accessibility of pornographic videos.[180]

The Task Force noted the paramount concern that although people had reported child sexual abuse to the police and relevant child protection authority, it had been to no effect.[181] It was advised that 'many people who commit atrocities against Indigenous children are not brought to justice'.[182] The lack of response was one factor that led to non-reporting; other factors included the fear of reprisal and shame.[183] In cases that did proceed, children experienced court as traumatic:

> One young woman, a witness for the Crown, was so upset by her court appearance that she vomited after leaving the witness stand. The psychological trauma of the experience caused her to become very angry with her mother whom she blamed for allowing her to appear. She later attacked her mother with a knife. [184]

Children felt overwhelmed by the court layout and the formality of the proceedings, the process of cross-examination, the presence of police and the feeling of isolation from support. It was accepted that the legal process meant that children 'can leave the court feeling further violated'.[185]

The violence in Queensland communities was recognised as the result of colonisation and cultural genocide, 'the greatest violence of all'.[186] Many emotional health problems were related to colonisation and the dysfunction that resulted had not been resolved.[187] The patriarchal nature of colonisation meant that women were unheard and equal gender representation on government boards and community councils should be endorsed.[188] Colonisation was ongoing, and the present justice system was 'characterised by cultural exclusivity'.[189] Aboriginal experiences of police involved acts of overt and covert racism and institutional racism in the police force.[190]

Similar to the Gordon Inquiry support for the One Stop Shop, it was considered that regional centres should be funded to develop resource and training packages and specific intervention approaches, including children's healing programs.[191] More women needed to be appointed as police, and children's shelters were required.[192] As the Task Force noted, it was vital to observe principles of best practice in relation to all programs addressing family violence in Indigenous communities. This included building on the skills of people at the community level, based on the belief and practice that any form of violence is unacceptable.[193]

The Task Force acknowledged alternative forms of justice, such as restorative justice, arguing that the justice system did not work with families to address the child or parents' underlying problems.[194] It considered the use of Sentencing Circles in Canada and an internationally acclaimed holistic healing model addressing child sexual assault, Hollow Water.[195] These approaches are examined in Chapter 7.

A systemic failure

We have witnessed more than a decade of government inquiries and reports — several headed by Aboriginal women — aimed at understanding the nature and extent of family violence and child sexual assault in communities and the adequacy of governmental responses. These reports have all revealed child sexual assault to be severe, endemic and a threat to the future wellbeing of Aboriginal children, communities and families.

Some important changes have resulted, but government responses have varied and failure to implement recommendations has been a major problem. Some states have taken a different direction, and have not followed the vision set out in these expert reports. This is most evident from the Northern Territory inquiry, which resulted in a major intervention but failed to respond to the key recommendation that the territory and federal governments develop a memorandum of understanding specifically in relation to Aboriginal child sexual assault.

One major concern is that Aboriginal communities (rather than non-Aboriginal government agencies) have largely not been empowered to address and respond to the serious problem of child sexual assault. For example, a particularly advanced community-based recommendation is ACSAT's final recommendation that government consult with community to develop a new model to address Aboriginal child sexual assault through the continuum of the legal process. This key recommendation appears to have been overtaken by the National Child Sexual Assault Law Reform Committee (a non-Indigenous body), which has recommended an Indigenous specialist Child Sex Offences Court be established.[196]

It is apparent that power and funding remain largely vested with non-Aboriginal government agencies, whose responses to child sexual assault have clearly been inadequate. Through the inquiry processes it can be argued that government departments Australia-wide have been culturally inept and negligent in their responses (or lack thereof) to Aboriginal child sexual assault. In Western Australia, for example, notwithstanding the wealth of the mining boom, Aboriginal children have been denied powerful systems advocacy through the appointment of a Deputy Commissioner for Aboriginal Children.

Aboriginal empowerment in relation to child sexual assault is critical to reflect the fundamental human rights principle of self-determination — Aboriginal people's knowledge and ability to determine our own futures in relation to our children and communities. All these expert reports reveal severe levels of criminal abuse of children and re-victimisation within the Aboriginal and wider community. It is also evident that the criminal justice system is systemically failing to respond appropriately to Aboriginal children who are being impacted by a most severe criminal offence and human rights abuse.

Chapter 5

The criminal justice response to child sexual assault

The role of male dominance in the law has been examined by many legal feminists. As Australian critical legal theorist Margaret Davies explains, men have made the legal world and the law is reflective of male values.[1] Child sexual assault is formally regarded in law as a serious criminal offence, but the responses of the law and legal system in practice are highly ambivalent, and have been described as perpetrating a form of secondary abuse on the victim. Despite law reform to address systemic issues facing child victims, problems remain. This has led to a questioning of the adversarial system itself, with some commentators arguing that it is not an appropriate model to address child sexual abuse.

Aboriginal child victims have their own unique experiences in the criminal justice system. Although the concept of judicial neutrality is fundamental to our legal system, Aboriginal victims of sexual assault can experience 'double discrimination' and judicial bias. There is little research concerning Indigenous child victims and the criminal justice response, but recent high profile cases from the Northern Territory and Queensland highlight the disparate treatment that Aboriginal child victims experience before the law. From these cases it can be seen that the rape of Aboriginal children has been unpunished and even sanctioned by the justice system — seemingly under the guise of Aboriginal 'culture' and judicial beneficial intent.

This chapter concerns the law's response to child sexual assault. It includes the limited research highlighting children's particular experiences and examines case studies of several high profile cases that were concerning Aboriginal children. It shows the law's failure to respond appropriately to child sexual assault, and indicates the level of human rights violations being experienced by Aboriginal children within the justice system under the guise of culture.

The ambivalent response of the criminal justice system

Within the Australian legal system, child sexual assault has not always been treated as a criminal offence. Academic Jan Breckenridge has detailed the enormous efforts of Australian feminists in the 1970s and 1980s to ensure that sexual abuse of children was properly regarded and responded to not as a 'private' matter, but as a serious criminal offence.[2]

Notwithstanding the significant reforms that have occurred, child protection expert Professor Chris Goddard argues that there is still 'considerable ambivalence' about the use of criminal law in response to child abuse.[3] Goddard refers to a study he conducted in Melbourne in 1987 over a ten-month period looking at a total of 205 cases — 104 in relation to child sexual abuse and 101 cases of physical abuse. Of the 205 cases, charges were laid in only 22 cases and convictions gained in 17 of those 22 cases.[4] Goddard's research showed a 'minimisation' at all stages of police and court involvement[5] and indicated that 'prosecution of perpetrators is not a priority'.[6] Only 3 of the 17 persons found guilty served a term of imprisonment, and in each of those three cases a child had died. In no cases of child sexual assault was a term of imprisonment ordered. There were even cases where the perpetrator had admitted abuse but no prosecution had followed. Goddard concluded that 'child abuse is not always treated as a crime and, when it is prosecuted, it is rarely treated as a serious crime'.[7]

The low attrition rate for child sexual assault offences was considered in Western Australia by the Legislative Assembly's Inquiry into the Prosecution of Assaults and Sexual Offences.[8] The inquiry found that although there has been a significant increase in the rate of reporting for sexual assault offences, it is still less likely to be reported than any other form of violence.[9] Delays were particularly common for children, who have fears of reporting; consequently it was normal for children to delay telling about their abuse for a considerable time (sometimes years).[10] Many cases are never disclosed. As the inquiry recognised, only 10% of sexual assault offences are reported, and only 1% of such cases result in a conviction.[11] The rate of attrition for children was significantly higher than for adults, with the prosecution of sexual offences against children under six years described as 'exceptional'.[12] The decision to prosecute is influenced by the prospect of securing a conviction; children are widely perceived to be a class of 'unreliable witnesses', prone to lying or fantasy, or easily manipulated with inaccurate memories, so few cases actually proceed to trial.[13]

Secondary abuse or re-victimisation

The responses of the criminal justice system to sexual assault have long been identified as problematic and inappropriate. The reporting of rape has been described as a form of 're-victimisation' — in no other crime is the victim/complainant subject to so much scrutiny at trial.[14] The Western Australian Sexual Assault Referral Centre has said that the requirements of the justice system 'are counter-therapeutic' and victims can be repeatedly traumatised through the justice system.[15]

In Australia the most comprehensive study of children's courtroom experiences in response to sexual assault was conducted by Christine Eastwood and published in 2003 by the Australian Institute of Criminology (AIC).[16] Eastwood acknowledged that significant research and findings (including the Australian Law Reform Commission and HREOC) had shown that child complainants were encouraged into a system that resulted in further trauma and abuse of the child.[17] The legislative reforms have been 'piecemeal' and have not addressed 'the real issue of abuse inflicted by the justice system itself and the manner in which children are disadvantaged in the legal process'.[18] Eastwood stated that important recommendations for reform have been ignored and unimplemented.[19]

The study by Eastwood involved 130 participants; 63 were child complainants and the remainder were family members, prosecution, defence lawyers and judicial officers. It involved three jurisdictions: Western Australia, Queensland and New South Wales. The research aimed to investigate, from the perspective of the child complainants, the process and consequence of involvement with the criminal justice system. When asked if they would ever disclose sexual abuse again following their court experiences, 33% of children in New South Wales, 44% in Queensland and 64% in Western Australia said, yes, they would report again.[20] Clearly, significant numbers of children believed that reporting was not worth what they suffered in court. They reported to Eastwood:

> It makes me feel like it is no good going to court … It is just a waste of time … They don't look after you. They couldn't care less. They are not interested … It is the hardest thing and it ruins your life. You never forget it.
> (NSW child, 14 years)
>
> We are supposed to be free after this but we are not free — we are even more caged up. It's a joke — don't put yourself through the trauma.
> (NSW child, 16 years)
>
> It's too hard. I wouldn't want to go through it again.
> (WA child, 16 years).[21]

Similar to the children themselves, a high proportion of legal participants were asked if they would want their own children to proceed in the criminal justice system in response to sexual assault. Only one-third of the legal participants said they would.[22] According to one member of the Queensland judiciary, 'Their rights have been invisible — they have been denied very basic rights … the trial process is flawed for anybody, but for children it is not only flawed — it is cruel'.[23]

Eastwood identified the three key areas of concern for child complainants: waiting for trial, seeing the accused and the cross-examination process.

Children found the waiting time from reporting to trial (the average time was 18.2 months) prevented them from moving on with their lives, and that 'it seemed like it took forever'.[24] There were serious psychological problems associated with waiting such a long time, including nightmares, suicide attempts, self-mutilation, self-hatred, fear of the offender, depression, inability to concentrate on school and fears about the trial. In Western Australia the practical remedy to address this problem has been the full pre-recording of children's evidence.[25]

Seeing the offender was a major cause of concern for child complainants. This problem can be eliminated through the use of closed circuit television (CCTV), but only Western Australia ensured that this was standard practice for all child complaints.[26] In Queensland, judges regularly refused to allow the use of screens (to separate the child witness from the offender in court), and not one child in Eastwood's study had been allowed to give evidence by CCTV.[27] In New South Wales legislation provided that children could give evidence by CCTV, but legislative exemptions (for example, the court considers it is not 'in the interests of justice' to do so) were frequently invoked and nearly half of all children were refused the use of CCTV.[28]

The experience of courtroom cross-examination by defence lawyers was a further issue, notwithstanding that all states have legislation designed to control offensive cross-examination.[29] The children reported cross-examination that continued for hours and even days as 'horrible, confusing and upsetting'.[30] Children were commonly accused of lying, which they found particularly hurtful. They were sometimes shouted at and asked questions that were 'intimidating, misleading, confusing, annoying, harassing, offensive and repetitive'.[31] Only in Western Australia are children cross-examined just once, for much shorter periods of time, and with the benefit of the physical separation from the offender as afforded by CCTV.[32]

Since Eastwood's study there have been significant law reforms in New South Wales to improve the process for child complainants. However, this legislation has not been adequate to address the problems, especially in relation to the cross-examination process. Eastwood concludes that 'reform must go beyond legislation, and must include a concomitant shift in culture, attitudes and beliefs about sexual abuse and about children'.[33] The consequences of failing to effect meaningful reforms are serious. If children refuse to report sexual abuse because of the damage of the criminal justice system, the abusers are allowed to act with impunity.

The 'counter-therapeutic' approach of the law was also critiqued. Although it is now well accepted that children who have been sexually abused require as a matter of priority 'acceptance and validation' for their psychological survival, the adversarial legal system is fundamentally predicated on undermining the child victim's credibility.[34] Eastwood argues the law must start to recognise the realities of child sexual abuse; by remaining 'deaf to the voices and needs of the children it purports to protect from harm, it fails by any measure of what constitutes "justice"'.[35]

Eastwood's study is supported by recent AIC research.[36] In her 2009 paper 'Child complainants and the court process in Australia', Kelly Richards outlines the problems facing children in the court system, in particular the traumatic nature of the cross-examination process, the bias of juries that often believe that children are unreliable witnesses, and that delays in reporting (common in cases of child sexual assault) affect jurors' perceptions of the child's credibility. The low likelihood of a conviction was related to the generally secretive nature of the offence, but also to the court's willingness to dismiss charges (even without a hearing).[37] Richards also examines the array of reforms implemented in Australia, such as courtroom modifications, use of CCTV, pre-recorded evidence, support persons, restrictions on cross-examination, improvement to interview techniques and child witness statements, and even the introduction of a specialist court in New South Wales.[38] Richards' troubling conclusion is that 'such provisions have been limited in improving the experiences of child complainants and in turn, increasing conviction rates'.[39]

Richards' research highlights that legislative changes to improve experiences for child victims are not readily being translated into practice, that judges' discretion to utilise measures was often not exercised, and that concern for the rights of the accused is at play.[40] In highlighting areas of future research, Richards asks whether provisions to support children could be effective, 'given that the western adversarial model of criminal justice is essentially unsuited to child complainants'.[41] Alternative approaches, such as therapeutic jurisprudence, were also supported for further research and examination.[42]

The Australian research findings discussed may be underlined by the contentions made by United States psychiatrists Cindy Veldhuis and Jennifer Freyd, that society has refused to condemn child sexual assault and, moreover, that 'Silence is reinforced, speaking is punished'.[43] The authors identified deeply pervasive cultural beliefs and values that allow the continued perpetration of abuse and deny victims a voice. This includes the patriarchal notion that parents, especially fathers, have the right to do whatever they please with their children, that family matters should be kept private, and that adults should be believed over children. Other common beliefs are that although child abuse happens, after a certain age the victim should just 'get over it'. Also, acts committed under the influence of drugs and alcohol are tolerated. Disturbingly, some people view children as having the ability to consent or not to sexual activity. Many believe that talking about abuse is worse than the abuse itself, and that children and women who allege abuse are themselves disordered. Others believe that memory, especially that of children and women and/or memory for abuse, is implicitly untrustworthy.[44]

Arguably, in Australia the serious flaws identified with respect to the legal system are informed by such negative societal values that effectively sustain child sexual assault.

A traumatic and unjust system

The traumatic and unjust nature of the criminal justice system as a response to child sexual assault was the subject of a 2003 AIC conference, 'Child Sexual Abuse: Justice response or alternative resolution'.[45] David Kerr, from the South Australia Victim Support Service, argued that cross-examination was too often traumatic for children and gave the example of a ten-year-old girl who was required to spend eight hours as a witness over three days.[46] He commented there was often inappropriate language used with children, language that they could clearly not understand.[47] He proposed the exploration of an inquisitorial model in the context of a 'child appropriate inquiry process' conducted by a judge sitting alone.[48]

At the same conference, Paul Rofe QC and Filomena Merlino from the South Australian Office of the Director of Public Prosecutions, argued that a 'century of jurisprudence' that regarded children as a 'suspect class of witness' (along with sexual assault victims) was not 'easily swept away by the legislative broom'.[49] They considered that the trial process traumatised children, especially during cross-examination, which was not 'a level playing field' for the child complainant.[50] Judges and courts frequently did not appear to understand a child's level of understanding, asking inappropriate questions that children could not reasonably be expected to answer.[51] They noted that cases were rarely resolved through a guilty plea for the simple reason that defendants were aware of the likelihood of acquittal. In the authors' view, consideration needed to be given (in cases of intra-familial abuse) to diversionary programs and treatment-based alternatives within and external to correctional facilities.[52]

Judge Hal Jackson, who at the time was a Western Australian District Court judge, detailed legislative reforms in Western Australia, commencing with the 1992 Child Sexual Abuse Task Force of the Western Australian Law Reform Commission. Reforms included the introduction of CCTV, support persons, child communicators, pre-recording of evidence, abolishment of committal hearings, and other support measures including judicial and legal professional education.[53] It is evident from Eastwood's study that these reforms have ensured that children's experiences in Western Australia are significantly better than those of children in other jurisdictions.

Judge Jackson acknowledged that the system was still not perfect. For example, there were technical problems in relation to CCTV, and while the process had some advantages, 'it can be a poor means for conveying the truth'.[54] There were 'gaps in the protective framework', including matters related to the general criminal law (such as the required corroboration warnings), and there needed to be further consideration of the admissibility of expert evidence in relation to child sexual assault and children's responses.[55] Notwithstanding the relative success of legislative reforms in Western Australia, Judge Jackson conceded that 'Perhaps the time has come to look at the whole question of the adversarial process in these matters'.[56]

Dr Caroline Taylor, in a 2004 study of child sexual assault trials, also confirmed the traumatic, and indeed abusive, nature of the trial process.[57] Taylor observed that truth seeking, however crucial to establishing fact, was simply irrelevant in the court process:

'Rather than looking for evidence that supports "truth-seeking" the judiciary often creates evidentiary rulings and practices that are "truth-defeating".'[58]

Taylor identified patterns in defence narratives and judicial rulings that indicated that 'a kind of legal template' is applied to sexual offence proceedings for the purpose of enabling and mobilising 'deeply held stereotypes and social myths' about women, children and sexual assault.[59] The trial process was often an abusive one that Taylor argued had 'the ability to reflect symbolically the same structural inequality and abuses of power the child experiences at the hands of the perpetrator'.[60]

Aboriginal women and children have unique experiences

Aboriginal women and children have their own unique experiences of the criminal justice system. Although sexual assault and violence against Aboriginal women and children has long been widespread and endemic, Aboriginal women and children have largely stood outside the law's protection.

The colonial legal system's apparent sanctioning of sexual assault towards Aboriginal women and children is evident from historian Jillian Bavin-Mizzi's study of rape cases before the Supreme Courts of Victoria, Queensland and Western Australia in the years 1880 to 1900.[61] The study indicates that sexual violence against Aboriginal women and children was simply not regarded as a criminal offence. Of 1200 or so complaints, only six concerned Aboriginal women and children (with three cases each respectively), a remarkably low figure given the widespread level of sexual violence associated with colonisation.[62] Only one defendant was convicted in those six cases, and, as Bavin-Mizzi points out, in that case evidence of the rape was also given by a white man, a farmer who witnessed the rape.[63] Bavin-Mizzi also notes that in the cases concerning Aboriginal women and children, offenders acted with impunity, seemingly unconcerned by onlookers and third parties.[64] The lack of court convictions showed that Aboriginal women and children were outside the law's protection and that rape was seemingly an aspect of colonial entitlement.

In the 1980s researcher Vivian Bligh asked why Aboriginal women were not using the Adelaide Rape Crisis Centre.[65] She spoke to approximately one hundred women and most (75%)

conveyed that there was a considerable amount of rape occurring in the Aboriginal community.[66] However, Bligh found that the cases involving Aboriginal victims were not treated as criminal and not worthy of legal recourse: 'Throughout the study I found only one case, which was in fact taken to court and the rapist was convicted and sentenced. All other cases I learned about from the women either did not reach the court or were thrown out of court because of insufficient evidence.'[67]

In 2005 AIC published the results of a national consultation with sexual assault victim survivors and support services, in which it examined women's help-seeking decisions and service responses to sexual assault.[68] AIC was unable to interview Aboriginal victim survivors, but interviews with Aboriginal sexual assault support workers led the report's author, Dr Denise Lievore, to conclude that 'Overall, the criminal justice system appears to be particularly unresponsive to Indigenous women's complaints of sexual assault'.[69] The report found that police did not treat Aboriginal victims as legitimate victims of sexual assault.[70]

Although support workers encouraged Aboriginal women and girls to speak to the police and report sexual assault, cases did not go past the police stage: 'the police always give one answer — there's no case — without explaining why there is no case.'[71] One sexual assault support worker observed that while police did not respond to sexual assaults against Aboriginal girls, they routinely criminalised Aboriginal girls for behaviour linked to the assaults:

> Girls who are 13 to 16 years old are appearing in court for drugs, stealing, drunkenness and repeat offences. This is often as a result of sexual assault, which they'll disclose if you can get them talking. But we go to the police to tell them about carnal knowledge and there's no action, even when the girls are pregnant. I know two 14 year olds who were repeatedly abused by their stepfather. I took them to the police over two weeks ago. I've been involved with court support for over two years and not one sexual assault has gone through in that time. They go no further than the police.[72]

Aboriginality was viewed as relevant in influencing the police decision to not act on complaints by Aboriginal women and girls, with intra-Aboriginal sexual assault likely to receive no criminal response at all:

'If it's a black woman sexually assaulted by a white man, they'll rarely proceed. A white woman sexually assaulted by a black man is more likely to proceed, but when both parties are Indigenous it won't proceed.'[73] Aboriginal women of light skin (and presumably non-Aboriginal ancestry) were also regarded as more likely than dark skin women to receive the benefit of a police response.[74]

Supporting the AIC research findings, a research report, 'What is the outcome of reporting rape to the police? Study of reported rapes in Victoria 2000–2003', reported that no criminal charges were laid with respect to any of the 16 reported rapes by Indigenous complainants.[75] My own experience of the legal system was consistent with this, resulting in no criminal charges. It may be surmised from the research that police today still do not treat Aboriginal victims of sexual assault legitimately as victims and still do not respond appropriately in a non-discriminatory manner.

Aboriginal victims face 'double discrimination' in the courts

In the event that charges are laid with respect to Aboriginal victims, there is further evidence that Aboriginal complainants are subjected to discrimination in court on the basis of gender and race. Aboriginal women adult complainants of child sexual assault, and Aboriginal girls, often encounter 'double discrimination' in the courts.

Notwithstanding the legal prohibitions of discrimination under the *Racial Discrimination Act 1975*, Aboriginal sexual assault victims experience marked discrimination in the courts. The experiences of Aboriginal women victims of sexual assault were recognised in a comprehensive 1996 study of sexual assault court matters by the New South Wales Department for Women.[76] The report, *Heroines of Fortitude*, included the cases of 17 Aboriginal women complainants, with offenders being both Aboriginal and non-Aboriginal males.[77] It was found that Aboriginal women (described as ten times more likely to be complainants of sexual assault than non-Aboriginal women) faced 'double discrimination in the criminal justice system' and were subjected to false and degrading stereotypes imputed on the basis of gender and race.[78]

The report found that Aboriginal victims were regularly asked more questions about alcohol and drug use, victim compensation and victim promiscuity.[79] They were also asked far more questions by the defence, which implied that they were lying or making up the story. The average non-Aboriginal woman was asked an average of seven questions about lying, while two cases involving Aboriginal women showed they were subjected to 29 and 70 questions about lying.[80] Almost every Aboriginal woman appearing in court was asked if she had made a false accusation for the purpose of victim compensation.[81] The longest ever cross-examination concerned an Aboriginal woman — it lasted five hours and 20 minutes.

The research also highlighted instances where Aboriginal women were regularly bullied, harassed and intimidated during cross-examination.[82] In one case the Crown Prosecutor commented in his closing submissions that the Aboriginal complainant was 'not very bright'.[83] Not surprisingly, the report found that Aboriginal women were very distressed as a result of their experiences at trial, with distress causing frequent interruptions and victims becoming ill and nauseated in the witness box, needing to take regular breaks, crying and being unable to give evidence.[84] The report concluded, 'The experience of these women goes beyond the testing of a complainant's evidence for its veracity and honesty and is insensitive, abusive and victimising of women'.[85]

Almost all of the cases studied that involved a hung jury (where the jury could not agree on a verdict) and retrials involved Aboriginal complainants.[86] Often the Aboriginal complainants would not turn up for the second or third retrial and were forced by the courts to attend through a subpoena. In such cases it was noted that the trial was then aborted and the accused acquitted.[87] Clearly the harassment and resulting distress of Aboriginal complainants contributed to their cases being less believed by juries that were unable to reach a verdict.

The report considered that myths and stereotypes of Aboriginal women as unsophisticated, vengeful and morally corrupt were all at play and evident in trial.[88] The credibility of many Aboriginal women was also attacked with the use of racist myths and stereotypes about Aboriginal culture.[89] In one case the defence questioned the complainant at some length (with permission from the judge) about her Aboriginal cultural laws and whether they permitted casual sexual relations. Although the complainant attempted to explain she had two religions, both her Aboriginal culture and the Catholic religion, the defence repeatedly attempted to infer to her that her Aboriginal culture permitted casual sexual relationships. Upon objecting to this racist line of questioning, the victim was admonished by the Judge.[90]

The discrimination experienced by Aboriginal women was also apparent at the sentencing stage. Only one accused person pleaded guilty and only 25% of accused persons were found guilty.[91] Cases involving non-Aboriginal complainants resulted in a much higher proportion of guilty pleas (26%), which were encouraged by recognition during sentencing, and also a higher conviction rate of 31%. Notwithstanding the differential in sentencing patterns, some judges were conscious of the issues; as one judge stated in sentencing, Aboriginal women are 'entitled to the protection of the law as much as anybody else'.[92]

The criminal justice system sanctions Aboriginal sexual assault as 'culture'

There has been a long line of cases in which the rape of Aboriginal women and children has been regarded as less than serious by the courts. In the 1980 Northern Territory case *Lane* (Unreported NT Supreme Court, May 1980), Justice Gallop commented in sentencing three Aboriginal men for the rape of an Aboriginal woman:

> There is evidence before me, which I accept, that rape is not considered as seriously in Aboriginal communities as it is in the white community ... and indeed the chastity of women is not as importantly regarded as in white communities. Apparently the violation of a Aboriginal woman's integrity is not nearly as significant as it is in a white community.[93]

Audrey Bolger's ground-breaking 1991 publication *Aboriginal Women and Violence*, noted that Aboriginal women were adamant that the violence towards women and girls taking place in their communities was not traditional.[94] Bolger reported that Aboriginal women were being affected by violence from Aboriginal men that would not have been countenanced in traditional society. One woman reported, 'There are now three kinds of violence in Aboriginal society — alcoholic violence, traditional violence, and bullshit traditional violence'.[95] Aboriginal women (and some men) were adamant that much of what was happening in communities was in no way traditional. Aboriginal legal aid defence lawyers brought up 'customary practices' to excuse assaults against women,[96] and the judiciary held preconceptions about Aboriginal culture and traditions that 'may influence the course of justice'.[97]

In 1989 anthropologist Diane Bell wrote that defence lawyers have constantly argued that rape is a light matter in Aboriginal society, and that male anthropologists have given expert evidence that the 'pack rape' of Aboriginal women had been authorised as traditional Aboriginal punishment.[98] These concerns were supported by Aboriginal lawyer Sharon Payne, who, in 1992, documented a Canberra case of Aboriginal men who raped an Aboriginal woman; in the case, evidence was given to mitigate sentences on the basis of 'extenuating' circumstances, these being the men's loss of culture and lands.[99] As Payne pointed out, 'Apparently the young woman had no such defence although she too had lost her heritage'.[100]

Academic Wendy Shaw supports these concerns, arguing that 'gendered colonialisms' have been reproduced in law.[101] Shaw's examination of cases in the 1970s and 1980s in which Aboriginal customary law was invoked in acknowledgment of the (alleged) cultural practices (violence and sexual assault) reveals that 'Although violence against women was repeatedly accepted as customary in Aboriginal societies ... no references to sources or authorities was unearthed'.[102] What Shaw found instead in the many transcripts and court cases she studied were statements that pointed to general understandings or opinion on subject matters. For example, the case of *R v M*, of the Northern Territory Supreme Court (1975) concerned a charge of 'carnal knowledge' of a 10-year-old girl, described as 'willing' and 'sexually precocious', in which the judge stated, 'I do not regard this offence as seriously as I would if both parties were white. This is of course not to say that the virtue of Aboriginal girls is of any less value than that of white girls, but simply that social customs appear to be different'.[103]

Shaw found no actual evidence as to the origin of this apparent relevant cultural difference, only the judge's own views of disgust at the purported 'sexual precocity in young Aboriginal girls'.[104] While the cases studied by Shaw failed to reveal the actual origin of any customary law being argued, judges' own personal understandings about what constitutes the 'traditions' are positioned to sit firmly within the discourse *about* Aboriginal cultures.[105] From the case study research, Shaw argues that courts and judges were engaged in a 'neocolonial manoeuvre', imposing their understandings of Aboriginal culture.[106] Moreover, in what appeared to be non-Aboriginal resistance to the imposition of dominant, non-Aboriginal values, the violent punishment of Aboriginal women and children is sanctioned by the Australian legal system.[107]

During the early 2000s two high profile decisions of the Northern Territory Supreme Court highlighted that sexual violence against Aboriginal girls is sanctioned by the criminal justice system as Aboriginal culture. A fundamental tenet of the legal system is that all who come before it are equal and entitled to its equal protection. However, these cases leave no doubt that sexual violence against Aboriginal girls has been excused in the name of 'culture'. I analyse these cases in some detail, and consider that they reflect ongoing colonial and racist assumptions that impact all Aboriginal victims of sexual assault.

Case study: Pascoe's case, 2001

Pascoe's case involved decisions and appeals from the Northern Territory Magistrates Court through to the High Court of Australia.[108] The facts of the case as reported were that on 20 August 2001, the defendant, Jackie Pascoe Jamilmira, a 50-year-old from Arnhem Land, took a 15-year-old girl, described as his 'promised wife', to his outstation, whereupon she was subjected to a violent beating and rape. The victim managed to escape with her family, although Pascoe objected by discharging his shotgun.[109]

Northern Territory Magistrate Vince Luppino heard the charges against Pascoe — not of rape but sexual intercourse with a minor, and discharge of firearms. According to the North Australian Aboriginal Legal Aid Service (NAALAS), the police initially charged the defendant with rape, but following investigations by the Director of Public Prosecutions (DPP) (the Crown) and 'negotiations' with NAALAS, it was agreed to reduce the rape charge to unlawful intercourse with a minor and firearms offences.[110] This decision flew in the face of evidence provided by the young victim in a police statement and reported in the national *Australian* newspaper:

> He started slapping my face and then punching me. He used his right and left hand to slap me in my face. He was hitting me real hard. He had that closed fist and he hit me eight times. I was feeling dizzy and he said to me 'let me look, so I can hit you again'. I said to him I want to go out and have a drink of water and wash my face. He said: 'No, you're not going anywhere, no phone call, no truck [out of there] for you'. He told me to take off my clothes, so I did. He grabbed me by my left arm and my right leg and threw me onto that mattress. He put his foot onto my neck and he was pushing me down on that mattress. He had my right arm and he was twisting it — it felt like he would break it. Jackie was wearing a long sleeved jacket, that grey one; it had blood on the back of it. The blood came from my nose. He was on top of me and he forced me, and I was laying down and I was trying to cross my legs.[111]

The victim's statement can be contrasted with that of the principal solicitor for NAALAS, Gerard Bryant, who maintained the behaviour complained of was not recognised by the Aboriginal community as unlawful: 'Rather it is viewed as appropriate and morally correct.'[112] The NAALAS spokesperson appeared to be arguing that violent rape of young girls is a matter of Aboriginal culture.

Notwithstanding the Crown's failure to prosecute a charge of sexual assault, Magistrate Luppino treated the case before him as one of sexual assault, sentencing the defendant to 13 months of imprisonment for the charge of unlawful intercourse and two months for firearm offences.[113] Justice Gallop of the Northern Territory Supreme Court overruled this decision, finding that a person could not be sentenced for an offence for which they have not been charged or convicted.[114] Justice Gallop also found that Magistrate Luppino had failed to give 'due weight' to the customary law practice of promised marriage. Astoundingly, the defendant's sentence was reduced to just 24 hours' imprisonment for unlawful intercourse with a minor, and 14 days' imprisonment for the firearm offences.[115]

Causing much controversy, Justice Gallop agreed with the 'expert' anthropological evidence concerning promised marriages, stating 'She didn't need protection [from white law] … She knew what was expected of her. It's very surprising to me [that Pascoe] was charged at all.'[116] This view stands in marked contrast to the view later stated by that United Nations that 'laws requiring the free and full consent of the intending spouses are necessary to protect the girl child against forced marriage. Such protection is enhanced by consistent implementation and monitoring of relevant national legislation and its enforcement'.[117]

The Full Court of the Northern Territory Supreme Court, in *Hales v Jamilmira* [2003] NTCA 9, overturned the Supreme Court decision, finding the sentence 'manifestly inadequate'.[118] The court increased the sentence for unlawful carnal knowledge from 24 hours to 12 months, but to be suspended after a period of only one month. The court considered anthropological evidence from non-Aboriginal male experts who argued that the promised marriage was 'the cultural ideal, sanctioned and underpinned by a complex system of customary law and practice'.[119] From the case decision it does not appear that any Aboriginal women Elders or women anthropologists were called to give evidence to support the young victim or her right to a chosen marriage, or to dispute the male view that sexual assault is culturally permissible.

On appeal, the Supreme Court noted that the charge was not one of rape or sexual intercourse without consent, for which a maximum penalty of life applies, accepting that the investigatory and prosecuting authorities must have concluded that none of those elements could be made out to the required degree.[120] In doing so the court effectively presented the discriminatory conduct against the young Aboriginal victim as an unbiased matter related to proof and evidence. As the DPP did not prosecute the charge of sexual assault, the account that was given originally by the young victim to the police became distorted and recast before the court as a matter of consensual sex. The so-called 'facts' as prosecuted erased the victim's testimony of a violent rape — presenting 'facts' as a matter of underage and consensual sex.[121]

In support of the defendant's argument that his sentence should be reduced (mitigated), it was argued and accepted by the court that he had a lack of prior convictions 'for offences of this type'.[122] However, the defendant's history of violence included the killing of a former wife, which was minimised by the court as a drunken fight between two apparently equal parties.[123] As revealed in the *Australian* newspaper account, the deceased was a highly respected Maningrida teacher in her thirties who was beaten with sticks by Pascoe and, according to pathologists, had about 75 bruises on her body post mortem.[124]

In the Pascoe case, the complainant is heard only through her court-mandated victim impact statement: 'I am angry for what he done. I was sad and upset. I think about it all the time. I always get angry with everyone. This makes me upset.'[125] It is clear that non-Aboriginal male lawyers for both the defence and the Crown actively silenced the young Aboriginal victim, and promoted a distorted narrative in which violence and rape disappeared behind the purported power and strength of Aboriginal men's customary law: 'Our law is like the ocean, it is vast and affects all parts of our lives, it never changes. Your law is like a puddle of water, it is ever changing. I am being punished for following my law.'[126]

Author Joan Kimm considers that until this case, the government and judiciary were reluctant to support women's rights as victims when customary law was involved, and that there appeared to be an acceptance that Indigenous defendants 'had a de facto claim of right to commit serious assaults on young girls when enforcing "the promise"'.[127] Kimm's argument that Pascoe's case recognised the rights of young Aboriginal sexual assault victims is surprising. In this case the victim's complaint of a violent sexual assault was distorted and recast as consensual underage intercourse. The victim's identity as an Aboriginal girl and the allegations of Aboriginal 'culture' were clearly the grounds by which the criminal justice system responded to her in such a highly discriminatory manner.

Notwithstanding the serious human rights implications of the cases, women's organisations, human rights groups and Aboriginal organisations were noticeably silent. With other Aboriginal women I felt compelled to condemn this case through media as abuse of culture and violation of the human rights of Aboriginal women and girls. I was contacted for a comment by ABC Radio. I considered it best if Aboriginal women from the Northern Territory commented on this case, but ABC Radio advised me that no one could be found who was prepared to make public comment. Although many Aboriginal women are opposed to violence, there is taboo, silence and even fear surrounding speaking publicly about sexual violence, especially when issues of culture are raised.

I felt that it was imperative to publicly condemn this case in the interests of all Aboriginal women and girls. The following radio conversation was broadcast by ABC Radio on 22 October 2002:

DAMIEN CARRICK: My understanding is that in the case there was anthropological evidence presented that promised marriages are morally correct and proper under traditional law.

HANNAH McGLADE: Well that may have been so. The question ... is whether that violence that was inflicted on the young woman is morally correct. Aboriginal women across Australia have said violence is not the traditional way, and it should not be described as customary violence. In fact Aboriginal women in the Northern Territory for many years have rejected that violence. I can't speak for the Northern Territory; Aboriginal women across Australia say 'It's not our traditional way' ...

DAMIEN CARRICK: I think the anthropologist said something along the lines of ... 'While such behaviour may be at variance with contemporary Western sensibilities, mores and laws, it in no way diminishes the fact that it was regarded as entirely appropriate, indeed morally correct conduct.'

HANNAH McGLADE: Well I don't think the young woman at all felt that that was entirely appropriate conduct. She fled from him. She was beaten and violated. I don't think she at all felt that that was appropriate conduct, or her family, who came to rescue her.

DAMIEN CARRICK: Do you think that Aboriginal men sometimes hide violence behind a pretext of customary law? ...

HANNAH McGLADE: Absolutely. I think that certainly violence has been normalised by Aboriginal men ... It's disconcerting that our own Aboriginal legal services have assisted ... by running defences where violence is said to be culturally acceptable or excused under some sort of cultural basis.

DAMIEN CARRICK: What do you say to the argument that Indigenous communities should be allowed to keep their customary law strong … and that whatever issues surrounding those practices are best left to the communities …

HANNAH McGLADE: But has this been left to the community or has it been left to the powerful members of the community, the men of the community, the people who have distorted, engaged in the distortion of traditional customary law?[128]

Case study: 'culture' revisited, 2005

The Northern Territory Supreme Court revisited the issue of child sexual assault as Aboriginal culture in a 2005 bush court session before Chief Justice Brian Martin in Yarralin. In this case, the defendant, a 55-year-old Aboriginal man (known only as GJ) beat the 14-year-old 'promised bride' victim with a boomerang and forced her to his outstation, where he lived with his first wife and where he violently raped the victim.[129] He was sentenced to two years' imprisonment with parole to be suspended after one month.[130] The Chief Justice defended his minimal sentencing: 'I must deal with the law as it is, and one of the criteria is to look to the individual's culpability. The court has said over many years that we need to take into account these matters which arise peculiarly from the ethnic or Aboriginal background.'[131]

It is clear in this case that the interests of the victim were again very much dismissed, and that Aboriginal 'culture' was relied upon to effectively excuse and sanction the violent sexual assault of an Aboriginal girl. In sentencing, the Chief Justice made it clear that GJ was not being charged with rape (even though the facts accepted involved a violent rape) and that he had 'a great deal of sympathy' for the defendant, who was unaware that his actions were illegal under the Northern Territory law.[132] The *Australian* reported the case as follows:

> The child kicked and screamed and resisted you. You lay her on a bed and asked her for sexual intercourse. She told you that she was only 14 years old. You hit her on the back. You then lay next to the child and remained there throughout the night. No act of sexual intercourse occurred.' According to the Chief Judge, the

following night GJ took the young girl back into the bedroom. 'You then pushed the child onto the mattress. The child was lying on her stomach. She told the police that you had a boomerang in your hand and that you were threatening her with it. While the child was laying on her stomach you had anal intercourse with her. During intercourse she was frightened and crying. You injured the child. You caused a deep laceration at the edge of her anus.' The child was later seen by a doctor and the examination also revealed painful areas over the child's body. The child later told the police that she was 'at that old man's place for four days', and that she was crying from Saturday to Tuesday. She knew that she was promised to you in the traditional Aboriginal way, but she did not like you. In the words of the child, 'I told that old man I'm too young for sex, but he didn't listen.'[133]

The court's imposition of a one-month prison sentence showed complete disregard for Aboriginal girls' right not to be raped, seemingly in 'cultural' deference to Aboriginal male Elders, who are regarded as important ceremonial men. Astoundingly, the Judge treated the defendant (whom he expressed a 'great deal of sympathy for') as the child, rather than the child rape victim.[134] This respect for the Aboriginal perpetrator was not supported by the local Aboriginal community, men and women who did not agree rape was acceptable 'culture', who were 'disgusted' by the rape, and who considered that the offender had impugned them all as Aboriginal people: as one local man stated, 'He should be ashamed of what he done'.[135]

The Northern Territory Court of Appeal, in *R v GJ* [2005] NTCCA 20, agreed with the DPP submission that the victim appeared to have been 'forgotten' in this case. It overturned the sentence as 'manifestly inadequate' and imposed an 18-month sentence.[136] In his written decision for the majority, Justice Mildren reaffirmed an earlier decision of the court that confirmed Aboriginal women and children's right to the protection of the law: 'The courts have been concerned to send what has been described as "the correct message" to all concerned, that is that Aboriginal women, children and the weak will be protected against personal violence insofar as it is within the power of the court to do so.'[137]

Notwithstanding the overruling of the Chief Justice's decision, as Justice Mildren pointed out, it was important to keep in mind that this was not a case where any charges of sexual assault had been laid. The charge concerned the offence of unlawful or underage sex and as such did not require any proof that the child did not consent.[138] Justice Mildren acknowledged that the facts or objective circumstances were serious for a number of reasons, including that the victim did all she could to impress upon the respondent that she was not consenting to him.[139] He further elaborated:

> Whilst it must be accepted that the respondent did not intend to have intercourse with SS without her consent, the reason for that lack of intent was to be found in his belief that intercourse was consented to, based on his understanding of traditional law and ignorance of territory law. Nevertheless, the respondent ought to have realised that he was mistaken and that she was not consenting.[140]

How do these legal arguments about rape actually operate in the circumstances of this case? Although the facts as accepted by the court clearly evidenced rape, Justice Mildren explained that both the Crown (the DPP) and Chief Justice Martin accepted that the respondent (GJ) believed that intercourse was acceptable because the child had been 'promised' to him, and that because of his tradition he would have believed she was consenting to sexual intercourse — apparently notwithstanding her clear objections, resistance and his use of violence. Justice Mildren speculated that the respondent was 'mistaken' in his understanding, but he still supported the underlying contention that the violent rape of an Aboriginal girl can be constructed to deny Aboriginal men any criminal intent (and legal responsibility) on the basis of their Aboriginal culture.

This reasoning is circular and self-defeating, promoting rather than rejecting the reasoning behind the court's wrongful decision in the first instance. This legal argument sanctions within the justice system discrimination against Aboriginal victims of child sexual assault. The fundamental right to equality under the common law is a core principle of the common law, yet one able to be denied to young, vulnerable Aboriginal rape victims in the context of the 'promised bride' scenario.

Aboriginal women publicly condemned the case and the abuse of the law in the name of Aboriginal culture. The views of Aboriginal women stand in sharp contrast to those of non-Aboriginal males. In an ABC Radio interview on 19 August 2005 about the case, Aboriginal Professor Boni Robertson condemned the distortion of Aboriginal culture. I was also interviewed, and my perspective was that legal discrimination against Aboriginal rape victims must end:

BONI ROBERTSON: This man has tried to stand behind an age-old traditional part of our culture which may or may not have relevance in today's society. To condone and to justify the abuse that he dealt upon that young girl is wrong and what is equally wrong is that the judge gave him a sentence that was nowhere near what one would expect.

ANNE BARKER: Isn't the judge right, though, that this man was less culpable because he genuinely didn't know his actions were against Northern Territory law?

BONI ROBERTSON: Oh, come on. We're living in the 21st Century. He's a 50-year-old man. People know what's right and what's wrong, you know? I don't buy that … Even though we have people who are living very, very traditional lifestyles and I respect absolutely everything that goes along with our culture in both traditional urban and rural environments … I really don't buy that. A violation is a violation.

ANNE BARKER: Some Indigenous women are now calling for further changes to the law to prevent such lenient sentences for what they say is nothing less than rape.

Traditional law is still a mitigating factor in sentencing in the Northern Territory, but Hannah McGlade, an Aboriginal human rights lawyer, says that has to change.

HANNAH McGLADE: You know, it's now well accepted by the legal system that white men can't rape their wives anymore, right? That's been a big struggle … but in the Northern Territory, we have the Supreme Court there blatantly discriminating against 14-year-old Aboriginal rape victims.

ANNE BARKER: What sort of message does this send now to other traditional men and even women …

HANNAH McGLADE: I think it's a real message out there that Aboriginal male rapists, their rights will prevail and that culture is an excuse for rape, because they're not going to get in serious trouble for it, are they?[141]

Culture is no excuse...in non-Aboriginal cases

The two case studies examined above may be contrasted with a 2005 decision by Justice Michael Groves of the New South Wales Court of Criminal Appeal.[142] This case concerned an appeal by three Pakistani Muslim brothers to have their sentences reduced for the rapes of two non-Aboriginal Australian teenage girls. The sentences imposed by the court were at the upper end of the sentencing scale: two of the brothers were sentenced to 22 years' jail terms, and the third to 16 years. All sentences were upheld on appeal and Justice Groves was very critical of the defence lawyer's attempt to blame the rapes on the defendants' ethnicity by describing one of the perpetrators as a 'cultural time bomb'. The linking of culture and rape was rejected by his Honour as inappropriate and inept: 'If it was intended to suggest that difference might be observed in behaviour in the respective cultures of Pakistan and Australia, there was, and is, not the slightest basis for concluding other than in both places all women are entitled to respect and safety from sexual assault.'[143]

Although the defence lawyer did not romanticise Pakistani culture in the same manner as those arguing the cultural appropriateness of sexual violence in the Northern Territory cases, the New South Wales court felt strongly that any cultural explanations for rape were simply unacceptable and could not be entertained before an Australian court of law. If we compare the cases, it can be surmised that if the victim is a non-Aboriginal Australian girl, an offender may not rely upon cultural arguments to minimise or mitigate sentence, but where the victim is an Aboriginal girl, cultural arguments may be used to deny even the charge of sexual assault. The race of the offender is also relevant. Whereas sexual assault perpetrated by Pakistani Muslims upon non-Aboriginal girls is viewed as extremely serious, the rape of Aboriginal girls by Aboriginal men is not considered serious and is unlikely to be seriously punished. The disparate responses confirm the law's gendered and racial nature, and the consequent lack of regard for Aboriginal girls' human rights within such a legal framework.

Case study: a case that 'bespeaks error', Aurukun, 2007

It should not be imagined that the human rights violations of Aboriginal sexual assault victims is limited to the Northern Territory and the practice of the 'promise bride'. A 2007 court decision in Aurukun, Far North Queensland, concerned a 10-year old Aboriginal rape victim's court experiences.[144]

In December 2007 it was reported that Judge Sarah Bradley had refused to impose any prison sentences on three adults and six juvenile males guilty of sexually assaulting the 10-year old girl.[145] Furthermore, Judge Bradley appeared to agree with the Crown prosecutor (note that these submissions in favour of the defendants were given not by the defence but by the prosecution) that no rape had occurred: 'I accept that the girl involved, with respect to all of these matters, was not forced, and that she probably agreed to have sex with all of you.'[146] Judge Bradley agreed with both the defence and the prosecution that no custodial sentences should be imposed and, furthermore, that the juveniles should not have a conviction recorded for the offence.[147]

Prominent Aboriginal women including Professors Boni Robertson and Marcia Langton immediately issued public condemnation of the decision. Professor Robertson called for Judge Sarah Bradley to stand down pending a full inquiry and rejected outright that any issues of Aboriginal culture were involved: 'There is no way that any culture could be used to claim that it's okay for nine men to sexually interfere with a 10-year-old child', she said.[148] The decision, Robertson said, 'defied any logic':

> To think that a judge, and a woman at that, would give such a lenient sentence, and didn't even record a conviction on some of them, is absolutely appalling. I think (the sentence) breaches every single moral, social, political and cultural code that you could even think of. What sort of message does that send to paedophiles and other people out there who think it's OK to go out and have sexual relations with children under the age of consent?[149]

Professor Marcia Langton described the judge as having 'expressed utter contempt for this little girl and for the basic norms of humanity'.[150] She pointed out that the judge had disregarded the Criminal Code of Queensland that prohibited sex with children who are deemed unable to give consent to sex, and she questioned whether it was 'acceptable in Queensland to suspend the laws of the state when dealing with convicted felons of Aboriginal ethnicity?'[151] She described the case as 'ultimate race hate practice' that rewarded offenders and placed victims and communities at increased risk.[152]

The then Aboriginal and Torres Strait Islander Social Justice Commissioner Tom Calma, responded by affirming the importance of the principle of equality before the law and the dire need for equal application of the law to Aboriginal people:

> Every Aboriginal person — woman, child and man — needs to be reminded that the justice system will apply to them, as perpetrator and will protect them as victims … All public officers — be they the judiciary, police, prosecutors, or service deliverers dealing with health, housing, care and protection or education — must be committed to providing equality of treatment for Indigenous peoples. Who said such officials could give up on Indigenous people and condemn them to unsafe conditions without the protection of the law?[153]

In the face of national and international media reporting and widespread concern and condemnation, including by then Prime Minister Kevin Rudd, the Queensland Government responded by standing down the Crown Prosecutor involved and instigating an inquiry into the prosecution of Aboriginal child sexual assault offences and an appeal by the Queensland Attorney General.[154]

The 2008 appeal decision of the Supreme Court of Queensland revealed a great deal about the court's initial decision.[155] The Supreme Court overturned the decision and noted that the Queensland Criminal Code's definition of rape under section 349(3) is that a child under 12 cannot give consent, and that under section 215(3), any person who has or attempts to have unlawful carnal knowledge with a child under 12 years of age is guilty of a crime and liable to imprisonment for life. The Supreme Court stated that these provisions of the Criminal Code reflect the gravity in which child sexual abuse is normally viewed in Australia.

The court held that the sentencing judge proceeded to sentence on a 'footing which did not recognise the gravity of the offence',[156] and it was well established by law that sexual offences committed by adults upon children under 12 years of age should attract a sentence of imprisonment, and that juveniles will also receive a sentence of detention in the absence of 'significant exculpatory circumstances'.[157] Accordingly, the three adult defendants were sentenced to six years' imprisonment, and the juvenile offenders received various sentences of probation, detention and compliance with program requirements.[158]

The sentencing judge did not record any reasons as to why there should be a departure from the established standards of sentencing and this was considered an error of law, which demonstrated there had been a miscarriage of justice in the sentencing process.[159] The Supreme Court also noted an 'astounding discussion' between the sentencing judge and prosecutor in which both parties appeared to agree that break and enter charges against two of the juveniles were more serious than the sexual assault of the 10-year-old.[160]

On appeal, the reasons why the sentencing judge engaged in a miscarriage of sentence were considered to have included the attitude of the prosecutor, the heavy workload in court that day (all nine matters were disposed of between 3.40pm and 5.03pm), the 'excessive haste' and 'all too summary fashion' in which the sentencing process was conducted, that the judge was not assisted by a victim impact statement, and that the judge was not assisted by either counsel as to appropriate sentences and actively led in to error.[161] It was concluded 'in the extraordinary circumstances of this case' that the sentencing process had miscarried, first, on the basis that the respondents were not sentenced on a basis that reflected the gravity of the crime and, second, that the judge erred in treating the respondents equally (where three were adults and six were juveniles) and that the completely suspended sentences imposed on the adults 'bespeaks error'.[162]

There was little acknowledgment of the victim in the appeal judgment. Although it was recognised the assault must have had a 'significant detrimental impact' on her, the court said that this was not established by evidence (such as a victim impact statement) either at the original sentence or on appeal.[163] Notwithstanding the wrongful lack of advocacy for the young victim, the Supreme

Court's sentencing of the offenders was based on the finding that there was no violence used or threatened, and no breach of trust.[164] The victim's aunty, however, described the victim as 'a little girl who has had the lights turned off in her life'.[165]

This finding was made even though one of the offenders admitted that the victim had not consented.[166] It may also be viewed alongside the fact that the oldest offender, who was 25, had previous convictions for unlawful carnal knowledge and aggravated assault on a female.[167] From the judgment it appeared that two of the respondents (aged 18 and 14 years) were cousins of the victim, and according to Aboriginal culture thereby had a care obligation towards their younger cousin.[168] Two respondents had previous assault convictions.[169] One had previously assaulted the young victim and was being cared for by his grandmother, who expressed concern for her own physical safety.[170]

The court did not identify race or Aboriginality as relevant to the miscarriage of sentence that occurred. However, the complete departure from the Criminal Code and the supporting facts in this case suggest that the Aboriginality of the offenders and the young victim was highly relevant. This was also suggested by arguments concerning 'Aboriginal community dysfunction' relied upon by the sentencing judge, and again on appeal on behalf of the respondents. As the Supreme Court noted, it was asserted by the defence lawyers that the non-custodial sentences 'can be understood and justified as an acknowledgement that the offending by the respondents was due to the dysfunctional nature of the community in which the respondents have been brought up, rather than to deviant criminality on their part'.[171]

Under this argument, sexual assault of Aboriginal children may be explained by reason of Aboriginal community dysfunction (for which offenders should not be held responsible) rather than any 'deviant criminality' (for which responsibility should attach). This argument was supported by expert psychological reports (tendered on behalf of the nine respondents) that emphasised environmental factors, including the breakdown of traditional laws and values resulting from colonisation and the resultant normalisation of underage sexual behaviour or 'experimentation' that they considered may be addressed by appropriate sexual education.[172] This evidence positioned Aboriginal child sexual assault as a consequence of colonisation and community dysfunction, acknowledging 'sexual assault and rape are not culturally accepted practices and are of significant concern to the Aurukun community'.[173]

At trial and on appeal it was suggested that what occurred in this case (and moreover in the community generally) had resulted from 'peer pressure' between children and young people.[174] This characterisation suggests conduct that is neither harmful nor characteristically criminal in nature. The emphasis on 'peer pressure' underplayed the seriousness of child sexual assault by positioning it as a matter between children and youth and an understandable aspect of contemporary yet dysfunctional Aboriginal cultural life.

The facts, on closer inspection, show that much more than peer pressure was at play. One offender, AAC (a 13-year-old at the time of the offence), had been exposed to domestic and extra-domestic violence (adult violence) from a young age.[175] He was sexually assaulted from the age of eight years and had sexually abused the victim four years earlier (for which they were both treated for sexually transmitted infections).[176] AAC had attempted suicide twice.[177]

The Supreme Court accepted that an offender's dysfunctional background was relevant to sentencing, but rejected the broader proposition that no custodial sentences were warranted as a result of that dysfunctional background.[178] To accept such a proposition 'would be to abandon the role of the courts and indeed, of the law in relation to the need for protection of the entire community, in Aurukun and beyond, by preventing or deterring the commission of crime'.[179] The comments of Justice Fitzgerald in a 1998 Queensland case were cited approvingly:

> It would be grossly offensive for the legal system to devalue the humanity and dignity of the members of Aboriginal communities or to exacerbate any lack of self-esteem felt within those communities by reason of our history and their living conditions … Aboriginal women and children who live in deprived communities or circumstances should not also be deprived of the law's protection … they are entitled to equality of treatment in the law's response to offences against them, not to some lesser response because of their race and living conditions.[180]

It was stated that a court must not take 'judicial notice' of the supposed effects of a community's dysfunction upon its members.[181] This is a form of stereotyping that 'diminishes the dignity of individual defendants' by consigning them 'to a category of persons who are less capable than others of observing the standards of decent behaviour set by the law'.[182]

It appears that Judge Bradley did not consult the local Aurukun Community Justice Group (set up by the state government to assist with law and justice matters), which was not consulted by the Crown Prosecutor or the sentencing judge. Despite the limited role and authority of the group, it should have been regarded as an important advisory body. Member Janine Chevathun said, 'We cannot understand her decision. It has mystified and deeply disturbed us. We want her to come here and explain why she ignored our group. We believed she was a good woman.'[183] In the appeal decision, the Community Justice Group confirmed that sexual assault and rape are not culturally accepted practices and are of significant concern to the Aurukun community.[184] The original exclusion of the group from the legal process and the continuing lack of justice afforded to the child victim confirms Wendy Shaw's argument that Australian courts have engaged in a 'neocolonial manoeuvre' and imposed their understandings of Aboriginal culture, sanctioning the sexual abuse of children at the same time as hypocritically maintaining the legal fiction of 'equality before the law'.[185]

Blaming the children — a Canadian example

The Queensland decision, in which the vulnerabilities of the child victim were erased and reconstructed as 'responsibility', resembles a high profile Canadian case concerning the sexual assault of a 12-year-old Aboriginal girl by three non-Aboriginal adult male offenders.[186] The *Edmondson* case caused great controversy as a result of sentencing comments by Judge Kovatch, who said that the young victim was 'not only a willing participant, but indeed, the aggressor'.[187] The victim was a homeless 12-year-old (with evidence that sexual abuse had occurred at home) and the three adult males had plied her with alcohol before the sexual assault occurred. Only one of the offenders was sentenced, and he received a two-year community supervision order.[188]

The case was strongly opposed by the Native Women's Association of Canada, which reminded the Canadian courts that children under 14 years are unable by law to give consent, and that children's sexualised behaviour or 'acting out' must not be used to mitigate sentence. Further:

> To reduce the blameworthiness of a person found guilty of sexual assault on a child for this reason only serves to deprive of the full protection of the law those members of society who are most in need of it. It is tantamount to making the Court complicit in the repeated abuse of children.[189]

In her assessment of the *Edmondson* case, academic Lise Gotell argued that the violation of Aboriginal women and girls is 'an ongoing repetition of the colonial encounter that is sanctioned by law'.[190] Gotell stated that the child complainant's vulnerabilities were erased and victim-blaming constructions were mobilised 'in a judicial narrative that reframes her as a sexual threat'.[191] By contrast, the adult male defendants were represented as posing no risk at all: 'He is depicted as a white citizen subject, tied to his family and the community.'[192] Gotell considered the case as an example of constructions of 'good/ credible victims' being tied less to chastity and sexual propriety than to exclusions that draw upon persistent race- and class-based ideologies in which vulnerability is reconstructed as responsibility.[193] In this way sexual assault has become individualised, depoliticised and reconstructed as a failure of individual responsibility, 'while the power relations that define sexual violence are obscured'.[194]

The abuse of culture

In Australia the courts have used Aboriginal 'culture' in a distorted and abusive manner that denies the harm of child sexual assault. Critical race expert Sherene Razack warns that the use of cultural arguments within a legal system that is deeply embedded with racist and sexist ideology is inherently problematic.[195] Moreover, 'The eagerness with which these theories of cultural difference are taken up in the justice system, while racism and sexism remain unnamed, is a reminder that culture is treacherous ground to travel in a white supremacist and patriarchal society'.[196]

Razack describes 'culture talk' in sexual violence cases as a 'double edged sword' that 'fragments sexual violence as what men do to women and takes the emphasis away from white complicity'.[197] Her study of culture talk cases reveals a lack of self-reflexivity such that 'White judges and lawyers seeking neat, culturally sensitive, un-gendered solutions to justice have not stopped to question their authority to interpret Aboriginal culture, history and contemporary reality'.[198] Her contention is that courts, by taking into account what they perceive as Aboriginal culture (or by extenuation Aboriginal dysfunction, perhaps even mere Aboriginality), have contributed to 'making invisible the harm that is done to Aboriginal women' (and clearly also children); also, in deeming Aboriginal men as inherently violent, they have confirmed the 'superiority of white men'.[199] According to Razack, such 'culturally sensitive' decision making serves the purpose of masking what white people have done to Aboriginal people and the role of sexual violence as a part of the colonisation process. White male judges and lawyers with little or no knowledge of history or anthropology continue to interpret Aboriginal culture and its relevance to the courts: 'Wrapped in a cloak of sensitivity to cultural difference and the recognition of colonisation, the anthropologising of sexual assault continues to have gendered overtones and to maintain white supremacy as securely as in days of more overt racism and sexism.'[200]

In 2006 the Australian Law Reform Commission rejected any suggestion that family violence or sexual assault of Aboriginal women and children was justified under Aboriginal customary laws.[201] At the same time, it agreed with the Western Australia Law Reform Commission that courts should be able to give consideration to customary law arguments in relation to violence and sexual abuse of women and children:

> while the Commission accepts the potential for Aboriginal customary law to be incorrectly argued as an excuse for violent and sexual offending, this should not prevent courts from considering Aboriginal customary law. The common law suggests that such arguments would today be likely to fail. Further, due

to the discretionary nature of sentencing, courts are able to balance Aboriginal customary law and international human rights standards that require the protection of women and children.[202]

This conflicts with court cases in which Australian courts have readily deprived Aboriginal child sexual assault victims of equality before the law. Furthermore, the assertion that courts will acknowledge international human rights law is not supported by the case law. In the 2005 case of GJ (see 'Case study: "culture" revisited, 2005' above), the HREOC applied to the court to make submissions with respect to international human rights law. The court refused this request.[203] In my view, the Australian Law Reform Commission (and the Western Australia Law Reform Commission) should be guided by international human rights law that condemns the use of any alleged 'customary law' to sanction violence against women and children.

Relevant United Nations human rights standards note that the Convention on the Elimination of all Forms of Discrimination against Women, adopted in 1979, calls upon state parties 'to take all appropriate measures, including legislation, to modify or abolish existing laws, regulations, customs and practices which constitute discrimination against women (article 2(f))'.[204] Also, the 1993 *Declaration on the Elimination of Violence against Women* requires states to condemn violence against women, and not invoke any custom, tradition or religious consideration to avoid their obligations with respect to its elimination. This clear enunciation of international human rights law is further supported by United Nations model domestic legislation concerning violence again women, which should expressly provide that no custom, tradition or religious consideration shall be invoked to justify violence against women.[205]

Aboriginal women (and some men) have long described the use of culture to justify violence and sexual assault of women and children as a gross abuse of culture. However, the 'double-edged sword' of culture has resulted in Aboriginal women's (and children's) voices being denied before the courts and the criminal justice system, and sexual violence being sanctioned and justified as an aspect of Aboriginal culture. Consistent with international human rights standards, domestic legislation should be enacted to prohibit any alleged customs or traditions to justify and sanction violence against women and children.

In 2007 the Australian Government, as part of the NTER, introduced legislation to prohibit the use of Aboriginal culture as a defence or in mitigation of a sentence.[206] This was a legislative response to the offensive case law excusing rape and violence against Aboriginal women and children under the guise of 'culture' (this case law is discussed in Chapter 5). The legislation was challenged by the North Australia Aboriginal Justice Agency (NAAJA) in the Northern Territory Supreme Court case of *R v Wunungmurra* [2009] NTSC 24. NAAJA accepted that the defendant had committed an aggravated assault on his wife (with the use of a weapon) but argued that he was merely acting as a responsible husband and carrying out his 'duties' in accordance with the Yolngu culture.[207] Once again a peak Aboriginal organisation was arguing that violence against women was justified as a matter of Aboriginal culture.

In this case Justice Southwood applied the legislation as he was bound to do so, but was very sympathetic to the defence arguments, criticising the legislation as 'unreasonable' and 'undesirable'.[208] These comments were taken up by NAAJA, which described the legislation as 'shameful' and 'leading to unjust decisions'.[209] In my opinion, NAAJA, as well as Rex Wild QC, who prosecuted the case (and previously co-chaired the Little Children Are Sacred inquiry), appeared to lack awareness or concern that gender-based violence is a serious violation of human rights and causes the suffering of many Aboriginal women, children and young people, resulting in immeasurable trauma and harm to Aboriginal families and entire communities.

There was no public response to this case. The silence was deafening. This case called for dialogue Australia-wide about the shocking impacts of violence in Aboriginal communities and the imperative of human rights to be fully accorded to women and children.

As a part of this important (but imagined) debate, we could ask how Aboriginal people can legitimately demand an end to race discrimination and the recognition of Indigenous rights (such as those contained in the *Declaration on the Rights of Indigenous Peoples*), while at the same time arguing in favour of rights violations of women and children on 'cultural' grounds, and rejecting the right of women and children to live free of violence and rape. Even if Aboriginal culture once sanctioned violence to women (as NAAJA and Wild

QC argued), why should that continue unchallenged today and not be rejected outright as a matter of human rights for our future wellbeing and existence as Aboriginal people?

An ambivalent system

Child sexual assault is a crime we abhor in principle, but in practice Australian children are let down by an ambivalent criminal justice system. Children, academic experts and legal professionals have all agreed that the criminal justice process is too often an abusive one. Legal reforms to improve children's experiences in court are important, but even significant reforms have not adequately addressed the problem. Fundamentally, our legal system has been particularly unresponsive to sexual assault, a crime largely perpetrated by men upon women and children. Arguably, the 'male' nature of law is conflicted in its response to victimised children, with the consequence that very often the 'rights' of male perpetrators prevail.

Aboriginal victims have unique experiences with the law, and it is evident that Aboriginality itself can operate to deny legal protection. The criminal justice system has wrongfully minimised and normalised Aboriginal child sexual assault in the name of Aboriginal culture, and Aboriginal 'dysfunction'. The cases in this chapter indicate the ongoing legacy of Australian legal history in which sexual violence against Aboriginal women and children was apparently sanctioned and permitted. Historically, Aboriginal women and children were not responded to as legitimate victims of sexual assault, and have experienced discrimination based on race, gender and age. Despite more than a quarter of a century of legal prohibition of discrimination, Aboriginal sexual assault victims can be readily deprived of legal rights and appropriate responses by the criminal justice system on such grounds.

Chapter 6

Close to home: Noongars taking
a stand in the courts

As a young mother nearly a decade ago I began my research concerning the experiences of Aboriginal women and children using the criminal justice system as a response to family violence and child abuse. At this time child sexual assault was not a matter discussed publicly or otherwise in the Noongar community. This was a far cry from the 'Stop the Abuse' campaign I experienced as a young woman in the late 1980s, in which some Aboriginal women bravely put the issue at the forefront. In Perth the leadership in our community appeared increasingly male dominated, and women's services, such as women's resource centres, were increasingly marginalised.

In the Noongar community the criminal prosecution of Aboriginal offenders was almost unheard of. This changed dramatically with several high profile cases and prosecutions, including some against prominent male offenders. While the previous chapter is national in focus, this chapter is localised. It concerns legal cases that represent a significant snapshot of our history, when Noongar people, Noongar women in particular, stood up against child sexual assault and fought it through the criminal justice system.

The chapter is based on three case studies and draws on interviews with two Noongar women, Donna Kickett and Ingrid Collard, about their court experiences. Both women spoke publicly and in detail to the media about their experiences, with Collard setting a precedent by waiving confidentiality of her identity as a complainant. Kickett was not a complainant but supported a young male family member through the process, speaking publicly about her experiences through the media. These interviews are complemented by a comprehensive analysis of a written court case decision, *R v Bropho* [2004] WADC 182.

All three cases occurred during the period 2004–06 and involved adult complainants (of varying ages) of child sexual offences. The cases highlight the responses of the legal system to Aboriginal victims of child sexual assault and their experiences within the criminal justice system. One of the cases resulted in a successful conviction of the offender, and two resulted in acquittals.

Case study: Donna Kickett warns courts are 'devastating'

This case study concerns the experiences of a young Aboriginal male complainant, whose experiences raise the issue of discrimination based on race. The court process is traumatic for Aboriginal males, although very little is known about this.

Aboriginal children's experiences of courts have not been documented. However, the inference can be readily drawn from research concerning non-Aboriginal children's experiences that secondary abuse and trauma resulting from the court process is common to all child complainants. Aboriginal children (and adults) using the criminal justice system as a response to child sexual assault may face additional difficulties on the basis of culture. Although the courts in Western Australia have promoted a level of cultural inclusiveness, the distinct 'culture' of the court remains non-Aboriginal and as such may be insensitive to Aboriginal people. The extent of cultural differences — and arguably the clash of cultures — is evident through a 2004 case closely observed by Donna Kickett, at the time an ATSIC regional councillor. I initially became aware of Kickett's concerns through media reports of her comments.[1]

Kickett described the trial process, which involved a young family member she supported, as a 'devastating experience for the victim and his family'.[2] She stated that after witnessing the court process she would be 'discouraging any other Aboriginal young people from coming forward'.[3] Kickett argued that there needed to be support before, during and after the court, and that it was the victim who was made to feel guilty.[4]

I interviewed Kickett in Perth in July 2005 and sought to explore her public condemnation of the court process. During the interview, Kickett identified (thereby confirming) issues recognised by the 2003 Australian Institute of Criminology (AIC) research by Eastwood (discussed in the previous chapter) concerning the difficulty in seeing the accused in court and also the cross-examination. This case also involved a re-trial (two actual court cases), with significant time delay taken to resolve the court matter, in favour of the defendant. Kickett identified many other issues of concern, discussed below, including:

- the complainant was not regarded as a special witness
- cross-examination (which can be a deliberately confusing practice and can produce 'forced errors')
- the 'gaps and silences' of not allowing the history of the defendant to be mentioned in court
- the fact that Noongar cultural matters were ignored
- the lack of acknowledgment of Aboriginal child-rearing practices, which may differ to European styles
- Aboriginal English
- the lack of previous contact with the assigned prosecutor
- limited victim support
- the failure of the legal process to empower the victim and address the abuse.

Children and adults testifying in Western Australian courts as victims of child sexual assault are regarded as 'special witnesses', and relevant court support processes are in place, including the use of CCTV. However, the Aboriginal complainant in this case was not accorded such protective status. Kickett said the complainant was not given the opportunity to provide his evidence by CCTV, and had great difficulty in physically facing the defendant in court.[5] This fear was heightened because the defendant was a person with 'links back to traditional tribal culture' and the issue of fear in relation to payback and retribution was present.[6]

Under section 160R of the *Evidence Act 1906* (WA), an adult may be declared a special witness and receive the benefit of measures to assist in giving evidence. The court may make such an order where it is likely that the complainant will (i) suffer severe emotional trauma, or (ii) be so intimidated or distressed as to be unable to give evidence or to give evidence satisfactorily by reason of age, cultural background, relationship to any party to the proceedings, the nature of the subject matter of the offence, or any other evidence the court considers relevant. The court has legislative ability (section 106RA) even once the prosecution has commenced to make an order that the whole of evidence of a witness be taken at a special hearing and recorded by CCTV. Some of these legislative reforms took effect in 2004 (when the case was heard) and it is possible that an order was not made on behalf of the complainant, or was refused by the judge.

Kickett described the cross-examination of the complainant during the trial as problematic. It was lengthy and considered 'twice as long' as the cross-examination of the defendant.[7] In addition, the defence lawyer's tactics appeared to be aimed at deliberately confusing the complainant — thus creating 'confusion' to achieve the level of doubt required for acquittal:

> The lawyer bamboozled this young man … he was using the same question but changing it a whole way around so different questioning the whole time, so it would be the same question but he used it in a different way, probably five or six times where the young man became confused. And in the end I don't think that went too well in his favour … because he started to become confused and obviously if you've got a white jury sitting there and they see this young boy becoming confused by the questioning, is there some doubt in his mind, not thinking that he's got no idea and he's not understanding what the question is, I think that certainly didn't do him any favours …[8]

Kickett said that the judge did not intervene to ensure that the complainant knew what was being asked, nor did he address the aggressive and intimidating tactics of the defence lawyer. The judge, in Kickett's view, failed to ensure that the victim had adequate understanding of what was happening during the cross-examination process: 'no wonder we've got so many Aboriginal people in the justice system who are going through and being convicted because they're not understanding the language and the terminology that's being used by professionals in the court room'.[9] Kickett said the complainant's confusion during cross-examination did not concern the actual abuse alleged, but peripheral matters unrelated to the abuse, such as 'the colour of the house, the layout of the house and having to recall fourteen years prior to what the house actually looked like'.[10]

Dr Caroline Taylor's important study of court trials showed that 'forced errors' were a common outcome of the adversarial systems process of cross-examination.[11] Taylor explains that most defence questions target not the actual abuse alleged but 'minute and peripheral' details connected to the charges. Sometimes the defence lawyer will repeatedly ask the same question hoping to receive a different answer that can therefore constitute a 'prior inconsistent statement' that undermines witness credibility.[12]

Consistent with Taylor's assessment that the legal process is not a truth-seeking process, Kickett observed that a considerable defence line of questioning was directed at the mother of the complainant (who was not on trial) and her ability as a mother. Kickett stated the defence lawyer 'focussed a whole lot on her abilities as a mother to actually care for the child and how many times she would drop him off [with her sister and the defendant]'.[13] This line of questioning was arguably an attempt to discredit the mother as 'bad'. This is consistent with the defence narratives identified by Taylor, which commonly include suggestions of motive and revenge in which the mother–child accusation is very common.[14] The mother–child collusion stereotype acts as an 'undercurrent' to the defence narrative,[15] one that is 'often promoted in legal narrative and judicial comment'.[16] Taylor identified the narrative of mother–child collusion as a discriminatory stereotype deployed to 'negate mothers' credibility and vitiate the credibility of the child's own evidence.'[17]

Defence cross-examination also focused on 'the direct actions of a 6-year-old immediately after being sexually abused' and the lack of complaint by the complainant as a young child.[18] This line of questioning is consistent with Taylor's identification of the 'favourite defence tactic' of implicit suggestion that yelling and screaming and immediate disclosure is expected of 'real' victims.[19] Research by child sexual abuse experts suggests that very often children do not disclose or seemingly even 'resist' sexual assault. As Roland Summit explained:

> Society allows the child one acceptable set of reactions ... Like the adult victim of rape, the child victim is expected to forcibly resist, to cry for help, and to attempt to escape the intrusion. By that standard, almost every child fails. The normal reaction is to 'play possum' ... Small creatures simply do not call on force to deal with overwhelming threat.[20]

Chris Goddard notes that the common perception of child sexual assault as non-violent fails to recognise the totality of violence in the family, which presents a 'major obstacle' to disclosure.[21] That perpetrators often use force to sexually assault children means that children's fears of the perpetrator are very real and may prohibit disclosure.[22] In the case at hand, it appears no explanation was provided to the court that the complainant as a child may well have feared the defendant, an adult perpetrator, and therefore lack of complaint was most understandable. This is one clear example of how the lack of expert evidence in relation to child sexual assault hinders the complainant and, ultimately, truth seeking. Expert evidence, if adduced, would have clarified the complainant's lack of response.

Kickett stated that the defendant had a history of sexually abusing other children in his family. He had previously been charged and served a term of imprisonment. However, this evidence was kept from the jury. Kickett said:

> You know, I'm not too sure as to how long he's been in prison for the other offences but that was another thing. They couldn't actually refer back to the fact that 'hey you know you sexually abused all these other women in the family', so that could never be mentioned in the courtroom. I've got no idea why, because to me that would be relevant to the case.[23]

Taylor identified that legal evidentiary rulings can 'result in the fragmentation of evidence, and gaps and silences are subsequently imposed on the complainant'.[24] In this case study the evidence of the defendant's history of sexually assaulting children was excluded on the basis of evidentiary rulings. While the complainant's (and his mother's) credibility was undermined through the cross-examination process, he was not permitted to speak truths very relevant to the case, namely the history of inter-generational abuse in the family (impacting many members) and the commitment of the victim and his supporting family to address that abuse in the court.

In 2004, at the time of the trial, the defendant's previous sexual offence convictions were excluded by High Court case law rulings that prohibited evidence relating to previous child sexual abuse as 'prejudicial' to the accused and outweighing any 'probative' value.[25] On 1 January 2005 section 31A of the Evidence Act was introduced, allowing previous convictions relating to the accused to be introduced into trial on a similar matter. In this case the complainant did not have the benefit of this important law reform.

At one point in giving evidence the male complainant requested a break. Kickett said this was to allow his mother and other women family members an opportunity to leave the courtroom. However, his request was denied by the judge. Kickett explained that under the Noongar culture, sexual abuse and sexual matters are not spoken of freely between the genders: 'That's not the sort of stuff that's talked about. Boys talk to their fathers about their male issues ... That's the culture as far as we're concerned and that's how we're brought up.'[26] The fact that women family members were present would have made it much harder for the complainant to give evidence.

In denying the victim's request for a break, the judge said, 'Young man, if you think it's hard now, it's only going to get harder. You might as well tell us'.[27] However, the judge showed no awareness of the cultural sensitivity involved in the circumstances and that the young man's request was considerate of women family members, his mother in particular, who then 'broke down' crying during his evidence.[28] The judge apparently individualised the complainant's request without understanding that a strong cultural norm was involved and should have been respected.

The explicit language used by the Crown prosecutor was also a concern. While the complainant attempted to use 'de-sensitised' language to describe the abuse (by using the correct anatomical descriptions), family members were shocked to hear the prosecutor paraphrase his evidence in a graphic manner, asking the complainant, 'Oh, so you're telling me he put his prick up your arse'.[29]

One serious issue arising in this case was the possibility of the victim experiencing retribution and 'payback' from the perpetrator, who was described as having links to traditional tribal culture.[30] Kickett explained that there was a psychological fear of being 'done in' or seriously harmed. Even though the charged offences took place in Noongar country, at one stage it was determined that the court hearing was set to take place in the country of the defendant (who had traditional tribal links on that country).[31] This decision understandably increased the victim's fear of payback.

Serious fears of payback are commonly reported, but are not responded to or accommodated in any way by the court system. According to Dr Dawn Bessarab, 'Spiritual realities are alive and well in the Aboriginal community and pervade the everyday lived experience of an Aboriginal person'.[32] Fears about payback are very real and form the backdrop by which 'culture can sometimes be used to control a woman, child or young person'.[33]

This case shows that fear of sorcery is not confined to remote communities but may operate whenever the offender is a person with known traditional links. In the case observed by Kickett, the court process did not exercise any sensitivity in relation to this matter and thereby heightened the fear of the complainant.

Kickett also expressed concern that the Noongar family kinship system was not understood during the court and that this was used against the victim's interests. She observed the defence lawyer subjected the complainant's mother to criticism for leaving her son in the care of her sister and her husband (the defendant):

> They focussed a whole lot on her abilities as a mother to actually care for the child, and how many times she would drop him off, and again as I said if you've got an all white jury sitting there not understanding the dynamic within a Noongar family ... and I guess that's one of the reasons why they acquitted as well.[34]

According to Kickett, the prosecutor did not attempt to explain to the non-Aboriginal jury that this was an acceptable cultural practice. As many Aboriginal people and anthropologists are aware, the relationship that may exist in these circumstances is akin to that of a 'second mother' and child-rearing responsibilities in such circumstances are not uncommon or socially unacceptable.

The ways in which Aboriginal people, as speakers of Aboriginal English, are subjected to serious disadvantage during the court process has been researched by sociolinguist Dianne Eades, who has observed, in particular, the issue of gratuitous concurrence, silence and eye contact.[35] Although the ongoing existence of 'Aboriginal English' is well understood by most Aboriginal people, most non-Aboriginal people do not understand Aboriginal English.[36]

Eades has illustrated through case studies how frequently used cross-examination strategies can and do create the ideal situation for gratuitous concurrence.[37] This is described as the tendency to say 'yes' to any question (or 'no' to a negative question) regardless of whether or not the person agrees with the question, or even understands it. This is a characteristic Aboriginal strategy for dealing with interviews, and particularly relevant in situations of severe power imbalance. Eades points out that the likelihood of gratuitous concurrence increases the more questioners raise their voice, an intimidation tactic frequently adopted in court. In the case Kickett observed it is very possible that gratuitous concurrence occurred and was influenced by the defence lawyer's 'quite aggressive' questioning.[38]

Eades also describes speakers of Aboriginal English as frequently using silence as 'a positive and normal part of conversation'.[39] In Aboriginal English silence is a perfectly acceptable way to begin to answer a question, but this is frequently misinterpreted at trial by non-Aboriginals who may invoke a negative connotation to silence.[40] In this case it appears that the complainant's quietness (or Aboriginal silence) was perceived negatively by the judge, who kept saying to him, 'Can you speak up?'[41] In addition to using silence constructively, many Aboriginal people have a naturally quiet demeanour. However, the courtroom layout ensures that the defendant, rather than the complainant, is the one seated close to the jury, thus making it physically difficult for the jury to hear the complainant's evidence. This explains the judge's repeated comments to the complainant, 'The jury can't hear you so you need to speak up'.[42]

Another sociolinguistic concern identified by Eades is the use of eye contact: 'In many Aboriginal societies throughout Australia, children learn that it is rude and disrespectful to make direct eye-contact with an older person with whom they are speaking.'[43]

Kickett also linked the aggressive defence lawyer's techniques with the complainant's eye contact, noting that he was 'really shyly looking at the ground, not wanting to look at anybody in the courtroom'.[44] In her view, the complainant spent much of the trial avoiding eye contact, and she considered that this was because of the defendant's presence in the court, the 'intimidation' of the defence lawyer, and the common Aboriginal response to avoid eye contact in such circumstances.[45]

The issues associated with the use of Aboriginal English were considered by the Western Australian Office of the Director of Public Prosecutions in its 2001 *Review of Services to Victims of Crime and Crown Witnesses*.[46] These matters were more recently identified in the *Aboriginal Benchbook for Western Australian Courts*.[47] However, there is no obligation on judiciary, defence lawyers or Crown prosecutors to ensure respect or any understanding of the cultural norms of Aboriginal complainants in court.

Another matter of concern in this case was a lack of prior contact with the DPP-assigned prosecutor, whom the complainant met only at the commencement of the trial. The problem of different prosecutors being assigned to the same case appears to be a common one and was raised during a Western Australian Legislative Assembly inquiry, which noted there are frequent changes of prosecutors handling cases, which understandably causes concern to victims. According to one submission:

> What I did struggle with was that at each and every court appearance a different DPP lawyer would be assigned ... that day. In a survivor's eyes the DPP lawyer is the only hope that their story will be told. It severely lessens your confidence to know your file will be handled by someone different for every court appearance.[48]

With the impact of staff turnover and other factors, DPP lawyers in only 50% of cases conduct the same matter from allocation to finalisation. This is, however, an improvement from previous years, where the figure was 5–10%.[49]

In Western Australia the Victim Support Service (VSS) works with the Department of the Attorney General and has a crucial role in supporting victims of crime. Unfortunately, in this case the level of victim support prior to the trial was considered limited and related solely to financial matters such as an allocated meal allowance, tea-making facilities and use of the court-designated victim support waiting room.[50] Family members felt they were not at all ready or 'braced' for the harsh reality of the cross-examination process.[51]

The complainant's limited experience with the VSS may be consistent with that of Aboriginal people more generally. According to a 2001 DPP report, Aboriginal people, although making up a large percentage of the victim population, 'are largely silent and infrequent consumers of services such as the VSS'.[52] Although it was stated that 'lack of interest' on the part of Aboriginal clients may well account for their under-use of support services, it was also recognised that 'services are not culturally appropriate, exacerbated by the fact that they are often provided by non-Aboriginal people with no understanding of Aboriginal ways and with no cultural sensitivity'.[53]

Overall, and regardless of race, it is a matter of concern that victims of sexual assault receive limited and inadequate support in their relationship to the courts. This was evident at the 2008 Western Australian Inquiry into the Prosecution of Assaults and Sexual Offences, which recognised that victims did not have constant legal representation (as contrasted with offenders, who were regularly represented, for example, by Legal Aid or Aboriginal Legal Service). There is a clear and established need for 'witness assistance officers' to help address victims' issues and to provide information about matters such as:

- facing the perpetrator in court
- fears of cross-examination and public exposures
- lack of involvement in the process and ensuing powerlessness
- threat of withdrawal of the case.[54]

Although the DPP in Western Australia had a formal protocol in relation to liaison with families of homicide victims, due to insufficient resources this did not extend to victims of sexual assault. The 2008 inquiry noted that witness assistance services are now commonplace in most DPP offices, and are required in Western Australia, where 'Victim dissatisfaction with services provided was a common theme in submissions and evidence to the Committee'.[55] Accordingly, it was recommended that the Western Australian Government 'establish a victim/witness assistance service team in the [Office of the DPP] based on a combination of New South Wales, Victorian and South Australian models. Indigenous victims and witnesses, and victims and witnesses with special needs, should be provided with officers dedicated to working with these groups.'[56] This recommendation, along with many of the inquiry's other recommendations, was not implemented or progressed.

The case considered was especially troubling in that the jury could not make a finding and a retrial was consequently ordered. The victim was required to go through another court experience, and initially he felt that he could not do that. Following the subsequent acquittal, the complainant's brother, who also identified as a victim of the defendant, decided that he would not proceed through the legal system as a result of his sibling's court experiences and the acquittal.[57]

Kickett described child sexual abuse as a 'sickness', which in Aboriginal communities was very often 'handed down' or inter-generational.[58] She also felt that in disclosing sexual abuse, young Aboriginal people wanted the abuse to stop and to be empowered by the process; however, the response of the agencies was to 'tear that family apart' and was one of disempowerment.[59] The statutory response involving police and child protection was perceived as not assisting in resolving the issue of sexual abuse in Aboriginal communities, nor working with and supporting the family.[60]

Kickett's experience supports Summit's 1980s argument for intervention on both a clinical and legal basis: 'The counsellor alone cannot expect co-operation and recovery in an otherwise reluctant and unacknowledged offender. The justice system alone can rarely prove guilt or impose sanctions without preparation and continuing support of all parties within an effective treatment system.'[61] Summit commented that a verdict of not guilty is 'tantamount to a conviction of perjury against the victim'.[62] Furthermore, the verdict of not guilty in effect maintains the offender's denial of the abuse: 'Neither the victim, the offender, the family, the next generation of children in that family, nor the well being of society as a whole can benefit from continued secrecy and denial of ongoing abuse.'[63]

Kickett's powerful advocacy of the court process coincided with significant law reforms introduced later that year. These reforms to the Evidence Act addressed the particular injustice associated with 'gaps and silences' in relation to the defendant's several prior convictions and the court's failure to allow a clearly vulnerable witness the protection of the special witness provision. Although the complainant did not experience personal justice, the legislative reforms introduced following this case allow for a more just response for other victims in these circumstances. It should be remembered, however, that the previous Western Australian state of law remains current in other Australian jurisdictions.

Case study: Ingrid Collard breaks the silence and asks 'who's on trial?'

In 2005 I became aware of a young Noongar woman, Ingrid Collard, who was speaking out publicly in the Noongar community about child sexual assault and the harm caused to her when she was growing up. I arranged to meet her and learnt that she had made a complaint to the police. Collard was keen to participate in my research and we met several times before, during and after the court case in 2005–06. She gave me permission to observe the court case, which resulted in successful prosecution and conviction of her grandfather, a now deceased Aboriginal Elder.[64]

In the Noongar and wider community, Collard bravely permitted herself to be publicly identified as a survivor. She spoke through television and print media, and advocated through her position on the Victims of Crime Reference Group.

Collard's case represents the small minority of cases of child sexual assault that result in a finding of guilt and a prison sentence. This case had an opposite outcome to the case observed by Kickett, but both cases show the traumatic level of re-victimisation that occurred throughout the court experience. Collard's case also highlights that even a guilty verdict may not address the offender's denial and the needs of the victim, offender, family and even the next generation to end the secrecy and denial surrounding child sexual abuse. This case importantly shows that interventions based on both a legal and therapeutic basis are needed.

In reporting the case, Collard identified issues including:

* deciding to report
* the inadequate police response

- failure by the DPP to engage in culturally appropriate practices
- her lack of awareness of VSS
- the need for more counselling supports
- her observations of her cousin's case and lack of justice
- support by some members of the Noongar community.

Collard decided to report in order to name and confront the abuse, which had been denied by certain members of her family. She had struggled to be heard about her victimisation as a child and consequently it was unaddressed in her life. The decision was made because she wanted to confront the abuse and have healing in her life:

> I think the initial reason I decided to finally take this through the courts was because I've had a lot of opposition … if the person was actually guilty or not. I was silenced for many years, I've been told that it would shame the family name by telling, what would happen, that old elders were allowed to do things like that to children. So I was perpetrated all these myths of why I shouldn't go ahead with it for many, many years and I think it got to a stage in my life where I couldn't ignore it anymore. I couldn't confront it because I knew that what happened to me was wrong. It was bad and it ruined my life for many years … I had more opposition from some of my family than actual support … I think what got me to the court process in the end was sort of realising within myself that it was wrong and something had to be done, because the longer I denied it the longer I let that monster walk around like that knowing what he had done to me, the longer I was making myself sick.[65]

Although Collard initially felt optimistic, the delay in the legal process became apparent. Collard signed her police statement in 2004. It took eight months for police to lay charges and another year later there had still been no court date set. In more than a year she received two telephone calls from the investigating officer.[66] There was no 'real follow up or concern' as to whether she was coping.[67] She believes that Aboriginal girls and women have particular fears about 'retribution' and police could respond better to that fear.[68] Notwithstanding the resulting court sentence, Collard sensed that police had reluctance with respect to responding to Aboriginal victims, perpetrators and communities: 'It seems [that] reporting sexual offences against Indigenous women or men or children ... in communities seems to be [an] extremely touchy subject that police I think tread too carefully in.'[69]

In addition to these delays, Collard had fears for her safety and believed that some family members were angry that disclosure had been made through the legal system.[70] She felt that some extended family members considered that a victim did not have the right to complain and that in disclosing she had 'thrown a big spanner in their works'.[71] Collard said she felt 'scared' and 'traumatised' after disclosing and was worried about 'what was going to happen next because of no real support'.[72]

Another issue related to the DPP was the lack of cultural sensitivity or appropriateness. A young non-Indigenous male prosecutor was assigned the case and was required to ask in-depth questions concerning the nature of the assaults.[73] Collard explained that for Aboriginal women graphic and anatomical descriptions of sexual abuse are 'women's business' and not something to be discussed with men.[74] However, she felt that she had no 'right to complain' or ask for a woman prosecutor to be assigned to the interview. She gave the information but felt very uncomfortable through the interview. Notwithstanding, Collard commented positively that the DPP lawyer was 'respectful in every single way' and that in her view each person's own style of relating and interacting was pivotal.[75] Her main concern was that she repeatedly requested a copy of her police statement, but it was not provided until two weeks before trial. This caused enormous stress because she had erroneously believed that she needed to memorise or know the statement by heart.[76]

No one assisted Collard to liaise with police or the DPP, or talked with her about the court process. In 2005, during our early conversation, I became aware that she did not know about the VSS.[77] Collard does not recall the police referring her to the VSS, or being given any pamphlets or information about the service.[78] Upon making contact with the VSS, the experience was perceived as very positive:

> Being with Victim Support for the whole way would have been really awesome in terms of helping me not stress out and be anxious about the whole process ... They told me all the things

you want to know, like how long does trial take? What am I expected to do in court? How do I speak? How do I do anything? … And to the point that the day before Court, they took me into the court rooms, they showed me around … they ran a few questions with me like how was I supposed to answer questions … They were just so unbelievably brilliant.[79]

Collard was aware of the Sexual Assault Referral Centre, but she said she felt uncomfortable as an Aboriginal person making initial contact with this agency, and said that it would be better if someone helped her by physically taking her to the centre, introducing her and making her feel comfortable.[80] I also understand from experience that many Aboriginal people will not simply access a non-Aboriginal support agency about which they know nothing. It seems there is an invisible barrier that relates to culture that needs to be pro-actively addressed, quite possibly by the kind of measures that Collard suggests. Although there was a 'little amount of counselling' offered through the Domestic Violence Advocacy Service, this was not enough to address the resurfacing trauma, especially in relation to the police statements.[81] The lack of adequate support meant that Collard felt that her life was put 'on hold' waiting for the court case:

It just puts this wet cloth around your bloody shoulders all the time. You can't take it off. You know you try to get on with your life like the police tell you to and the counsellors tell you to, but how do you get on with your life if there's no support?[82]

The abuser was a close family member, which understandably caused great emotional pain and conflict in the family. Even though her immediate family was very supporting, Collard considered this was very emotional and 'really heavy gear on everybody' and that 'neutral support' from outside the family was needed for all the immediate family.[83] In the lead up to the trial there were high levels of stress on her, with her health being impacted and self-harm attempts resulting.[84]

I asked Collard if she believed her abilities as a person with bicultural skills, having both Aboriginal and non-Aboriginal parents, helped her in any way with the court. She said that was 'absolutely' the case and also that she 'feels sorry for Noongar girls who don't have much contact with *wadjella* [non-Noongar] lives and have grown up in Indigenous environments and Indigenous values and cultures … It's a very different world.'[85]

Collard perceived that some people positioned her as 'mad' — and therefore not believable — and appeared to consider Graylands Hospital (a well-known Perth mental institution) as an appropriate response to her childhood victimisation:

Taylor's research documented the 'mad' and 'bad' narratives as dominant themes used to discredit sexual assault complainants in court.[86] As Collard explained, the 'mad' narrative was clearly used to discredit herself and to cause fear in her for disclosing child sexual assault. These fears surely contributed to the trauma Collard experienced, and spoke of as being heightened during the criminal justice process.

While dealing with enormous stress, Collard also experienced support from the local Noongar community. She received messages of support from people she didn't know, including Donna Kickett:

> Somehow people find out who I am and what's going on and say 'look we're here for you'. And that was fantastic because I don't know these people … I've got word, I've had messages sent up from Rockingham Noongars, down from Midland Noongars, a lot of different Noongar communities around Perth who tell me that they give me their utmost support, very proud of me for what I'm doing, very brave.[87]

This noticeable level of community support shows that many Noongar people are concerned about child sexual abuse, which is clearly seen as very much against our culture. There is a need for victims to come forward and disclose, and a role for community members in supporting that process.

In relation to the court experience, Collard identified issues including:

- fear and intimidation
- abusive and deliberately confusing cross-examination
- the importance of a woman judge.

The court experience was marked by fear and intimidation. During the three years prior to the case she was 'scared', not knowing what the end result would be.[88] The courtroom itself was felt as 'surreal'.

One of the defence lawyer's 'tricks' was to try to get Collard to look at her grandfather in court by using hand gestures and pointing towards him. Collard perceived this as a deliberate intimidation tactic:

So he was actually trying to get me to look at [my grandfather] to intimidate me because he knew that [he] scares me and intimidates me. But I refused to look … because I knew that I wasn't strong enough then to be able to look at him and go through that process.[89]

The questions asked by the defence lawyer were deliberately confusing. Specific language and wording were used to confuse her. At one point she responded, 'You are asking me a question that I cannot possibly answer'.[90] The judge intervened and noted that the defence had asked a two-part question and only allowed her to respond in part.[91] After this session, Collard described the approach adopted by the defence as very abusive, but after the trial she realised that the defence lawyer's approach was not substantial in a legal sense, and that 'all he had was tricks'.[92]

The defence lawyer attempted to undermine Collard's character through questioning that sought to portray her as promiscuous — with many irrelevant references and questions about boyfriends and men. In Collard's own words, the defence line of questioning was aimed at insinuating that she had the 'Sexual life of a slut, pretty much'.[93] While the defence did not actually use these offensive words, this was the clearly perceived inference being made through the line of questioning, questioning that I also observed in court and that appeared irrelevant and undermining.[94] Along with this suggestion, the defence lawyer also alleged drug use.[95]

At one point during the cross-examination, the defence made an astounding accusation that, because Collard was studying Aboriginal cultural studies, the complaint against the defendant was made purely as 'a political stand for Aboriginal women'.[96] We talked about that question later and she laughed at first, but then on a serious note explained:

I think that claim says to me, do Indigenous women have a right to come out [and], you know, make a political stand about this sexual abuse? … It's like well, yeah, we do because it's such a problem and some people still want to abuse children and young women and young boys, and I think one of the main reasons why nothing gets done is because not enough people want to stand up strong and loud and say this is what happened to me, it's wrong and it's about time the rest of us … start standing up and saying the same thing and believing it too.[97]

The cross-examination process sought to demean Collard and, moreover, insinuated that Aboriginal girls and women are generally untrustworthy, deceptive and dangerous perjurers in regard to sexual assault allegations. This degradation, sanctioned by the court, has some correlation to the actual cycle of abuse, in which victims (including Collard) are routinely re-victimised as 'liars' and 'trouble-makers' for disclosing.

The effect of the cross-examination process on Collard was clearly one of re-victimisation and trauma. Understandably, she was very angry at the defence, at one point asking the pertinent question of the court and the defence lawyer, 'Who's on trial?'[98] Although the prosecutor and judge intervened several times to address the defence lawyer's line of questioning, Collard stated that it was important to note that 'when you go in there as the victim you end up somehow feeling like the perpetrator, the way they victimise you in there'.[99]

The cross-examination lasted several hours and I observed the impact on Collard. At court completion she ran from the courtroom, screaming and crying before collapsing. This court experience was such that, notwithstanding the strength she showed in court, her family had to physically support her out of the court building. The legal process was experienced by her as attack, abuse and victimisa-tion, coming at the end of years of such behaviour.[100]

One of the few perceived positives of the trial experience was the presence of a woman judge. Although Collard did not feel that men lacked capacity to understand sexual abuse, she felt that a woman judge's presence was consistent with the Aboriginal cultural under-standing that child sexual abuse (and her own identity as a woman and girl child) raised the issue of 'women's business'.[101] Collard was impressed with the judge's sentencing comments, especially the fact that she did not 'mince her words'. She was pleased to hear the judge condemn the sexual abuse of a young family member as 'a gross abuse of trust', and to describe his unwillingness to admit guilt as offering little hope for his rehabilitation.[102]

The aftermath of the ordeal and trauma of the court experience required some re-adjustment time: 'Even after court it took a good month to come back to normal even though I won.'[103] Collard described having a 'lot of mixed feelings of guilt' for taking legal action that resulted in the incarceration of the 'head of the family'.[104]

Ingrid Collard powerfully broke the silence on child sexual assault in the Noongar community, recognising the extent of the problem and encouraging others to come forward; 'I know there's a lot of other girls out there who know how I feel … And I just want to give that message of hope to these girls. You've got to say something 'caus otherwise if you keep silent that is how these people get away with it!'[105]

Notwithstanding the traumatic impact of the justice system, Ingrid believes her actions and the court outcome allowed her to move forward in her life. Today she is a powerful advocate for youth leadership, empowerment and cultural integrity.

Case study: *R v Bropho* [2004] WADC 182

In September 2004 I received a telephone call from Lillian Passmore (now deceased), who was working for the Victim Support Service of the Department of Justice. Passmore was the first Aboriginal Victim Support Officer, an important position created by the Gordon Inquiry (this position appears to have now been disbanded). Along with other Aboriginal community-based victim support workers, she encouraged members of the Noongar community to attend a court verdict in a criminal case concerning a prominent Aboriginal Elder and leader charged with child sexual assault offences.

Why was it important for members of the community to come to court for the verdict? I understood from Passmore (and other Aboriginal support workers) that Noongar people were being called to attend this court verdict to show support for Noongar victims of child sexual assault, and raise awareness that this is not acceptable to our culture and community. There was a clear intention to raise awareness and break down the 'private' nature of child sexual abuse, and to encourage exposure of the issue into the wider Noongar community. In a similar manner, Aboriginal sexual assault workers consulted nationally by the Australian Institute of Criminology described the importance of encouraging awareness: 'At a local level, people are standing up and saying this behaviour is not acceptable. This is powerful for victims to see.'[106]

Upon attending the court I was informed by court officials that the court was not yet open to the public and I should wait in the public waiting area. I soon realised that I was seated in the presence of at least 20 to 30 people, Aboriginal and non-Aboriginal, who were there to support the defendant. In the court it was soon apparent that neither the victim nor her family attended court at all. I wondered how they would have felt in the face of so many of the defendant's family and supporters. Personally, I felt uncomfortable as an observer only.

Seated in court I noticed the judge's associate, a young white male, warmly acknowledge the defence barrister, whom I recognised as a well-known former town mayor. Judge Mazza soon entered the courtroom and the case was over in no time as he promptly handed down his verdict of 'not guilty'. The defendant's supporters gave victory shouts in court. Then I heard the judge refer to 'other matters' pending. I was not sure what this meant, but I was informed this involved other charges of child sexual assault. It shocked me that even with this information, people were prepared to support the defendant and were jubilant at the verdict. Outside the court, the defendant's high profile barrister spoke to the media, claiming that the DNA (deoxyribonucleic acid) evidence used against the defendant was not sufficient in the case, and that it may also be insufficient in similar cases involving Aboriginal people. I could hear him urging the DPP to appeal the case.

Passmore and I talked briefly immediately after the case, and we surmised that surely the DPP would appeal if there were grounds to do so. However, a quick read of *R v Bropho* [2004] WADC 182 suggested to me that the DPP had not prosecuted the case in the best possible manner — and an appeal was therefore unlikely. For example, the judge found that no evidence was given on three of the original counts of rape and unlawful assault.[107] It was unclear why the DPP would have prosecuted charges in relation to which it did not provide any evidence. As she photocopied the judgment for me, Passmore said there was concern expressed that the DPP had 'handballed the case around the office'.

A reading of the decision shows that it turned on the DNA evidence introduced by the prosecution to show that the defendant was the biological father of one of the complainant's children. Although this DNA evidence was not evidence of the rape itself, if accepted it would have supported the complainant as a credible witness. That is, the DNA evidence about her child's biological father also supported the truthfulness of her account of sexual assault by the defendant. According to the DPP the child was at least 3134 times more likely to be the biological child of the defendant and not the child of another man who was unrelated to him.[108]

However, very complex scientific arguments surrounding DNA and Aboriginal people were presented to the court, with an expert for the defence disputing the DPP's expert evidence on the basis that it was not scientifically valid to 'estimate the frequency of Aboriginal men who could have been the biological father'.[109] The judge accepted the complex scientific evidence to the effect that the state government's DNA processes were not appropriate in relation to Aboriginal people.[110] His Honour also said the DPP should have excluded near relatives as possible offenders in this case, and that the DPP's failure to exclude a man once nominated by the complainant as her child's father was a significant omission.[111]

This decision was a controversial one. Forensics expert Simon Walsh, from the University of Technology Sydney, described the DNA evidence showing that the defendant was the biological father of the complainant's child as 'very convincing'.[112] Walsh stated that for the purpose of the Family Court of Australia, the evidence of paternity in this case was well above what is generally required, and certainly would have established paternity in a civil matter.[113] This strong evidence of paternity was not enough to convince Judge Mazza, who instead accepted the defence's expert evidence questioning the reliability of DNA evidence for Aboriginal people across Australia.

The National Institute of Forensics Scientists (NIFS) considered this case to be 'problematic' and 'seriously counter-productive if initiated'.[114] It initiated a swift national response providing a 'scientific counter-point' to the decision that was soon being relied upon to launch legal challenges in Western Australia, South Australia and the Northern Territory to reject Aboriginal DNA evidence, including in matters of sexual assault.[115] As part of its response, NIFS convened an expert committee that included the defence expert from this case. According to Margaret Cunneen, senior New South Wales Crown prosecutor, the NIFS report has since been independently reviewed and statistically validated outside Australia, with the conclusion being reached that the statistical factor used in the case is a sufficiently conservative figure to be applied even in relation to Aboriginal people.[116] This expert international response meant that 'The prosecution evidence on DNA in *Bropho* was therefore proved to be correct'.[117]

In addition to the rejection of this DNA evidence, a significant factor relied upon to dismiss the criminal charges concerned the complainant's history of mental illness. The judge relied upon evidence introduced by the defence about the complainant's hospitalisation as a result of her mental illness, without acknowledging the context of abuse: 'I cannot exclude the possibility that a possible alternate offender was one of Mr Bropho's brothers and that as time has worn on and whilst labouring under the effects of her mental illness the complainant has wrongly nominated Mr Bropho as the offender.'[118]

No expert testimony was adduced on behalf of the complainant to explain the impacts of child sexual assault, nor the context of mental illness in this case (for example, one hospital admission occurred during the week the complainant's daughter made allegations of sexual abuse to police in relation to an indecent and physical assault). Her mental state and hospital admission were related to both her own and her daughter's history and disclosure of sexual abuse, and, if anything, expert knowledge of the psychological impacts of child sexual abuse may have suggested that such evidence supported credibility rather than weakened it.

Another important legal issue raised by this case concerned the issue of corroboration. Traditionally, sexual assault cases under common law have included warnings about 'uncorroborated' evidence; that is, evidence not independently supported by another person or witness. In sexual assault cases a judge was traditionally required to make a warning to the jury that it would be 'dangerous' to convict on the uncorroborated evidence of a sexual assault complainant. This evidentiary rule was developed by the common law in response to a deep-seated bias and stereotyping of women who made complaints of sexual assault.[119]

In Western Australia section 50 of the Evidence Act was amended to provide that judges did not need to issue a corroboration warning 'to the jury unless the judge is satisfied that such a warning is justified in the circumstances'. Notwithstanding such progressive legal reform, *Longman v The Queen* (1989) 168 CLR 79 (a decision of the High Court of Australia) established that where there is a long delay between the alleged offence occurring and the reporting of the offence and trial, a warning must be given. The *Longman* warning, as enunciated by the High Court, requires judges to warn a jury that a long delay means that the fairness of a trial has been impaired, and that it would be dangerous to convict on evidence of the complainant alone unless the jury is satisfied of the truth and accuracy of the evidence after scrutinising it with great care, considering the circumstances relevant to its evaluation and paying heed to the warning.

In *Christopher v The Queen* (2000) 23 WAR 106, Judge Owen in the Supreme Court of Western Australia stated the 'Longman direction' is a rule of practice that applies notwithstanding the enactment of section 36BE (now section 50) of the Evidence Act and it is not a conventional corroboration warning. Rather, 'It arises because of the overriding obligation of a trial judge to ensure that there is a fair trial and avoid a perceptible risk of miscarriage of justice occurring, again because of the circumstances of the particular case'.[120]

In the *Bropho* case the judge acknowledged that there was some 'controversy' in relation to corroboration warnings and as to whether a jury should be directed to use the word 'dangerous'; however, he also decided to direct himself that it would be 'dangerous' to convict on the complainant's evidence alone.[121] He also considered that there were other matters that impacted negatively on the complainant's credibility. He stated that these included the great delay in making the complaint, the apparent unlikelihood of the alleged acts taking place in the places nominated (being public places) and the complainant's uncertainty about when the incident actually occurred. Also, he referred to a card that was signed by the complainant. Although not written by the complainant, the card expressed sentimental thought that was contrary to her testimony that she hated the accused. Further, the judge said that her initial allegation was made on the date of her daughter's funeral and at that time she had feelings of blame towards the accused.[122]

Having made such adverse conclusions, his Honour was then required to consider section 36BD ('Lack of complaint, jury warning about') of the Western Australian Criminal Code, which stipulates that in relation to sexual offences, a judge shall:

(a) give a warning to the jury that absence of complaint or delay in complaining does not necessarily indicate that the allegation of the offence is false; and

(b) inform the jury that there may be good reasons why a victim of an offence may hesitate or refrain from making a complaint of that offence.

The complainant's delay in making the complaint was considered by the judge to have been understandable in view of her young age, the position the accused held, her affection for her aunty, her feelings of shame and being 'low and dirty' about what happened, and that, because of not wanting to alienate herself from the family and the recognition that her own mother at that time was struggling with alcoholism, 'she had no significant adult in her life to whom she could complain'.[123]

However, the presiding judge failed to recognise a primary factor — fear — that the complainant voiced in her testimony: 'Why didn't you tell anybody? Because I was frightened. What were you frightened off? My family.'[124] It appears that the complainant was not asked to elaborate in court about her fears and those fears were ignored by the judge, contrary to section 36BD.

Notwithstanding the recognition of (some) of the reasons for the delayed complaint, the judge concluded that the delay meant 'the fairness' of the trial had been impaired:

Had the allegations been made soon after the alleged event and reported to the authorities it would have been possible to explore much better than now, the detail of the circumstances surrounding the commission of the alleged offences and perhaps obtain evidence throwing doubt upon the complainant's version of events or confirming the accused's denial.

Had the complaints been made promptly, there is little doubt that a medical examination of the complainant, an examination of the alleged crime scene and forensics analysis of clothing would have occurred which may have exonerated the accused.

The accused, had the complaint been more promptly made, would have been better able to account for his movements and, perhaps, establish an alibi.[125]

These findings are made despite the facts accepted by the judge — namely, that the 'alleged offences' occurred in 1975 and 1976 when the complainant was 13 years of age. She had no mother to turn to at that time and she lived with her aunty and her uncle, a man who she later disclosed had sexually abused her. Their children were her cousins and, according to Aboriginal kinship, had a relationship akin to cousin-siblings. She was a homeless Noongar girl from a background of poverty, family dislocation and sexual assault. Who could she realistically have made such a complaint to? It was recognised that the complainant had no significant adult in her life to whom she could have complained, but lack of complaint was still used to draw conclusions that undermined her credibility. It was related to the conclusion that she was not a reliable and truthful witness, unlike the defendant, whose evidence was described as 'plausible'.[126]

It is evident from this case that progressive law reform and legislative intervention had no real effect on the case and the ultimate decision. The *Longman* warning (which is not characterised as a corroboration warning) was required (and heeded). The judge regarded the delayed complaint as being 'dangerous' evidence, regardless of the legislative reforms that have rejected corroboration warnings and recognising that there are good reasons why a complaint of sexual assault may be delayed. Legal academic Dorne Boniface, in her analysis of judicial directions and warnings in sexual assault cases, has considered the somewhat contradictory directions permissible in the case of delayed complaint.[127] On the one hand, juries are told there can be good reason for delay and it does not mean the allegations are false. On the other hand, they are also told that they can take that delay into account when determining whether to believe the complainant. As Boniface points out, 'The two directions together can be nonsensical'.[128] Furthermore, 'If there are good reasons for a complainant to delay in complaining, how can that delay then relate to their credibility?'[129]

In the *Bropho* case, the judge's view was that the delayed complaint meant 'the fairness' of the trial had been impaired. At the practical level this decision undermined the legislative reforms that acknowledged that there are good reasons for delayed complaint in relation to matters of sexual assault, particularly child sexual assault. The court decision revealed the lack of impact of law reforms and moreover that the judge's own personal views conflicted with the progressive legislative reforms: 'It is a matter of common experience that the longer a person believes something to have happened the more convinced that person is that it actually happened';[130] 'I suspect that the truth of these matters has been lost in the sands of time.'[131]

The reluctance of the judge to adhere to the spirit of legislative intention was not unusual. Corroboration warnings were considered in some detail by the New South Wales Department for Women, which found that regardless of the legislative reforms, warnings were overwhelmingly given by judges hearing sexual assault cases.[132] In a study of 150 cases of the New South Wales District Court over a 1 year period, it was found that the older style of warning (that it is 'dangerous' to convict on the evidence of the complainant alone) was given in 40% of cases, and a newer style warning ('scrutinise her evidence with great care') was given in 59% of trials.[133] In 14 cases no warning was given by the judge, and in 19 cases the judge gave both warnings.[134]

Disturbingly, the New South Wales report also found that judges were still giving corroboration warnings (both old and new) in cases where evidence of a complainant's medical injuries had been accepted by the court.[135] For example, in one case the Crown prosecutor asked the judge to direct the jury as to the evidence that corroborated the complainant, including a neighbour's evidence that she had heard her screams, and medical evidence about a broken limb and her state of hyperventilation at a medical centre. The judge refused to do so and instead went on to warn the jury, using the old style warning, about the dangers of convicting an accused person on the uncorroborated evidence of the complainant.[136] However, the report also found there were some cases that evidenced a changed attitude on the part of some members of the judiciary. For example, in one case concerning the sexual assault of an Aboriginal woman by a group of men, the judge refused to make the corroboration warning, and commented to members of the jury that they should examine the evidence of the accused person with great care rather than the evidence of the complainant.[137]

Although the District Court rejected the complainant's evidence in the *Bropho* case, as indicated at the verdict I observed, other cases were progressing. In 2008 Judge Nisbet of the Western Australian District Court sentenced Bropho to three years' imprisonment relating to child sexual assault charges.[138] The defendant appealed this sentence, but a cross appeal by the DPP, claiming that the sentence imposed was 'manifestly inadequate', was upheld by the Court of Appeal in *Bropho v The State of Western Australia* [No 2] [2009] WASC 94. This case also involved DNA evidence (resulting from children fathered) but it was clear that the higher court agreed with Judge Nisbet, who rejected the same scientific evidence that Judge Mazza accepted in 2004.[139] Judge Nisbet pointed out that the basis of that 'expert' evidence — that the appellant belonged solely to the Noongar sub-population — was incorrect.[140] On appeal, the court also agreed with the DPP submission that the sentence was inadequate, and increased the sentence to six years' imprisonment.

The apparent lack of knowledge in 2004 on the part of the Crown prosecuting the case, namely that the defendant's genealogy extended beyond the Noongar sub-population, illustrates my concern as to the marginalisation of Aboriginal people in the administration of the justice system. The DPP must ensure the employment of Aboriginal prosecutors with localised knowledge who are better placed to prosecute such cases. It has always been well known in the community that in the *Bropho* case the defendant's family history went beyond Noongar country, and therefore that the basis of the scientific evidence upheld (and seemingly unquestioned by prosecution) in 2004 was negligible. Notwithstanding its Reconciliation Plan, the DPP employs no Aboriginal prosecutors. Failure to ensure Aboriginal people's proper participation clearly disadvantages Aboriginal victims whose cases rely on a measure of successful cross-cultural ability. In a sense, the inadvertent exclusion of Aboriginal people perpetuates a form of systemic discrimination, where Aboriginal victims are likely to receive less favourable treatment in the prosecution of their court cases.

The decision in *R v Bropho* [2004] WADC 182 reflects the pervasive and racist stereotype that Aboriginal women and girls cannot be raped, and thus have no need for protection and recognition under the law. Although the court failed to afford recognition to the human dignity of the complainant, to my mind and many others she will always be seen as a brave Noongar woman. From my knowledge of this case and time in Noongar history, it is evident that she rejected the insidious silencing of victims in families and communities, and paved a way forward for others to stand bravely against violence and abuse of children. Others did follow in her footsteps and their cases eventually resulted in the incarceration of a once-powerful Aboriginal man.

Although I met the complainant in this case some years after the trial, I was not able to interview her as anticipated because she had left the state shortly after this decision. I became aware that this was not an unusual response and that other Aboriginal victims had fled the state for their own safety.

This chapter shows how members of the Noongar community have sought to address child sexual assault through the criminal justice system and raises questions about the high costs associated with 'justice'. Victim survivors have often not experienced justice, nor support, acknowledgment or outcomes conducive to healing for themselves and their families. The complainants in the case studies all experienced and were disadvantaged by the criminal justice system's lack of respect for Noongar people and culture, the 'male' nature of the law that has seen an undermining of law reforms to support victims, abuse and lack of support for victims, high levels of re-victimisation and trauma to victims, and more. Aboriginal child sexual assault is a serious problem, but the response of the criminal justice system is sadly lacking.

Chapter 7

Looking forward:
Aboriginal victims at the centre

This chapter explores the future development of Aboriginal models to address child sexual assault. Aboriginal people have both the right and responsibility to be an important part of the law's response to child sexual assault and the criminal abuse of children. The responses of the non-Aboriginal criminal justice system have been discriminatory, traumatic and largely ineffective, and fail to address holistically the needs of victims and families. There is an urgent need for legal responses developed by Aboriginal people and supported by the criminal justice system. Such models should aim to address the grave harm caused to victims, ensure greater prospect of accountability and rehabilitation of offenders, and break the traumatic, unhealthy cycle of abuse that has become entrenched (even normalised) within our communities.

There has been considerable support for the development of new Aboriginal models to address child sexual assault by governments in partnership with Aboriginal communities. This support reflects the growing awareness of the extent of Aboriginal child sexual assault and the critical understanding of Aboriginal self-determination. As a matter of human rights, Aboriginal people have an important role to play.

In 2007 the New South Wales Aboriginal Child Sexual Assault Taskforce (ACSAT) acknowledged that many Indigenous people believe that improving the situation for Indigenous victims of child sexual assault requires a holistic process of community healing, and that 'restorative justice' approaches are needed to support community healing and genuinely empower people.[1] The ACSAT final recommendation is that the New South Wales Government should, 'In consultation with the Aboriginal community, research, develop and implement a new model to address child sexual assault in Aboriginal communities through the continuum of the legal process from initial investigation through to sentencing'.[2]

The 2007 report of the Northern Territory Board of Inquiry into the Protection of Aboriginal Children from Sexual Abuse also supports alternative Aboriginal models. The inquiry acknowledged that the current criminal justice approach to Aboriginal child sexual assault results in only 'a small percentage' of offenders being identified, arrested and convicted.[3] It also agreed that the present approach results in 'institutional trauma' to the victim and family, and outcomes that may not be viewed in a positive manner by the victim and family.[4] The inquiry noted that many submissions argued the need for a model that placed less emphasis on the criminal justice system.[5] It was considered that jail was not a deterrent and did not rehabilitate,[6] and recommended:

> the government to commence meaningful dialogue as soon as possible with Aboriginal communities aimed at developing alternative models of sentencing that incorporate Aboriginal notions of justice and rely less on custodial sentences and more on restoring the wellbeing of victims, offenders, families and communities. Further, where these models can demonstrate probably positive outcomes within the relevant community that are suitable to the needs of victims, promote rehabilitation to offenders and promote harmony within the broader community, the government commit to the ongoing support of such programs and to legislative changes necessary to implement such changes. Any model which is developed may only be utilised with the consent of the victim.[7]

Although child sexual assault is a major issue confronting Aboriginal communities, neither of these critical recommendations has been implemented or seemingly even progressed. Most recently, it appears that the National Child Sexual Assault Reform Committee, a national non-Aboriginal advisory body, has implicitly rejected these key recommendations. In 2010 the committee recommended a 'less adversarial pilot study' of one hundred Indigenous child sexual assault cases in the District Court.[8] This recommendation does not appear to have resulted from any consultations or dialogue with Aboriginal communities, and is unlikely to have Aboriginal support in view of the New South Wales ACSAT holistic recommendation.

In exploring these key recommendations and Aboriginal responses to address child sexual assault, I consider international approaches adopted by Indigenous people of Canada and the United States. In Canada the concept of 'justice as healing' — and one model in particular, the Community Holistic Circle Healing of Hollow Water — has been widely recognised internationally and in Australia. In the United States, the Native American tribes have adopted an approach that could be described as Indigenous 'specialisation' as evident from the award-winning Navajo Child Special Advocacy Program.

'Justice as healing': the case of Hollow Water

There has been a great deal of international attention generated by the Community Holistic Circle Healing (CHCH) program of Hollow Water, Canada. This model was acknowledged and supported by ACSAT and the Board of Inquiry into the Protection of Aboriginal Children from Sexual Abuse. The foundation of CHCH is located within the Indigenous Canadian paradigm of justice as a form of healing.

In 2006 I travelled to Canada to study the Canadian Aboriginal concept of 'justice as healing' — the development of legal respon-ses that are premised on both justice and healing. According to Aboriginal Canadian Judge Turpel-Lafond, healing is an Aboriginal justice principle that is becoming merged into Canadian criminal law through the use of sentencing circles and community-based diversion programs.[9] The significance of healing to justice as a matter of human rights is articulated by Patricia Angus-Monture, a Mohawk law professor, who believes that Aboriginal peoples' healing is the foundation upon which we must build our human rights claim of Indigenous self-determination: 'Healing is ... about taking responsibility. It is about re-learning how we are supposed to be. Without knowing what traditional responsibilities are, then the right to self-determination means nothing. Healing is about learning to act in a good way ... '[10]

At the University of Saskatchewan, Saskatoon, I visited the Native Law Centre, which has been a leader in the field of justice as healing. The co-ordinator of the Native Law Centre and author of *Justice as Healing Indigenous Ways*, Wanda McCaslin, suggested that I learn about the CHCH model, which addresses child sexual assault and was developed in a neighbouring province, Manitoba, in the community of Hollow Water. I travelled to Manitoba and met Valdie Seymour, a founder of CHCH.

I was taken back at how far Aboriginal people had come to address the traumas resulting from colonisation, and the achievements and understandings they held. The level of understanding, insight, capacity, commitment and responsibility to individual and community healing was not something that I had ever encountered in Australia. The healing process in Canada was supported and influenced by the Canadian government's commitment to reconciliation with Aboriginal people, a commitment that clearly stalled in Australia under the Howard government. Since 1998 the Canadian government has supported the Aboriginal Healing Foundation to support many community-based healing initiatives of Métis, Inuit and First Nations people, who were directly or indirectly affected by the legacy of physical and sexual abuse in residential schools.[11]

More than a decade later in Australia our government has learned from Canada and established a healing foundation, recognising that 'International experience shows that healing practices result in positive changes in peoples' lives if those practices have strong roots in Indigenous traditions, values and culture, while also incorporating Western and mainstream practices'.[12]

My understandings of CHCH have been influenced by being on country and meeting and talking with many people including leaders, academics, Elders, and men and women working for community healing. I was also very fortunate to participate in Canadian Aboriginal cultural practices such as the healing circles, the sweatlodge ceremony and smudging, and to experience the vital role of Aboriginal cultural and healing practices.

The CHCH model of Hollow Water, Canada, was formed in 1987 as the community began to learn that sexual victimisation and inter-generational sexual abuse was at the core of the poor wellbeing of many individuals and families.[13] From the community's experience, the non-Indigenous adversarial legal system could not understand the complexity of this issue and what was needed for a community to break the cycle of abuse that impacted upon so many of its members. The community developed the model in an effort to take responsibility for what was happening, to work to restore balance and to make the community a safe place for future generations. In developing the model, the community held the following beliefs:

(a) that victimisers are created, not born;
(b) that the vicious cycle of abuse in communities must be broken — now; and
(c) that, given a safe place, healing is possible and will happen.[14]

Hollow Water does not support the incarceration of offenders:

What the threat of incarceration does do is keep our people from coming forward and taking responsibility for the hurt they are causing. It reinforces silence and therefore promotes, rather than breaks, the cycle of violence that exists. In reality, rather than making the community a safer place, the threat of jail places the community more at risk.[15]

Within the CHCH process, offenders are instead held directly accountable to those most affected by the victimisation: the victims, families and the wider community.

The CHCH program uses principles traditionally used to deal with victimisation. These principles allow the community:

1. To bring it out into the open.
2. To protect the victim, so as to minimally disrupt the family and community's functioning.
3. To hold the victimiser responsible for his or her behaviour.
4. To offer the opportunity for balance to be restored to all parties of the victimisation.[16]

Hollow Water founder Berma Bushie explains the process as one that works in conjunction with the Canadian criminal justice system. Following a disclosure of sexual assault, a team consisting of a CHCH team member, a representative from the Child and Family Services department and a representative from the police come together to investigate and record the victim's story and ensure safety.[17] If it is determined (beyond reasonable doubt) that the abuse has taken place, the abuser is confronted and charged. At the same time, a member of the CHCH team encourages the person charged to admit to the abuse and agree to participate in the healing program.[18]

As explained by Bushie, only victimisers who agree to plead guilty and fully co-operate with the healing process are accepted into the program.[19] The CHCH team makes it clear that those who do not agree will not receive support, but will instead be abandoned to the courts (with jail as a possible outcome). Abusers who agree to 'the healing road' and participation in CHCH are mandated to the program, where they may remain for several years.[20]

The CHCH model entails the development of a 'healing contract' that offenders must agree to be bound by; the contract involves healing circles held separately with the victims and perpetrators and their families; the sentencing circle in which victims, victimisers, families and the wider community are brought together and in which a non-custodial sentence is imposed on the offender; and a final 'cleansing' ceremony held to acknowledge the offender's participation within the program and reintegration back into the community.[21] Fundamentally, the CHCH process 'lives within' and is guided by the Anishinabe sacred teachings (the seven sacred teachings given by the Creator for Aboriginal people), which are honesty, love, courage, truth, wisdom, humility and respect.[22] It is also apparent that CHCH uses both contemporary and traditional cultural practices, including the circle, prayer, smudging, the sweat-lodge ceremony and herbal medicines.

To understand CHCH it needs to be recognised that it was developed by individuals who are survivors of child sexual assault and the success of the process is considered to be founded directly on the team members' own personal knowledge and healing. The personal healing of team members is 'foundational, extensive and inclusive' and authenticity in both personal and public life is essential.[23] Rupert Ross, an experienced Crown prosecutor, writes that unhealed people cannot bring healing to others, and the creation of the healing team at Hollow Water took many years of personal dedication.[24] Some members are also former perpetrators who have successfully completed the program and they are considered to have an important role to play, especially because of their understanding of an abuser's denial system.[25]

Ross states it is this personal and very real understanding of the emotional, mental, physical and spiritual complexities of sexual abuse that gives the team 'an extraordinary rapport' with victims and victimisers alike.[26] Through healing circles, the CHCH team members speak openly about themselves and their histories and understandings as both victims and victimisers. They confront abusers and work with them to address the anger, denial, guilt, fear, self-loathing and hurt that surround sexual assault and which must be faced.[27] Ross argues that the Hollow Water concept promotes offenders to take responsibility for their acts, and that this process is not just a mental acknowledgment — it is aimed at trying to make offenders actually feel some of the pain, grief, sorrow, outrage or other emotions that they have caused in others.[28] During the process an offender's past victimisations are dealt with 'so that their influence is diminished' — but this past abuse is never permitted to stand as an excuse for the offending.[29]

At the same time, a team member is assigned to work closely with victims, and to support their families in coming to terms with the abuse. Victims are assured that the abuse was not their fault, and within the CHCH process they are encouraged to face abusers and work towards healing.[30] According to Bushie, 'Victims receive a great deal of care, love and skilled therapeutic attention in dealing with the trauma of their abuse'.[31]

CHCH is a process of 'building up' the victim who has been harmed and 'stripping down' the victimiser to redress the imbalance caused by sexual assault.[32] The CHCH team praises and celebrates the courage of victims and acknowledges their pain.[33] Bushie acknowledges the CHCH team members are battling generational silence — and the generational blaming of the victims: 'If it hadn't been for them disclosing their parents would still be in denial or their victimisers would still be in denial. So it's very much their courage that is celebrated that day.'[34]

As Ross notes, the Hollow Water model offers victimisers (offenders) the possibility of a future free of the shame of their past.

Offenders who successfully complete the program are not shunned forever by the community but, rather, are seen as an important resource with the ability to 'get under the skin' of offenders and 'disturb the web of lies that have sustained them'.[35]

The model has reported achieving a remarkably low recidivism rate of offenders who participate in the program. According to one study, of 107 offenders who had participated in the program, only two have re-offended.[36] CHCH has been described as having a reported rate of success with offenders that 'is nothing short of spectacular' and not comparable to that of mainstream non-Indigenous approaches.[37]

An independent evaluation of CHCH also concluded that the values and teachings had been embraced in the wider community, and the community's own spiritual, emotional, physical and mental wellbeing had improved significantly since its establishment.[38] This was reportedly reflected in various ways — happier children and better parenting, more disclosures and empowerment of victims, women feeling empowered, community actions and responsibility, respect, broadening of resources, responsiveness, openness and honesty, strengthening of traditions, harm reduction, and violence being controlled.[39] Without the CHCH model and process, community members said they felt that there would be 'utter chaos': 'It would become silent again', and 'The communities would fall apart. Suicides would be common. Many people would deny they need help.'[40]

Ross has made some important observations concerning the problems associated with the criminal justice system and the benefits of CHCH. Many victims, especially Aboriginal victims, are reluctant to report abuse to police and this is referenced to the problem of shame (whereby individuals perceive that they were somehow at fault) and communal shame, particularly the 'conspiracy of silence' that surrounds sexual abuse.[41] When the abuse is within families there is the problem of divided loyalties and what the criminal process will do, and this may be heightened for Aboriginal people who 'face special pressure not to involve police'.[42] Ross argues that the lack of reporting is one of the most striking, unacknowledged failures of the criminal justice system: 'a great many victims, especially Aboriginal victims, chose not to use it'.[43]

The Hollow Water team developed CHCH as an alternative to the court, which it felt was too traumatic on child victims and heightened the abuse already experienced: 'Crown Attorney's, to make their case, put the victims — often children — on the witness stand and expect them to participate in a process that in many ways ... further victimises them. The court room is not a safe place for the victim to address the victimisation.'[44]

Ross agrees that the criminal justice system does not help victims to move beyond anger. Instead, it requires them to participate in an adversarial system in which their truthfulness is attacked and their feelings are substantially irrelevant. The criminal justice approach therefore contributes to the anger caused by sexual assault.[45]

Another seldom acknowledged problem is that even after victims disclose and charges are laid, suspects who exercise their legal rights and call for a trial stand a higher than average chance of being acquitted. In Ross's experience, Aboriginal victims struggled to testify in a 'convincing manner', especially before non-Aboriginal judges and juries, and every verdict of 'not guilty' is 'corrosive', with abusers 'laughing at the system that could not touch them'.[46] Victims realise and feel understandably aggrieved that their disclosures took them through an agonising process for seemingly no purpose or good whatsoever. Ross reported that some victims after reporting abuse have been ostracised, punished and driven out of their community never to return.[47]

The Australian context

Hollow Water's CHCH has great possibilities that should be explored in the Australian context. The participation and empowerment of victims in the process, the potential of healing and rehabilitation of perpetrators, the involvement of the community, the positive benefits to the community, and the re-establishment of traditional culture and spiritual values appear to all be highly valuable outcomes of CHCH. The current approach of the criminal justice system (in which Aboriginal people are marginalised and have virtually no role) offers little to none of these benefits to Aboriginal people and communities.

Many problems associated with the nature of Aboriginal child sexual assault and the response of the criminal justice system as identified by Hollow Water and Ross, were evident from comments made at a 2007 meeting with Aboriginal practitioners in Perth to discuss the development of therapeutic communities for abused Aboriginal children and their families.[48] The following comments made by practitioners illustrate similar problems to those once faced by the community of Hollow Water:

> There is confusion over the law and excuses are being made. We are talking about kids of eighteen months with [sexually transmitted infections] and 12-year-olds having babies.[49]

> It takes courage to stand up and be counted and to maintain a cause and continue to fight takes huge courage. A lot of people in the community knew about [sexually transmitted disease] in children but no one spoke up. But one of us carried her voice on. Not enough of us do that. There is not enough support for the messenger. When two families opened up on abuse there were three men charged and now 8 to 10 people have been charged. Unfortunately some of those people who took action have had to be relocated as the community has turned on them.[50]

> The laws of evidence don't work in child protection. There is criminal law but it is too hard for the cops. They try but they say: 'It's too hard, we can't do anything, we can't find the evidence or we're not being given enough by the family to be able to do anything.'[51]

> And when the wife finds that sexual assault is occurring — say an uncle is abusing her daughter — her husband says shut up or you'll cause an argument.[52]

> What happens in the smaller centres when children disclose? Who protects them and the family when they talk about abuse especially when it [the claim] is against an elder? Support is needed before, during and after the court process and support is needed if it doesn't go to court as well. The alleged offender can get bail or remand and go back into the community. It might be two years until the trial and if the [alleged offender] is well liked or connected there can be intimidation involved for the child and family.[53]

CHCH may be regarded as controversial as a diversionary model not based on incarceration of offenders. However, it should be recognised that Australian courts have released offenders on suspended sentence without any supervision, treatment or rehabilitation measures. This situation was apparent in a cluster of cases before the Broome District Court in 2009 involving two Aboriginal victims aged 12 years and three separate adult male offenders aged 39, 51 and 20 years.[54] Furthermore, it is clear that there is a very high attrition rate for sexual assault offences (especially concerning children), and offenders who plead not guilty and put children through a court process have a very good chance of acquittal.

Some Aboriginal people appear ambivalent about whether Aboriginal child sexual assault should be addressed outside the criminal justice system. For example, in a 2005 address Mick Gooda, then Chief Executive Officer of the Cooperative Research Centre for Aboriginal Health, said that he has 'come down firmly on the rights of children taking precedence over all others', but he also said:

> The frontline of Aboriginal child protection is Aboriginal families and communities themselves. It is essential that we take on this responsibility ourselves because if governments do intervene they often do so through the criminal justice system with the result that more of our people go to gaol. I am not defending perpetrators of child abuse here but simply making the point that protection of children is generally best organised by that child's community rather than the often clumsy hand of state intervention.[55]

On a similar note, Australian criminologist Harry Blagg has argued for interventions that 'open pathways to healing, with minimum intervention by the criminal justice system'.[56] Aboriginal men, Blagg considers, should be diverted from 'unnecessary contact' with the criminal justice system and towards community-based systems of control.[57] Blagg states that diversion should be dependent on the seriousness of the offence and the victim's willingness,[58] but does not specifically address child sexual assault.

ACSAT supported Blagg's assessment that 'peacemaking and healing' opportunities aimed at diverting offenders into Indigenous community-based systems of control were needed.[59] At the same time ACSAT found that Koori Sentencing Circles, which involve local Aboriginal communities in the court process and incorporate 'peacemaking and healing' in their approach, were not appropriate for child sexual assault matters.[60]

As a matter of human rights, Aboriginal responses to child sexual assault arguably must incorporate the criminal justice system. According to the United Nations Convention on the Rights of the Child, the criminal nature of the offence is envisaged:

> *Article 19* states parties shall take all appropriate legislative, administrative, social and educational measures to protect the child from all forms of physical or mental violence, injury or abuse, neglect or negligent treatment, maltreatment or exploitation, including sexual abuse, while in the care of parent(s), legal guardian(s) or any other person who has the care of the child.

Child sexual assault is a serious criminal offence and the criminal justice system will always have an important role to play for that very reason. The independent organisation Save the Children affirms that alternative or additional systems must be guided by the legal system.[61] This was seen as especially important in order to protect the best interests of the child, and ensure that the family is not tricked, or threatened by the abuser to withdraw its claims of justice.[62]

Other compelling arguments for the role of the criminal justice system were made some years ago by United States child sexual abuse medical experts, who argued that the 'greatest lapse of societal concern for the sexually abused children lies in the failure to link punishment of the convicted offender to treatment'.[63] These experts were convinced that the criminal justice system had an important role to play, noting that many perpetrators, although initially willing to enter therapy and treatment, often lost interest without external pressure, and 'the capacity of the criminal justice system to intervene positively must be encouraged'.[64] They saw the authority of the criminal justice system as 'absolutely essential' in treating intra-familial child sexual assault.[65] The question posed long ago by these experts has ongoing relevance: 'Why do we ignore compelling evidence that an authoritative incentive to change his or her behaviour is absolutely essential for the adult perpetrator of child sexual abuse?'[66]

CHCH is supported by the criminal justice system

One of the main reasons why CHCH works well is because it is supported by the Canadian criminal justice system. The victimisers, upon being charged by the police, are given the option to admit to the charges, disclose fully the offence and undertake CHCH, in which case, imprisonment will not result. CHCH has developed protocols and strong working relationships with the police and Crown prosecutors, and its direct involvement in the initial investigatory stage is considered critical to the success of the program.

Although Hollow Water did not require any transfer of jurisdictional authority, it is clear that the CHCH model is supported by an overarching Canadian legal framework that has embraced Aboriginal and restorative justice models and processes. Aboriginal Judge Mary Ellen Turpel-Lafond has explained the significant changes to the Canadian legal system.[67] In the 1999 case of *R v Gladue* the Supreme Court of Canada considered amendments to the Canadian Criminal Code (section 718.2), which required judges to consider all available sanctions other than imprisonment for offenders that are reasonable in the circumstances and with particular attention to Aboriginal offenders. According to Judge Turpel-Lafond the *Gladue* decision is an 'important turning point' in Canadian criminal law, and the interpretation of this provision 'clearly endorsed the notion of restorative justice and a method of sentencing that emphasises "healing"'.[68] This case followed more than a decade of scrutiny of the criminal justice system and its discriminatory impact on Aboriginal people, particularly significant government inquiries such as the Royal Commission on Aboriginal Peoples and the Manitoba Aboriginal Justice Inquiry.[69]

Judge Turpel-Lafond stated that the *Gladue* decision (in accordance with section 718.2) adopted restorative justice and a philosophy of personal and community healing. In her view this included an approach to remedying crime in which it is understood that 'all things are interrelated and that crime disrupts the harmony which existed prior to its occurrence, or at least which it is felt should exist'. According to the Supreme Court decision, Aboriginal victims are clearly considered to be a part of the restorative justice process: 'The appropriateness of the particular sanction is largely determined by the needs of the victims and the community, as well as the offender. The focus is on the human beings closely affected by the crime.'[70]

Judge Turpel-Lafond has argued that the sentencing practices that result from the *Gladue* case must interact with strong concerns from Aboriginal women and that 'the needs of victims should not be disregarded in the healing enterprise'.[71] In considering alternatives to incarceration, Turpel-Lafond maintains that the courts have to weigh whether the victim's interests are properly protected by a non-custodial sentence.[72]

Critical concerns — victims must be properly protected

Aboriginal people in Australia considering the development of our own model/s to address child sexual assault must also recognise the concerns expressed in relation to CHCH and other Aboriginal and restorative justice responses. Leading Canadian Aboriginal scholar Professor Emma LaRocque has been critical of Aboriginal justice models such as CHCH, arguing that they are offender oriented, that they promote leniency for the offender (who is treated as a 'victim'), that they pressure victims to 'forgive' and that they are detrimental to victims' overall wellbeing.[73] LaRocque expresses the view that restorative justice and healing circles are influenced by Christian and new age concepts, and are not consistent with traditional Aboriginal punishments that were quite often severe.[74]

LaRocque's concern that models are biased and oriented towards offenders was supported by a 1996 study of CHCH that found only 28% of victims viewed the Hollow Water sentencing circle process as a positive experience, as compared to 72% of offenders.[75] According to the survey, victims felt that they received less help than they needed and participated in fewer processes than offenders. Although it was appreciated that CHCH gave them a place to report victimisation, they reported that they needed more ongoing help than what was provided. Victims were also concerned that offenders were not dealt with appropriately and about one-third (34%) of victims surveyed said that the community was not usually supportive of them after going through the program.[76]

Concerns with restorative justice were also the focus of a 2001 report by the Canadian Aboriginal Women's Action Network (AWAN).[77] Research participants expressed tremendous concern that the widespread adoption of Aboriginal restorative justice measures was based on a premise that presupposed a healed community, but a radical transformation of existing structures of gendered domination within Aboriginal communities had not yet happened.[78] Women feared that the restorative justice reforms failed to address the under-lying power inequity that was rife in communities after years of oppression.[79]

The silencing of victims and normalisation of violence in commu-nities was regarded as a serious issue, as were sexual harassment, nepotism and discrimination.[80] Participants were also concerned that 'unhealthy elders' (with a past history of abuse) were frequently engaged in leadership roles and activities such as healing circles and spiritual ceremonies.[81] It was felt that there needed to be more learning around the actual dynamics of sexual abuse before restora-tive justice or alternative forms of Aboriginal justice were used.[82] Notwithstanding, the AWAN report considered that the Aboriginal justice reforms had some potential to address Aboriginal crime in a way that the existing justice system did not.[83]

The focus on Aboriginal male offenders rather than victims has clearly prevailed within Aboriginal Canadian justice reforms, and is evident from criticisms by academics and Aboriginal women's groups. Within these justice models, it has been argued that Aboriginal male offenders, rather than Aboriginal female victims, have come to represent the interests of the Aboriginal community. This dynamic has been criticised by LaRocque:

> With respect to violence, the argument for community is trans-parently a case of favouring one individual (offender) over another (victim), elevating the offender's interests to 'collective rights' while reducing the victim's interests to 'individual rights'. It remains a puzzle how offenders, more than victims, have come to represent 'collective rights'. Besides disregarding all contemporary discourse on justice and ethics, the premise that individual rights should be sacrificed for the supposed good of the community has no substantiation. It is as if individuals are not part of the collec-tive good, as if the only way to ensure 'collective rights' is to subvert individual ones, or at least those of certain individuals. However, it cannot be good for the collective to disregard indi-vidual rights or well-being.[84]

Restorative justice expert Rashmi Goel's study of Canadian Abori-ginal sentencing circles supported LaRocque's concern that the interests of women victims of violence were silenced within the circle process. Goel's research caused her to consider that violence against victims was being overshadowed by the issue of racism and the male offenders' experiences of racism: 'the victim is obscured by a central focus on the offender as a victim of colonial society.'[85] Within the judicially convened sentencing circles, Indigenous male perpetrators have been able to deflect and/or minimise culpability by constituting themselves as victims of white colonisation. Australian academic Professor Kathleen Daly states that the problem is not the acknowledgment of the impacts of colonisation, but rather the obscuring of the victim that takes place in the process: 'when an offender makes a discursive shift from offender to victim, the actual victim is obscured. The zero sum game is played out with an offender taking the place of both offender and victim, with the actual victim having being removed (discursively) from the game.'[86]

Daly argues that Indigenous justice practices can be improved by 'bringing the voice or perspective of the victim into the process'.[87] This may be easier said than done if we consider the research on the Canadian sentencing circle. Canadian researchers Angela Cameron and Emma Cunliffe, in their examination of judicially convened sentencing circles, rejected circles as a restorative approach to intimate violence.[88] From their study, rather than facing and seeking to heal the harm done to survivors, the circles minimised and denied the harm.[89] From written court decisions, little attention was paid to the effects of the violence, or the decision of the circle, on the survivors: 'Women's lived experience of violence is being silenced within these decisions, and women's expertise about their own needs is being denied.'[90]

The research also found that survivors were coerced into participating in the circles, and their needs for safety and wellbeing were 'overwhelmingly' disregarded.[91] Judges simply had not listened to Aboriginal groups that they should not proceed with sentencing circles on the basis of concern that this will undermine 'the continuing struggle of Aboriginal women to have violence against them taken more seriously'.[92] Cameron and Cunliffe argue that, paradoxically, Aboriginal Canadian women's experiences of intimate violence were excluded from the circles ostensibly convened to heal violence in their communities.[93]

LaRocque rejects 'traditional' justice models and the CHCH approach on the basis that such models typically emphasis 'the harm done by colonial forces to men, without due regard to the damage done to women, not only by colonial forces but also by the sexually violent offender'.[94] She argues that colonial oppression has not been equally experienced within Native communities, but that women 'bear the greatest brunt of social disintegration' at the same time as 'being alienated from decolonisation efforts'.[95] LaRocque's criticism of Hollow Water supports the need to protect victims from further exposure to attackers.[96] In her view, offenders should be placed into alternative institutions incorporating traditional healing practices at the same time as restricting offender movement 'until such time as offenders prove themselves worthy of societal engagement'.[97]

The research concerning CHCH is unclear as to whether cases are declined on the basis of an offender's risk of recidivism and community safety. Community-based treatment models (where offenders are treated but largely unsupervised) may be unsuitable due to the high risk that offenders may continue to pose to children. Unsupervised and high-risk offenders endanger children, as high-lighted by a 2009 case in Broome, Western Australia. In this case the magistrate granted bail to a 23-year-old Aboriginal man (described by police as a 'serial sexual predator'), even though he faced three child sex offences.[98] Six weeks later, on bail, police alleged the offender lured a 4-year-old Broome girl from her home and raped her. It was reported that the offender was ordered out of the Kimberley town by the magistrate, and reported to Broome police as part of his bail conditions only 30 minutes after the alleged rape.[99] This case shows that Aboriginal offenders are released by courts into communities without any treatment or therapy (posing a serious risk to children), and that Aboriginal community-based models may not be suitable if children's safety is put at risk.

This does not diminish (but rather emphasises) the need for the provision of culturally appropriate offender treatment for incarcerated Aboriginal offenders. As analysis of a Western Australian Supreme Court case urges, we should also consider Aboriginal Canadian Healing Lodges for sexual assault offenders, ensuring the safety of community and improved outcomes for offender rehabilitation.[100]

Healing for victims an 'afterthought'

Research by the Canadian Department of Justice's Policy Centre for Victim Issues has supported the validity of the concerns about Aboriginal justice models.[101] Aboriginal people were being re-victimised by colonisation, 'this time indirectly as colonisation is turned inside out by Aboriginal people victimising themselves and where women and children bear the brunt of such trauma'.[102] Although the report recognised restorative justice and Aboriginal justice had the potential to benefit both offenders and victims, the literature was concerned with the offenders and ironically 'healing of the victim is a secondary thought if mentioned at all'.[103] The circumstances of Aboriginal offenders and their needs were well considered, but it was noted that 'there is little information on the impact of such Aboriginal justice initiatives on victims and communities'.[104]

The Policy Centre for Victim Issues also stated that research was needed to determine the perception in the Aboriginal community about the appropriate processes for Aboriginal offenders, and the degree to which Aboriginal people actually advocated rehabilitation and healing processes for offenders over punishment and societal protection (imprisonment).[105] It was not clear how much support existed for healing processes, nor the certainty of the claim that Aboriginal society was typically restorative as opposed to punishment oriented.[106]

The report acknowledged criticisms made by Aboriginal women and organisations such as AWAN, but cautioned against an assumption that all Aboriginal justice initiatives are problematic in perpetuating Aboriginal women's inequality and needs as victims in male-dominated communities. The report stated that there were examples of programs that seriously take into account the perspectives of victims in addressing violence against women, and acknowledged Hollow Water, but with the cautionary comment that 'More research … needs to be undertaken from the perspective of the victim and victim satisfaction with such processes'.[107] Overall, it concluded that there must be an assessment of Aboriginal justice processes in meeting the needs of victims and their ability to reduce the rate of victimisation,[108] and warned, 'If victims, primarily Aboriginal women and children, are to be protected there is a real need to ensure that community processes have certain precautions that recognise the gender imbalances that often exist in Aboriginal communities'.[109]

Most importantly, it was recognised that from a victim perspective, adequate protection of abused Aboriginal women and children is integral to program design.[110] This means that issues such as gender imbalance in the community and the effects thereof, the normalisation of violence, and women and children's safety must be considered and responded to in the design of the program and at all times.

Some Indigenous women reject 'healing' approaches

Assistant Professor Sarah Deer, victim advocate and legal specialist, states that both the Anglo-American and 'peacemaking' models are an inappropriate response to child sexual abuse.[111] Deer's criticism of peacemaking, including CHCH, is that the primary focus appears to be on the perpetrator rather than the victims.[112] From the CHCH literature, she also considers there is a message to victims that prison sanction is a form of genocide, with the suggestion that victims who pursue that course of action may also be complicit in genocide.[113] Deer rejects the assumption that survivors' wellbeing appears predicated on the perpetrators' ability to empathise and that their healing is dependent on their response. In her opinion, peacekeeping and restorative justice present issues of safety, coercion, re-victimisation, the excusing of criminal behaviour, and recidivism.[114]

Deer emphasises the support networks needed for survivors of sexual violence, but she disagrees with the popular notion that survivors of sexual assault need to be 'healed': 'What we need is justice. Justice has different forms, and certainly healing can be part of justice, but I always want to resist the labelling of victims as damaged or defective.'[115] I agree with Deer's concern that too much emphasis on healing diverts attention from those accountable for the violence and places the onus of the experience on the victim survivor.

A further argument made by Deer is that rape is linked to colonisation and genocide, and the applicability of peacemaking in cases of sexual violence is questionable: 'It is doubtful that a peacemaking model would be appropriate in cases of genocide and colonization; therefore it is questionable whether peacemaking is culturally appropriate in cases of sexual violence.'[116]

This view is similar to LaRocque's perspective that 'Sexual offence cannot be reduced to a "two-sided conflict" nor trivialized to an issue of "healing"'.[117] Rather, 'It is a particularly noxious violation against human dignity and must be treated accordingly'.[118] LaRocque has also reminded people of the very serious impacts of child sexual abuse and rape, including flashbacks, nightmares, poor health, low self-esteem, isolation, fear, anger, depression and suicide, all symptoms of post-traumatic stress disorder.[119] I believe that both Deer and LaRocque have made compelling arguments that question prevalent themes of Indigenous 'healing' approaches in the interests of Indigenous victims of sexual assault.

Lessons for Australia

In an Australian context, a bias towards Aboriginal male offenders has been evident and often this overwhelming focus on offenders has effectively rendered invisible the harms suffered by victims, predominantly women and children. It has now been recognised that major justice inquiries such as the Royal Commission into Aboriginal Deaths in Custody (RCIADC) failed to acknowledge the high rate of homicide of Aboriginal women, which far outnumbered the deaths (predominantly of men) that occurred in custody. Dr Elena Marchetti has analysed the gender bias nature of this inquiry, which heavily influenced the course of government policy.[120]

Marchetti compares the RCIADC with the Aboriginal Justice Inquiry of Manitoba, which took place at a similar time.[121] While the Aboriginal Justice Inquiry included an entire chapter discussing the relationship between Aboriginal women and the Manitoba justice system, the RCIADC gave only minimal consideration to Aboriginal women and ultimately only five of the 339 recommendations made any reference to women.[122] As noted by Marchetti, some Aboriginal women, including lawyer Sharon Payne, publicly criticised the gender natured bias of the RCIADC.[123] Marchetti agrees that there was very little discussion of family violence in any of the RCIADC reports, arguing that despite the alarming level of violence against Aboriginal women, 'ultimately the problems concerning Indigenous women were (as is often the case) overshadowed by the problems facing Indigenous "people", which in reality equated to problems facing Indigenous men'.[124]

Aboriginal people are vastly over-represented as victims of crime but the focus on Aboriginal offending and male offenders is prevalent. One may well wonder if this reflects a form of racial stereotyping (that is, Aboriginality as bad) coupled with the hierarchical race/gender power structure in which Aboriginal women and children's interests are often minimised and even denied. In my experience the traditional focus on offenders often overshadows the imperative of justice and healing for victims.

The most important lesson we can learn in Australia from the Canadian Aboriginal responses is that the interests of victims, of women and children, must at all times be acknowledged and protected. This difficult task requires that Aboriginal communities address the longstanding bias concerning male offenders, and begin a re-orientation towards the needs of the Aboriginal women and children being victimised.

This is made more difficult because, as Aboriginal commentator Noel Pearson has pointed out, 'Aboriginal policy is weighed down with confusion'.[125] Pearson notes that the progressive response to the situation of Indigenous offending has been to provide legal aid to offenders, whereas Aboriginal victims of crime — particularly women — have no support: 'So while the needs of offenders are addressed, victims and their families remain vulnerable.'[126] The positioning of Aboriginal male offenders as victims has very detrimental consequences:

> The truth is that, at least in the communities that I know in Cape York Peninsula, the real need is for the restoration of social order and the enforcement of the law. That is what is needed. You ask the grandmothers and the wives. What happens in communities when offenders are defended as victims? Is it any wonder that a sense soon develops that people should not take responsibility for their actions. Why is all of our progressive thinking ignoring these basic social requirements when it comes to black people?[127]

Pearson views this as linked to what he describes as 'victim politics', in which excuses and justifications ('Don't blame the victim') are routinely made to negate the personal responsibility of Indigenous peoples who are not required to accept the consequences of their actions. This description of victim politics highlights how such politics also operate along gendered lines, particularly to the detriment of women and children, whose serious, direct forms of victimisation are indisputable. Unfortunately, within victim politics the interests of male perpetrators and Aboriginal men at large, rather than women and children experiencing direct victimisation, are given priority and weight.

Native American tribal approaches

The approach of the United States appears markedly different from Canada and should also be considered by Aboriginal people in Australia. In the United States federal legislation (the *Children's Justice Act Partnerships for Indian Communities*) has been enacted to provide grants directly to tribes to establish victim assistance programs and to improve tribal investigation, prosecution and handling of cases in a way that limits trauma to victims.[128] According to Professor Larry EchoHawk, now an advisor to President Obama and member of the Pawnee Indian Tribe, one of the most destructive problems facing children in 'Indian country' is sexual abuse.[129] EchoHawk's analysis focuses on federal responsibility, legislative responses and practices, and acknowledges the critical importance of tribal responsibility:

> What is most important to securing a promising future for genera-tions to come? The answer should be that *children* are a tribe's most valuable resource and that their well-being is of critical importance to achieving a better future in the world. Tribal leaders must continue the fight to protect sovereignty, lands and natural resources, but nothing is more important than protecting the health, safety and welfare of their children. Without physically and mentally healthy children there is no bright future.[130]

EchoHawk's understanding of the impact of child sexual assault is impressive and progresses insightfully beyond a strict legal analysis. For example, he considers that while it is impossible to measure the impacts on victims, 'it stands to reason that the sexual abuse of a child who already suffers from being a part of the most disadvant-aged ethnic and racial group in America is likely to have a greater cumulative impact'.[131] The devastating impact of child sexual assault, described as 'the murder of innocence',[132] is recognised to affect the child victim, who is likely to suffer more aggravating trauma, but moreover 'the future of the tribe is further jeopardized when a youthful tribal member suffers potential long-term harm'.[133] For the tribe to overcome the detrimental past effects of 'seven generations' of colonisation and abuse, EchoHawk believes it is essential that perpetrators are caught and prosecuted, and that child victims are not victimised in this process but are healed through effective counselling and treatment.[134]

As documented by EchoHawk, the backdrop of legislative responses by Congress included the widespread sexual abuse of Indian children in reservation schools by non-Indigenous teachers and employees of the Bureau of Indian Affairs.[135] A special investigation by the Senate Select Committee on Indian Affairs revealed a 'pattern of callous disregard for the safety of Indian children in [Bureau of Indian Affairs] schools'.[136] The damning findings led to the passage of new legislation, the *Indian Child Abuse Prevention and Treatment Act*, and other laws to address child sexual assault in Indian countries.[137]

According to EchoHawk, the most important programs have occurred through the *Victims of Crime Act*. In 1987 the responsible office declared services to Native Americans a top priority. Accordingly, programs (including the *Children's Justice Act* (CJA) Program for Native Americans) have been developed for Native American victims to improve investigation and prosecution of child sexual abuse cases.[138] The Office for Victims of Crime has responsibility for administering the Victim Assistance in Indian Country Grant program, which provides grant awards directly to Indian tribes for the purpose of establishing reservation-based victim assistance programs in remote Indian areas.[139] Unfortunately, according to EchoHawk, despite commendable efforts, many legislative acts remain unfunded and Congress seemed reluctant to fund the programs mandated by its own legislation.[140]

EchoHawk is critical of the funding allotted under the CJA program (less than US$1 million), but this amount appears to have been increased by the government. In 2009 the Tribal Policy Clearinghouse stated that there was US$2.5 million available to federally recognised Indian tribes and non-profit tribal organisations to help American Indian and Alaska Native communities develop, establish and operate specialised services and procedures to improve the investigation, prosecution and overall handling of cases of child abuse, and to address the needs of child abuse victims in a manner that lessens the trauma to the victims and increases culturally appropriate service provision.[141] According to the Tribal Law and Policy Unit, the Office for Victims of Crime statutorily reserves 15% of the first US$20 million of funds from the Crime Victims Fund to make grants under the CJA program.[142]

The goal of the CJA grant program is to improve the capacity of tribes to respond to cases by developing specialised services and procedures that address the needs of American Indian child victims. Activities funded through CJA include:

- Establishment, expansion, and training for multidisciplinary teams.
- Revision of tribal codes to address child sexual abuse.
- Provision of child advocacy services for children involved in court proceedings.
- Development of protocols and procedures for reporting, investigating, and prosecuting child sexual abuse cases.
- Improved coordination that minimises the number of child interviews.
- Enhanced case management and treatment services.
- Specialised training for prosecutors, judges, investigators, and other professionals who handle child sexual abuse cases.
- Development of procedures for establishing and managing child-centered interview rooms.[143]

The level of specialist Indigenous tribal response to child abuse (promoted through allocated and substantial government funds) is impressive, and unfortunately not comparable to the situation in Australia. The legislative reforms strongly suggest that both Indian tribes and their federal government support important activities that suggest the development of Indigenous 'best practice' responses.

Navajo Child Special Advocacy Program

The approach of the United States is clearly oriented towards improving legal responses and is akin to Indigenous 'specialisation'. This approach involves increased penalties for offenders[144] and stands in contrast with the community-based diversionary approaches such as that adopted by CHCH in Canada and recently supported in

Australia. One of the most well-known Native American programs supported by the CJA is the Navajo Child Special Advocacy Program (NCSAP) based in the Navajo Nation, Window Rock, Arizona. This program was recognised by Harvard University in 2000 as part of the Honoring Contributions in the Governance of American Indian Nations (Honoring Nations).[145]

NCSAP was formed in 1990 after shocking revelations of abuse of children at the Hopi reservation by federal government-employed teachers. This prompted a self-assessment of social services by the Navajo Nation, which realised that victims and their families had few resources for help, that social and legal services that existed were disorganised and unstructured, that treatment was fragmented and that criminal investigations were handled inconsistently and often inappropriately.[146]

NCSAP provides comprehensive outpatient therapeutic services to children who have been traumatised by sexual abuse. It has a number of offices in the Navajo Nation, and employs social workers and master-level therapists and traditional counsellors — all of whom are Navajo people. The service is based on both Western clinical treatment and therapy and trauma reduction counselling, as well as Navajo-based treatment and services, including Indigenous diagnosis and referral to traditional healers. In addition to the therapy, NCSAP conducts the forensic interviews of child victims, which are used in legal proceedings by prosecutors. NCSAP works closely as part of a multi-disciplinary team of representatives of the various agencies responding to child sexual abuse. NCSAP also engages in community outreach and education to inform people of its services and to raise awareness of the problem of child sexual abuse.

In recognising NCSAP, the Honoring Nations Project said:

> NCSAP's very existence is an outstanding achievement. Recognising that effective self-governance requires tribes to confront even the most highly stigmatised and difficult social problems, the Navajo Nation acted upon its solemn responsibility to foster a safe and healthy environment for its most vulnerable citizens, its children. The Navajo Nation accepted the challenge of responding to an issue that many communities would rather keep secret. Indeed, good governance mandates that Indian

nations respond to compelling social problems that threaten the welfare of its citizens.[147]

Four aspects of NSCAP were identified as warranting particular attention. First, meticulous data collection and management allowed NSCAP to gain a clearer picture of the scope and patterns of child sexual abuse, allowing it to measure progress and structure services to better meet program objectives. Second, the NCSAP program was tailored to meet the specific needs of Navajo people and demonstrated through their practices that culture is an important consideration in service provision. Third, NCSAP developed effective interview processes that enhanced the ability of prosecutors and, since taking on the role of forensic investigator, the process has resulted in more care for victims and increased conviction rates.[148] Lastly, NCSAP co-ordinated the efforts of separate agencies and formed a core group, including criminal investigators, prosecutors, social workers, therapists, physicians and mental health staff, school authorities and professionals in other Native governmental departments. The multi-disciplinary team meets on a monthly basis and its approach has improved service delivery and allowed for NCSAP and the Navajo Nation to take greater responsibility for processes that were previously managed exclusively by the Bureau of Indian Affairs and the Federal Bureau of Investigation.[149]

Facilitating change

This chapter has examined the possible development in Australia of Aboriginal justice models to address Aboriginal child sexual assault. The international approaches of Canada and the United States, although contrasting in objectives, provide important guidance. Future Aboriginal Australian approaches must be fully informed and developed from the 'grassroots' by communities, and also in close co-operation with the criminal justice system. As has been argued in the Canadian context, it is not the model per se, but the 'quality of the process element that is key, and the part that is instrumental in facilitating real change in communities'.[150]

At the same time, there are clearly some lessons to be learned. In particular, any responses must be based on the empower-ment of women and children, and must address re-victimisation.

Overseas literature shows that 'healing'-based models have capacity to re-perpetuate oppression and victimisation of women and children.

In Australia, in marked contrast to both Hollow Water and Native American tribal approaches, Aboriginal people and our communities occupy very little (if any) presence within the response of the criminal justice system to child sexual assault. The New South Wales Aboriginal Child Sexual Assault Taskforce made important recommendations, but the lack of government response was been criticised by the former Aboriginal and Torres Strait Islander Social Justice Commissioner Tom Calma, as not being 'treated with the urgency and priority that it deserves'.[151] This situation must be radically altered for Aboriginal communities to be a part of the solution of effectively addressing child sexual assault, and breaking the cycle of abuse and trauma in our families and communities.

Chapter 8

Knowing from the heart

The topic of Aboriginal children's human rights is highly charged and controversial. At times my advocacy concerning Aboriginal child sexual assault is critical of male-dominant institutions and structures (Aboriginal and non-Aboriginal) that have seemingly thought little of victims, predominantly women and children. 'Speaking up' for human rights in this way is ethically unquestionable, but because of gender oppression and taboos surrounding child sexual assault it can be highly contentious, and can result in serious censure and ramifications. When I commenced this research I was perhaps naively unaware of how contentious child sexual assault actually is.

As a Noongar woman speaking against child sexual assault, it is apparent to me that this is simply not acceptable in society. As a result of my advocacy I have experienced intimidation and abuse, as well as alienation and marginalisation. I have to agree with MacKinnon's observations — women are silenced because they cannot tell the truth of what they know and survive: 'Those within and outside the academy who know that male power in all its forms remains entrenched also know that they face defamatory attacks and potential threats to their economic survival if they say so.'[1]

My experiences are consistent with those identified by MacKinnon, who argues that even in one's own critical community, one risks being shunned for raising issues of the sexual subordination of women of colour.[2] These have been the unforeseen and unintended consequences of my research, and I now understand why there are very few Aboriginal researchers specifically addressing child sexual assault in their work.

It is also important to acknowledge the changing landscape of Aboriginal child sexual assault. In Western Australia the establishment of police taskforce operations in remote regions since 2007 has shown that offences against Aboriginal children are now being regarded seriously and responded to by the criminal justice system. Aboriginal children are now seen as deserving the protection of the law. At this stage it is unclear whether police operations will be extended into settled regions, and whether other (perhaps 'less frontier') parts of the state will also experience improved police and investigative responses.

In 2007 Western Australia Police established taskforce operations in the far north Kimberley region to actively investigate and prosecute Aboriginal child sex offenders. This was long overdue. Offenders, many of whom held powerful positions in communities, had acted with impunity for too long. Aboriginal children disclosing were publicly attacked, including by some women community leaders.[3] Aboriginal male leaders and peak organisations also condemned these prosecutions as 'political'.[4] The Aboriginal Legal Service of WA acted immediately to defend male perpetrators (in accordance with government policies that prioritise criminal defence matters), but there were very few voices heard for children. I know from my own experience that asking a simple question — who will act for the children? — was fraught with controversy and resulted in censure and abuse from Aboriginal men and women.

Some Aboriginal women leaders spoke up bravely. In the Kimberley Mary-Ann Winton, chairwoman of the Kununurra Waringarri Aboriginal Corporation, welcomed the police prosecutions, stating, 'It's time it happened and it's up to Aboriginal people to admit they are doing wrong and make some changes, to support one another'.[5] Winton said that the key to stopping child sexual abuse in Aboriginal communities was supporting the victims, and more health education to recognise the signs of abuse: 'The victims are your main assets. If we can help them mentally and emotionally and support them and encourage them to get through this, they are the people who will stop it.'[6]

In response to the unprecedented level of police prosecution, justice authorities established the Indigenous Justice Taskforce.[7] The main focus was the expedition of cases, but other matters actively under consideration included the availability of defence, prosecution lawyers and judicial officers, the standard of court facilities, offender supervision, the ability to support victims and victim safety measures, and communication of sentencing outcomes to community.[8] The Taskforce included judicial members, the Aboriginal Legal Service and representatives of the Justice Department. Aboriginal women were not included or represented in this significant institutional response to the prosecution of offenders.

In the two years from April 2007 to April 2009, the Taskforce reported that 132 persons were charged with a total of 601 offences; 96% of persons charged were male, 70% of those charged were adults, 91% of victims were female, 61% of charges related to children more than 13 years of age and 39% related to children under the age of 13 years.[9] Consistent with the high attrition rate for sexual assault offences, the majority of the cases were dismissed.[10] Of those offenders convicted, 50% were released into the community without imprisonment.[11]

The Indigenous Justice Taskforce has now ceased and Operation Leeds in the Pilbara region has begun. In May 2010, I was at a Pilbara Aboriginal women's bush meeting in which 'specialist' officers of the Western Australia Police child abuse unit stated that their approach had shifted from active investigations to building community relations, and encouraging the confidence of community members to come forward and disclose. Some officers felt that the approach in the Kimberley had brought the abuse out 'into the open' but had left the community to 'pick up the pieces'. They said that they wanted to work differently this time around. I asked if there were any Aboriginal officers in the child abuse 'specialist' response unit, but there were none and it seemed to me they did not even like the question being asked. Non-Aboriginal agencies were actively addressing child sexual assault, yet they did not seem to think that Aboriginal people had to be an important part of the criminal justice system's response.

Aboriginal women at the gathering spoke first-hand about child sexual assault, and their knowledge was unquestionable. One woman talked to me about her experience as a young person of 15 in the courts when she sought to have prosecuted a now well-known serial repeat offender: 'White man's justice was nothing for me', she said, and after all these years I understood her well. Aboriginal women, especially victim survivors, go largely unheard and unseen, yet Aboriginal women's powerful knowledge and philosophies are maintained regardless. As a Pilbara woman leader told us at the meeting, there are two types of knowledge — knowledge from the head and knowledge from the heart. As Aboriginal women we should lead with our hearts and always be known to our communities. Aboriginal women's traditional culture embraces care, empathy and concern grounded in our connections at the community level — key qualities needed to effectively address child sexual assault in communities that are yet to be properly acknowledged and respected.

Notwithstanding the significant prosecutions of many offenders in Western Australia, there have been few discussions in either Aboriginal or non-Aboriginal contexts in relation to child sexual assault and improved justice responses. The response of the state Aboriginal legal service was to publicly attack the prosecutions and aggressively defend perpetrators by using technical legal arguments to secure a number of acquittals. Aboriginal women were (offensively) excluded from the Indigenous Justice Taskforce, which considered matters such as community education and the future possibility of Aboriginal sentencing courts in relation to such offences.[12]

Although child sexual assault is clearly a serious human rights violation of the child, it is not readily characterised as such. One main reason why is because Aboriginal human rights discourse has been set by Aboriginal men, and works seemingly to men's advantage. Child sexual assault is largely perpetrated by men upon predominantly girl children, thereby raising the uncomfortable issue of Aboriginal men's participation in human rights abuses against Aboriginal children. The biased nature of Aboriginal human rights discourse has unfortunately negated recognition of child sexual assault as a serious human rights matter.

In this context, the importance of 'knowing' from the heart means an honest, empathic acknowledgment of the pain and suffering being caused to children. There is a real challenge in how we encourage Aboriginal people, especially our male leaders, who predominantly hold positions of power in our communities, to also 'know from the heart' and fully acknowledge and respond to child sexual assault as a serious human rights abuse of the child. In turning a 'blind eye' (as frequently happens), it seems that Aboriginal leaders are mirroring the dynamic of abuse based on lack of concern and empathy to vulnerable children.

Addressing child sexual assault means we need to reject the *gammon* culture of human rights that has become prevalent in Aboriginal human rights discourse. I use the Aboriginal concept *gammon* — a word and concept that has gained universal understanding across Aboriginal Australia — to refer to pretence and lack of truth and reality: in other words, a lie. *Gammon* human rights are false, inauthentic human rights and according to Aboriginal culture *gammon* is not something to be very proud of. The *gammon* culture of Aboriginal human rights (involving and supported by Aboriginal and non-Aboriginal people) neglects to recognise — and undermines — the acknowledgment of women and children's fundamental human right to live free from violence and abuse.

Rejecting *gammon* Aboriginal human rights requires a rights dialogue and commitment from Aboriginal people (and non-Aboriginal human rights experts) that Aboriginal women and children's rights are significant human rights. In promoting genuinely Aboriginal human rights discourse and understanding we can affirm international human rights law that unequivocally denounces all violence against women and children as a breach of human rights.

Child sexual assault is a serious human rights violation, and responses by Indigenous people need to be developed in accordance with standards of international human rights law. The development of Aboriginal models to address child sexual assault is supported by Article 34 of the *Declaration on the Rights of Indigenous Peoples*, which provides that Indigenous peoples have the right to 'promote, develop and maintain their institutional structures … juridical systems or customs, in accordance with international human rights standards'. Article 7 affirms the right of children and young people to life, physical and mental integrity, liberty and security of person. In Australia we can start to develop understanding about these important human rights standards through educative responses such as a 'Charter of Aboriginal Children's Human Rights'.

As a matter of some urgency, the current criminal justice responses must be developed in a more inclusive manner towards Aboriginal women and children. The internationally acclaimed CHCH model has shown that women (victim survivors) have great ability and leadership to respond to child sexual assault, and in turn increase the empowerment of women in communities. According to Canadian academic Angela Cameron, Aboriginal women should be placed in positions of leadership and decision making, designing criminal justice process, rather than being subject to them.[13] I could not agree more. Also, as Native American feminist Sarah Deer has pointed out, 'Native women who have survived rape and who have advocated on behalf of rape victims should be at the centre of the response to sexual violence. Our voices will guide communities in developing responses that take into account both safety and dignity for the survivors'.[14]

Future responses need to also include children, most especially the children who have experienced victimisation. Children are silenced by abuse but their capacity to speak about abuse should be recognised and respected. Society's attitude to children has left them with little status, no voice and no political power, and this is especially so for Aboriginal children. Children's powerlessness is a key factor underlying child sexual assault, and this powerlessness should be addressed in all responses to child sexual assault. Even with increased acknowledgment of Aboriginal child sexual assault, there seems very little understanding that children's voices must be heard. The biased *gammon* nature of Aboriginal human rights has neither recognised nor respected Aboriginal children's human rights.

The lack of acknowledgment of Aboriginal children's human rights was evident in the federal government review of the Northern Territory Emergency Response (NTER), which was based solely on consultation with adults and neglected to provide any means of children's perspectives and participation.[15] Children's voices were also ironically absent from the shadow report condemning the NTER, *Will They Be Heard?*, which was launched by the former head of the Family Court of Australia, Alastair Nicholson.[16] Children's voices and their participation in policies and programs are critical to an Aboriginal human rights framework of understanding.

In Australia there has been no real recognition of the voices of the many Aboriginal children impacted by child sexual assault. The work of the international children's human rights agency Save the Children, highlights the importance of children's voices in addressing child sexual assault. This work provides valuable guidance in Australia as we seek to address Aboriginal child sexual assault. In its Global Submission to the United Nations Study on Violence against Children, Save the Children affirmed the significance of forming strong alliances with children impacted by child sexual assault:

> In children experiencing and surviving such childhoods, vulnerability and resilience exist side by side. They become like trees on windy islands battered by storms, bent over, but clinging on determinedly, adapting to live. These are the children we as adults need strong alliances with to start 'breaking the silence'. We have to first gain their trust and respect, and they must be in no doubt of ours.[17]

Article 22(2) of the *Declaration on the Rights of Indigenous Peoples* requires that 'States shall take measures, in conjunction with indigenous peoples, to ensure that indigenous women and children enjoy the full protection and guarantees against all forms of violence and discrimination'.[18] The Australian Minister for Indigenous Affairs, Jenny Macklin, has stated that government must work in partnership with Aboriginal people to find solutions to the problems and 'ensure that the most vulnerable people in the Australian community, Indigenous women and children, are the central focus of government policy'.[19]

It is very apparent that greater attention is necessary within the national and international context.

In my view, ensuring that women and children are a central focus of government policy requires established mechanisms through which women and children's voices (specifically in relation to Aboriginal children's human rights) are actually heard and thereby responded to.

In 2009 the federal government released an Australian National Plan of Action to address violence against women and children. The report, *Time for Action: The National Council's Plan for Australia to reduce violence against women and their children, 2009–2021*,[20] made key recommendations about Aboriginal violence. We need to hold government to account for the implementation of this report and the important commitments made, which include support for Aboriginal Healing Centres throughout Australia.[21] The National Council also proposed a National Centre of Excellence for the Prevention of Violence against Women to lead thinking, broker knowledge, and co-ordinate a national research agenda.[22] A National Centre of Excellence should aim to be non-discriminatory and supportive of substantive equality for Aboriginal women and children. It could intelligently lead national direction addressing violence against Aboriginal women and children. Such an approach would indicate a governmental response that is truly excellent in standard.

As pointed out by Amnesty International Australia, the United Nations General Assembly has recognised the necessity of states to 'ensure that diverse strategies that take into account the intersection of gender with other factors are developed in order to eradicate all forms of violence against women'.[23] The Australian Government has established the National Congress of First Peoples to provide advice concerning Aboriginal affairs, and the Congress has set an important precedent in ensuring women's equal representation.[24] At the same time, additional strategic and specialised responses are required to ensure more effective responses to violence against Aboriginal women and children.

During consultations with Amnesty International Australia in 2008, I submitted that the National Plan of Action should include a national-level body of Aboriginal women experts empowered to undertake research, build capacity and drive policy in relation to efforts to end violence against women and children. This recommendation was taken up by Amnesty[25] and could be considered within the proposed National Centre of Excellence. Such a body could support the development of Aboriginal justice models to address child sexual assault, a difficult but not impossible task.

In April 2012 the Commonwealth Government announced that a Children's Commissioner will be created to promote the protection and rights of children and young people. This significant national committment was announced by the Attorney General, Nicola Roxton, and will include a focus on Aboriginal children and family violence.

Colonisation has effectively denied Aboriginal people the legal authority to protect children. However, we must continue to affirm our right to take responsibility for protecting Aboriginal children who are at increased risk of child sexual assault. This requires absolute resistance to the ongoing silencing that surrounds Aboriginal child sexual assault and greater recognition of the harm to child victim survivors and, moreover, to Aboriginal people as a whole. There should be an immediate concession from non-Aboriginal society that Aboriginal people's participation in the administration of the criminal justice system is essential to protect children.

At both the national and state levels, Aboriginal child sexual assault has been 'brought out into the open'. Yet I am suspicious that there are racial underpinnings to the responses. I have sensed harmful and racist concepts such as 'black guilt' and 'white innocence', 'white authority' and 'Aboriginal disempowerment', as being present today. Historically, and in times not so long past, Aboriginal child sexual assault was closely linked to colonisation and the subordination of Aboriginal people — most especially women and children. It is not altogether clear that this link has been broken. Some evidence suggests that it is being re-perpetuated, albeit in changed forms today. There is a great deal that can still happen to ensure that Aboriginal child sexual assault is responded to in a manner that reflects a spirit of recognition of Aboriginal equality, self-determination and reconciliation. These matters are fundamental to the recognition of Aboriginal children's human rights and our nation's greatest challenge.

Abbreviations

ACSAT	Aboriginal Child Sexual Assault Taskforce
AIC	Australian Institute of Criminology
ALP	Australian Labor Party
APY	Anangu Pitjantjatjara Yankunytjatjara
ATSIC	Aboriginal and Torres Straits Islander Commission
AWAN	Aboriginal Women's Action Network
CCTV	Closed circuit television
CCYP	Commission for Children and Young People
CHCH	Community Holistic Circle Healing
CJA	*Children's Justice Act*
DCD	Department of Community Development
DNA	Deoxyribonucleic acid
DoCS	Department of Community Services
DPP	Director of Public Prosecutions
HREOC	Human Rights and Equal Opportunity Commission
NAAJA	North Australia Aboriginal Justice Agency
NAALAS	North Australian Aboriginal Legal Aid Service
NCSAP	Navajo Child Special Advocacy Program
NIFS	National Institute of Forensics Scientists
NPY	Ngaanyatjarra Pitjantjatjara Yankunytjatjara
NTER	Northern Territory Emergency Response
RCIADC	Royal Commission into Aboriginal Deaths in Custody
SARC	Sexual Assault Referral Centres
SNAICC	Secretariat of National Aboriginal and Islander Child Care
VSS	Victim Support Service
WHO	World Health Organization

Notes

Foreword

1. Robinson, Shirleene, *Something like Slavery?: Queensland's Aboriginal child workers, 1942–1945*, Australian Scholarly Publishing, Victoria, 2008.
2. Roth, Walter Edmund, *The Queensland Aborigines Vol. 11 Bulletins 1–8 North Queensland Ethnology from the Home Secretary's Department — Brisbane 1901–1908*, Hesperian Press, Melbourne, 1984.
3. For more information see the Child Wise website at www.childwise.net/.

Preface

1. United Nation General Assembly, Human Rights Council, Thirteenth session, 'Rights of the child: the fight against sexual violence against children', 2010, p. 1.
2. Anzaldúa, 'Speaking in tongues', 1981.
3. See Delgado and Stefancic, *Critical Race Theory*, 2001.

Chapter 1 — Facing the challenge

1. Finkelhor, *Childhood Victimization*, 2008, p. 3.
2. SNAICC, *Through Young Black Eyes*, 2002, p. 56.
3. Cited by Hill Collins, *Black Feminist Thought*, 1990, p. 188.
4. See further, Haebich, *For Their Own Good*, 1992, pp. 90–127.
5. See *Bropho v The State of Western Australia* [No 2] [2009] WASC 94; see also Taylor, 'Land campaign hid child sex abuse', 2008.
6. Taylor and Guest, 'Aboriginal camp boss Robert Bropho dies at 81', 2011.
7. See McGlade, 'Race discrimination in Australia', 2004.
8. See McGlade, *Treaty*, 2003.
9. United Nations Non-governmental Liaison Service, 'International Expert Group meeting', 2012, p. 1.
10. ibid., p. 7.
11. Kwast and Laws, *United Nation's Secretary-General's Study on Violence against Children*, no date, p. 3.
12. ibid, p. 13, emphasis in the original.
13. Save the Children, *Listen and Speak Out*, 2005, p. 11.
14. ibid.
15. UNICEF, See *From Invisible to Indivisible*, no date, for further information.
16. Save the Children, *Listen and Speak Out*, 2005, p. 11.
17. Sanderson, *Counselling Adult Survivors*, 2006, p. 16.
18. Summit, 'The child sexual abuse accommodation syndrome', 2000, p. 168.
19. Andrews, Gould and Corry, 'Child sexual abuse revisited', 2002.
20. ibid.
21. SCRGSP, *Overcoming Indigenous Disadvantage*, 2011, p. 22.

22. SNAICC, *Through Young Black Eyes*, 2002, pp. 45–6.
23. ibid., p. 46.
24. ibid.
25. Kelly, Regan and Burton, 'Sexual exploitation', 2000, pp. 77–8.
26. Save the Children, *Listen and Speak Out*, 2005, p. 14.
27. SNAICC, *Through Young Black Eyes*, 2002, p. 56.
28. ibid., p. 47.
29. ibid., p. 53.
30. Langton, 'The end of "big men" politics', 2008, p. 13.
31. ibid.
32. Cited by Olafson, 'When paradigms collide', 2002, p. 71.
33. ibid., p. 75.
34. Save the Children, *Listen and Speak Out*, 2005, p. 7.
35. SNAICC, *Through Young Black Eyes*, 2002, p. 1.
36. Sanderson, *Counselling Adult Survivors*, 2006, p. 41.
37. ibid., p. 44.
38. ibid., p. 55.
39. ibid., pp. 53–62.
40. ibid., p. 63.
41. ibid., pp. 44–5.
42. SNAICC, *Through Young Black Eyes*, 2002, p. 51.
43. ibid.
44. Sanderson, *Counselling Adult Survivors*, 2006, pp. 21–2.
45. Northern Territory Government, *Little Children Are Sacred*, 2007, pp. 16, 82.
46. O'Neill, 'Our leader is listening', 2007, p. 1.
47. McGlade, *Indigenous violent victimisation*, 2009.
48. ibid.
49. Children's Commissioner Northern Territory, *Annual Report 2008–2009*, 2009, p. 31.
50. Langton, 'The end of "big men" politics', 2008.
51. Price, 'I have seen violence', 2009, pp. 149–51.
52. ibid.
53. Price, 'Against change for the wrong reason', 2009.
54. Yu, Duncan and Gray, 'Executive summary', 2008.
55. Human Rights Committee, Ninety-fifth session, 2009.
56. Australian Government, *Stronger Futures in the Northern Territory*, 2012.
57. Harrison, 'Call for NT intervention policy to face human rights test', 2012.
58. ibid.
59. ibid.
60. See, for example, the introductory comments of the former Chief Justice of the Family Court, Alastair Nicholson, in Nicholson et al., *Will They Be Heard?*, 2009.
61. Committee on the Rights of the Child, *Indigenous Children and their Rights*, p. 9.
62. Northern Territory Coroner, Inquest into the death of Kunmanara Forbes.
63. Complaints were made to the ABC Independent Complaints Review Panel that Smith's *Lateline* program was 'poorly researched and full of lies and misinformation'. These complaints were dismissed. See Smith, S., 'Sexual abuse reported in Indigenous community', 2006.
64. ibid.

65. ibid.
66. Northern Territory Coroner, Inquest into the death of Kunmanara Forbes, p. 9.
67. ibid., p. 8.
68. ibid., pp. 13–14.
69. ibid., p. 18.
70. ibid., p. 22.
71. Cited by Olafson, 'When paradigms collide', 2002, p. 71.
72. Cited by Summit, 'The child sexual abuse accommodation syndrome', 2000, p. 168.
73. Burgess et al., *Sexual Assault of Children and Adolescents*, 1978, p. xv.
74. McGlade, 'Sacred yet unprotected', 2010.
75. Children's Commissioner Northern Territory, *Annual Report 2008–2009*, 2009, p. 38.
76. ibid., p. 40.
77. ibid., p. 34. The Commissioner notes rates increased from 29 in 2004–05 to 60 in 2008–09.
78. Kelly et al., *Living on the Edge*, 2009.
79. ibid., p. 20.
80. Crenshaw, 'Mapping the margins', 1995, p. 361.
81. ibid., pp. 361–2.
82. ibid., p. 362.
83. AIDA, *Submission to the Northern Territory Emergency Response Review Board*, 2012, no page numbers.
84. Robinson, 'Dogmatic about outcomes', 2009.
85. FaHCSIA, *Overview of Monitoring Data*, 2009; see also Statham, 'Sex abuse reports soar', 2010.
86. Libesman, 'Indigenous children and contemporary child welfare', 2008, p. 333.
87. ibid., p. 347.
88. ibid., p. 337.
89. ibid., p. 338.
90. Candy, 'Alternative paradigms', 1989, p. 7.
91. Davies, *Asking the Law Question*, 1994, p. 148.
92. Tenets of critical legal studies are examined in Leiboff and Thomas, *Legal Theories*, 2004, p. 283.
93. Discussed, for example, in White and Perrone, *Crime, Criminality and Criminal Justice*, 2010, pp. 107–29.
94. ibid., p. 107.
95. Leiboff and Thomas, *Legal Theories*, 2004, p. 253.
96. MacKinnon, *Women's Lives, Men's Laws*, 2007, p. 257.
97. ibid.
98. ibid.
99. ibid., p. 129.
100. ibid., p. 118.
101. ibid., p. 59.
102. ibid.
103. For the theory of black feminist thought, see hooks, 'Theory as liberatory practice', 1991; Hill Collins, *Black Feminist Thought*, 1990.
104. Hill Collins, *Black Feminist Thought*, 1990, p. 24.

105. ibid., p. 33.
106. ibid., p. 106.
107. Delgado and Stefancic, *Critical Race Theory*, 2001.
108. ibid., pp. 6–9.
109. ibid., p. 43.
110. Leiboff and Thomas, *Legal Theories*, 2004, p. 29.
111. ibid., p. 295.
112. Lawrence, 'Foreword', 2002, p. 2.
113. Brayboy, 'Toward a tribal critical race theory', 2005.
114. Cho and Wesley, 'Historicizing critical race theory's cutting edge', 2002, p. 52.
115. Wing, *Critical Race Feminism*, 2003, p. 7.
116. See Harris, 'Race and essentialism', 2000.
117. ibid., p. 270.
118. ibid., p. 271.
119. Crenshaw, 'Mapping the margins', 1995, pp. 357–83.
120. ibid., p. 360.
121. ibid., p. 360.
122. ibid., p. 368.
123. ibid., p. 377.
124. Cited by Lawrence, 'Foreword', 2002, p. xviii.
125. Cho and Wesley, 'Historicizing critical race theory's cutting edge', 2002, p. 51.
126. ibid.
127. Yamamoto, 'Critical race praxis', 1997, pp. 821–900.
128. ibid.
129. ibid., p. 872.
130. Su and Yamamoto, 'Critical coalitions', 2002, p. 387.
131. MacKinnon, *Women's Lives, Men's Laws*, 2007, p. 3.
132. ibid., p. 6.
133. ibid.
134. Williams, 'Vampires anonymous', 2000, p. 621.
135. ibid., p. 618.
136. ibid., p. 621.

Chapter 2 — Understanding colonisation and trauma

1. Stanley, Tomison and Pocock, 'Child abuse and neglect', 2003, p. 2.
2. ibid., p. 3.
3. Save the Children, *10 Essential Learning Points*, 2005, p. 50.
4. Memmott et al., *Violence in Indigenous Communities*, 2001, p. 11.
5. ibid., p. 13.
6. ibid., p. 11.
7. ibid., p. 24.
8. McRae, Nettheim and Beacroft, *Indigenous Legal Issues*, 1997, p. 124.
9. McGlade, 'Native Title, "tides of history" and our continuing claims for justice', 2003, pp. 118–37.
10. ibid.
11. Watson, 'Naked peoples', 1998, p. 4.
12. ibid.

13. Cunneen, 'Racism, discrimination and the over-representation of Indigenous peoples', 2006.
14. Keating, 'The Redfern Park speech', 2000, p. 61.
15. For a consideration of frontier violence and the myth of peaceful settlement, see Reynolds, *Why Weren't We Told?*, 1999.
16. See Chesterman and Galligan, *Citizens without Rights*, 1997.
17. HREOC, *Bringing Them Home: Report*, 1997, p. 275.
18. Dodson, 'Violence dysfunction Aboriginality', 2003, p. 2.
19. ibid.
20. Atkinson, *Trauma Trails*, 2002, p. 80.
21. ibid., pp. 59–73.
22. ibid., p. 50.
23. ibid., pp. 80–1.
24. ibid., p. 51.
25. ibid., p. 85.
26. Memmott et al., *Violence in Indigenous Communities*, 2001, p. 11.
27. ibid., p. 17.
28. ibid.
29. ibid., p. 14.
30. Bryant and Willis, *Risk Factors*, 2008, p. 4.
31. ibid., p. 4.
32. ibid., p. 5.
33. ibid., p. 5.
34. ibid., p. 5.
35. Pearson, *Up from the Mission*, 2009, p. 179.
36. ibid., p. 174.
37. ibid.
38. Northern Territory Government, *Little Children Are Sacred*, 2007, p. 162.
39. ibid.
40. ibid., p. 165.
41. Pearson, *Up from the Mission*, 2009, p. 175.
42. Wundersitz, *Indigenous Perpetrators of Violence*, 2010, p. 43.
43. ibid., p. 45.
44. Atkinson, *Trauma Trails*, 2002, p. 227.
45. ibid., pp. 227–8.
46. Goodall and Huggins, 'Aboriginal women are everywhere', 1992, p. 415.
47. ibid, p. 415.
48. Daylight and Johnstone, *Women's Business*, 1986, p. 240.
49. Atkinson, *Trauma Trails*, 2002, pp. 61–2.
50. ibid., p. 61.
51. ibid., p. 62.
52. Atkinson, 'Stinkin' thinkin'', 1991.
53. Attwood, *Telling the Truth*, 2005.
54. Windschuttle, *The Fabrication of Aboriginal History: Volume One*, 2002, p. 384.
55. Windschuttle, 'Flawed history', 2010, p. 6.
56. ibid.
57. Reynolds, *With the White People*, 1990, p. 207.
58. ibid., p. 74.

59. Paisley, *Loving Protection?*, 2000, pp. 84–5.
60. ibid., p. 85.
61. ibid., p. 129.
62. ibid., p. 127.
63. ibid.
64. ibid., p. 121.
65. Keating, 'The Redfern Park speech', 2000; House of Representatives, *Apology to Australia's Indigenous Peoples*, 2008.
66. HREOC, *Bringing Them Home: Report*, 1997, pp. 27, 37.
67. ibid., p. 278.
68. HREOC, *Bringing them Home: A guide to the findings and recommendations*, 1997, p. 33.
69. Haebich, *For Their Own Good*, 1992, p. 83.
70. ibid., p. 85.
71. Powell and Kennedy, *Renee Baker*, 2005.
72. HREOC, *Bringing Them Home: Report*, 1997.
73. ibid., p. 3.
74. ibid., p. 287.
75. ibid., p. 162.
76. ibid.
77. Simon, Montgomerie and Tuscano, *Back on the Block*, 2008, p. 41.
78. ibid.
79. HREOC, *Bringing Them Home: Report*, 1997, pp. 115–18.
80. ibid., p. 116.
81. ibid.
82. ibid., p. 117.
83. ibid.
84. Choo, 'Sister Kate's Home for "nearly white" children', 2002.
85. HREOC, *Bringing Them Home: Report*, 1997, p. 420.
86. See McGlade, 'The Sister Kate's Home Kids Healing Centre', 2008; McGlade, 'The "fair skinned" children of Sister Kate's', 2007.
87. HREOC, *Bringing Them Home: Report*, 1997, p. 195.
88. ibid.
89. ibid.
90. ibid., pp. 222–8.
91. Atkinson, *Trauma Trails*, 2002, p. 85.
92. ibid.
93. ACSAT, *Breaking the Silence*, 2006.
94. ibid., p. 50.
95. ibid.
96. ibid., pp. 50–1.
97. Steele, 'Psychodynamic factors', 2000, p. 261.
98. ibid.
99. ibid.
100. ibid.
101. ibid.
102. ibid., p. 268.
103. Summit, 'The child sexual abuse accommodation syndrome', 2000.

104. ibid., p. 163.
105. Goddard, *Child Abuse and Child Protection*, 1996, pp. 64–5.
106. ibid., p. 65.
107. ibid., p. 64.
108. Boyd, 'Young people who sexually abuse', 2006, p. 4.
109. Herman, *Trauma and Recovery*, 1997, p. 111.
110. ibid., p. 113.
111. David Finkelhor cited in Itzin, *Home Truths*, 2000, p. 9.
112. Spatz Widom, 'Does violence beget violence?', 2000.
113. ibid., p. 318.
114. ibid., p. 343.
115. ibid.
116. Browne and Finkelhor, 'Impact of child sexual abuse', 2000, p. 225.
117. ibid.
118. Boyd, 'Young people who sexually abuse', 2006, pp. 4–5.
119. Steele, 'Psychodynamic factors', 2000, p. 264.
120. Save The Children, *10 Essential Learning Points*, 2005, p. 109.
121. ibid.
122. Dodson, 'Violence dysfunction Aboriginality', 2003, p. 2.
123. ibid., p. 3.
124. Atkinson, *Trauma Trails*, 2002, pp. 49–50.
125. ibid.
126. ibid., p. 7.
127. ibid., p. 42.
128. ibid., p. 40.
129. Kimm, *A Fatal Conjunction*, 2004.
130. ibid., p. 44.
131. ibid., p. 105.
132. ibid., p. 64.
133. ibid., p. 105.
134. ibid.
135. ibid., p. 82.
136. Atkinson, Review, undated, p. 4.
137. ibid., p. 5.
138. ibid.
139. Nowra, *Bad Dreaming*, 2007, p. 7.
140. ibid., p. 14
141. ibid., pp. 9–24.
142. ibid., p. 25.
143. ibid., p. 89.
144. Scutt, 'Invisible women?', 1990, p. 4.
145. Watson, 'Aboriginal women's laws and lives', 2008.
146. ibid., p. 17.
147. ibid.
148. Nowra, *Bad Dreaming*, 2007, p. 91.
149. ibid., p. 92.
150. ibid., p. 93.
151. Robertson, Mundine and Cunneen, 'Three commentaries', 2007.

152. ibid.
153. ibid., p. 9.
154. ibid., p. 10.
155. Jarrett, *Violence*, 2009.
156. ibid., p. 9.
157. ibid., p. 36.
158. ibid., p. 37.
159. ibid., p. 43.
160. Kearney and Wilson, 'Raping children part of "men's business"', 2006, p. 1.
161. ibid.
162. Bessarab, 'A socio-political perspective', 2003, p. 96.
163. Overington, 'Sex abuse part of culture, boys told', 2006, p. 7.
164. ibid.
165. SNAICC, *Through Young Black Eyes*, 2002, p. 47.
166. Watson, 'Naked peoples', 1998.
167. Haebich, *For Their Own Good*, 1992, p. 116.
168. Personal communication with Mingli Wanjurri McGlade, 20 June 2009.
169. Hassell, *My Dusky Friends*, 1975.
170. Baines, 'Seeking justice', 2001, pp. 56–91.
171. ibid., p. 73.
172. ibid., p. 85.
173. ibid., p. 85.
174. Kimm, *A Fatal Conjunction*, 2004, p. 82, describes the perspectives of Aboriginal woman Sharon Payne as being 'from a contemporary and revisionist' viewpoint, seemingly on the basis that Payne (as with many Aboriginal women) does not accept the accuracy of the 'ancient cultural practices' such as 'sacred rape'.
175. Save the Children, *10 Essential Learning Points*, 2005, p. 111.
176. UN General Assembly, *The girl child*, p. 5.
177. ibid., p. 5.
178. Smith, *Conquest*, 2005, p. 13.

Chapter 3 — Patriarchy, and women and children's oppression

1. Gale, *We Are Bosses Ourselves*, 1983.
2. Green, *Making Space for Indigenous Feminism*, 2007.
3. ibid., p. 23.
4. ibid.
5. Breckenridge and Carmody, *Crimes of Violence*, 1992, p. 24.
6. ibid.
7. Itzin, *Home Truths*, 2000, p. 95.
8. MacKinnon, *Women's Lives, Men's Laws*, 2007, p. 240.
9. ibid., p. 242.
10. ibid., p. 241.
11. ibid., p. 246.
12. ibid., p. 242.
13. Blagg, 'Restorative justice and Aboriginal family, 2002, p. 193.

14. ibid.
15. See, for example, the report of the 6th Annual Indigenous Family Violence Prevention Forum: Centre for Domestic and Family Violence Research, *The Big*, 2009, p. 9. The forum was held in May 2009. While child sexual assault was not a focus of the conference, the harmful effects of the Northern Territory intervention were.
16. Breckenridge and Carmody, *Crimes of Violence*, 1992, p. 219.
17. Calma, *Addressing Family Violence and Child Sexual Assault*, 2006.
18. Australian Domestic and Family Violence Clearinghouse, *Australian Domestic & Family Violence Clearinghouse comment*, undated.
19. Huggins et al., 'Letters to the editor', 1991, p. 507.
20. Behrendt, 'Aboriginal women and the white lies of the feminist movement', 1993, p. 42.
21. Blagg, 'Colonial critique and critical criminology', 2008, p. 134.
22. Lucashenko, 'Violence against Indigenous women', 1997, p. 149.
23. ibid.
24. Langton cited in Memmott et al., *Violence in Indigenous Communities*, 2001, p. 30.
25. Egan, 'Black jail terms "low"', 2002, p. 6.
26. ibid.
27. Charlesworth and Chinkin, *The Boundaries of International Law*, 2000, p. 233.
28. ibid.
29. ibid., p. 235.
30. MacKinnon, *Women's Lives, Men's Laws*, 2007, p. 133.
31. Sculthorpe, 'Review of domestic violence resource materials', 1990, p. 19.
32. Secretariat of the Permanent Forum on Indigenous Issues, *State of the World's Indigenous Peoples*, 2009, p. 172.
33. See McGlade, 'Aboriginal women and the Commonwealth Government's response to Mabo', 2001, pp. 150–1.
34. O'Shane, 'Is there any relevance in the women's movement for Aboriginal women?', 1976, pp. 31–4.
35. Bolger, *Aboriginal Women and Violence*, 1991, p. 44.
36. Moore cited in Stanley, Tomison and Pocock, 'Child abuse and neglect', 2003, p. 12.
37. Wundersitz, *Indigenous Perpetrators of Violence*, 2010, pp. 35–7.
38. ibid., p. 36.
39. ibid., p. 37.
40. ibid., p. 34.
41. ibid.
42. ibid., p. 57.
43. ibid.
44. Greer, *On Rage*, 2008, p. 76.
45. Aboriginal and Torres Strait Islander Social Justice Commission, *Social Justice Report 2002*, 2002, p. 136.
46. Meuleners, Hendrie and Lee, *Measuring the Burden*, 2008, p. 4.
47. Aboriginal and Torres Strait Islander Women's Task Force on Violence, *The Aboriginal and Torres Strait Islander Women's Task Force on Violence Report*, p. 60.
48. Rule, 'Geoff Clark: power and rape', 2001.
49. Tickner, *Taking a Stand*, 2001, p. 48.

50. See McGlade, 'Aboriginal women and the Commonwealth Government's response to Mabo', 2001, p. 145.
51. Davis, 'A woman's place...', 2009.
52. Personal notes from ATSIC Board email, 2001.
53. Kingston, 'The sound of values clashing', 2001.
54. Stephen, 'What's behind the media campaign against Geoff Clark?', 2001.
55. Cited in Kingston, 'Rape and racism', 2001.
56. ibid.
57. *ABC Lateline*, 'Fallout continues', 2001.
58. ibid.
59. Kingston, 'Ending the cover-up', 2001.
60. ibid.
61. *ABC AM*, 'Geoff Clark won't be charged with rape', 2002.
62. Kissane, Berry and Doherty, 'Vindication at last', 2007.
63. Crenshaw, 'Mapping the margins', 1995, p. 371.
64. ibid.
65. Bargh, 'Hypocrisies', 2001.
66. ibid.
67. Western Australia Legislative Council, *Report of the Select Committee*, 2004, p. 3.
68. *ABC Lateline*, 'Preventing violence in Aboriginal communities', 2006.
69. ibid.
70. Western Australia Legislative Council, *Report of the Select Committee*, 2004, p. xix.
71. ibid., pp. 88–9.
72. ibid., p. 149.
73. ibid.
74. Gibson, 'How probe into child sex abuse went awry', 2005, p. 40.
75. Western Australia Legislative Council, *Report of the Select Committee*, 2004, p. 158.
76. ibid., p. 78.
77. ibid., p. 7.
78. ibid., p. 8.
79. Greens WA, 'Reinstate community', 2004.
80. Greens WA, 'Ease ordeal of rape survivors says MLC', 2004.
81. Western Australia Legislative Council, *Report of the Select Committee*, 2004, pp. 216–17.
82. *The State of Western Australia v Bropho* [2008] WADC 30.
83. United Nations Special Rapporteur on Racism, personal communication, Perth, 18 August 2009.
84. Bell and Nelson, 'Speaking about rape is everybody's business', 1989.
85. ibid., p. 403.
86. ibid., p. 404.
87. ibid.
88. ibid., p. 410.
89. ibid., pp. 410–11.
90. ibid., p. 415.
91. Jackie Huggins et al., 'Letters to the editor', 1991.
92. ibid., p. 506.
93. ibid.
94. ibid.

95. ibid.
96. ibid., p. 507.
97. Bell, 'Intraracial rape revisited', 1991.
98. Bell, 'Letters to the editor', 1991, p. 508.
99. Bell, 'Intraracial rape revisited', 1991, p. 386.
100. ibid., p. 391.
101. ibid., p. 389.
102. ibid., p. 386.
103. Transcript of interview with Denise Groves and Marie Andrews, Perth, 13 August 2005, p. 3.
104. ibid., p. 3.
105. ibid., p. 20.
106. ibid., p. 11.
107. ibid., p. 9.
108. ibid., p. 17.
109. ibid., p. 16.
110. ibid., p. 10.
111. ibid., p. 19.
112. Itzin, *Home Truths*, 2000, p. 5.
113. ibid., p. 1.
114. Moreton-Robinson, 'Tiddas talking up to white women', 2003, p. 67.
115. ibid.
116. ibid., p. 77.
117. ibid.
118. ibid.
119. Moreton Robinson, 'Tiddas talking up to white women', 2003, p. 77.
120. Howe, *Sex, Violence and Crime*, 2008, p. 157.
121. Howe, 'Addressing child sexual assault', 2009.
122. ibid., p. 57.
123. ibid., p. 61.
124. ibid., p. 60.
125. ibid., p. 60.
126. Watson, 'Aboriginal women's laws and lives', 2008, p. 27.
127. Dudgeon, 'Mothers of Sin', 2011, p. 103.
128. Dodson, 'Healing body, mind and spirit', 2002.
129. Anzaldúa, 'La conciencia de la Mestiza', 2001, p. 99.

Chapter 4 — A decade of government reports and inquiries

1. Mullighan, *Children on APY Lands Commission of Inquiry*, 2008, p. xi.
2. ibid.
3. ibid., p. xii.
4. ibid.
5. ibid., p. xi.
6. ibid., p. xiii.
7. ibid.
8. ibid., pp. 38–9.
9. ibid., p. 35.

10. ibid., p. xiii.
11. ibid., p. 56.
12. ibid., pp. 48–9.
13. ibid.
14. ibid., p. 47.
15. ibid., p. 72.
16. ibid., p. 49.
17. ibid., p. 80.
18. ibid., p. 66.
19. ibid., pp. 50–5.
20. ibid., p. 51.
21. ibid., p. 52.
22. ibid.
23. ibid., p. 110.
24. ibid., p. 112.
25. ibid., p. 73.
26. ibid., p. 217.
27. ibid.
28. ibid.
29. ibid., p. xiii.
30. ibid., p. 30.
31. ibid., p. 143.
32. ibid.
33. ibid.
34. ibid.
35. ibid., p. xx.
36. ibid., p. 243.
37. ibid., p. 222.
38. ibid., p. 217.
39. ibid., p. 242.
40. ibid., p. 67.
41. ibid., p. 251.
42. ibid., p. 113.
43. ibid.
44. ibid.
45. NIITF, <www.crimecommission.gov.au/our_work/determinations/niitf. htm> accessed 10 December 2009.
46. Northern Territory Government, *Little Children Are Sacred*, 2007, p. 41.
47. ibid.
48. ibid., p. 16.
49. ibid., p. 240.
50. ibid., p. 241.
51. ibid., p. 242.
52. ibid., p. 50.
53. ibid., p. 13.
54. ibid., p. 82.
55. Toohey, 'Last drinks', 2008.

56. ibid.
57. Northern Territory Government, *Little Children Are Sacred*, 2007, pp. 57–73.
58. ibid., p. 62.
59. ibid., p. 76.
60. ibid.
61. ibid., p. 77.
62. ibid., p. 78.
63. ibid., p. 84.
64. ibid.
65. Personal communication (telephone conversation) with Indigenous staff member of the Department of Family and Community Services and Indigenous Affairs, 6 April 2009.
66. Northern Territory Government, *Little Children Are Sacred*, 2007, p. 97.
67. ibid., p. 104.
68. ibid., p. 105.
69. ibid.
70. ibid., p. 140.
71. ibid., pp. 229–30.
72. ibid., p. 230.
73. ibid.
74. ibid.
75. ibid.
76. ibid., p. 158.
77. ibid., p. 160.
78. ibid.
79. ibid., p. 175.
80. ibid., p. 176.
81. ibid., p. 185.
82. ibid., p. 188.
83. ibid., p. 186.
84. ibid., p. 122.
85. Children's Commissioner Northern Territory, *Annual Report 2008–2009*, 2009, p. 38.
86. ibid, p. 12.
87. ACSAT, *Breaking the Silence*, 2006, p. 3.
88. ibid.
89. ibid., p. 49.
90. ibid., p. 3.
91. ibid., pp. 50–1.
92. ibid., p. 51.
93. ibid.
94. ibid.
95. ibid.
96. ibid., p. 55.
97. ibid., p. 52.
98. ibid.
99. ibid.
100. ibid., p. 53.

101. ibid., p. 54.
102. ibid., p. 53.
103. ibid., p. 54.
104. ibid.
105. ibid.
106. ibid., p. 55.
107. ibid., p. 56.
108. ibid., p. 57.
109. ibid.
110. ibid.
111. ibid., p. 24.
112. ibid., p. 110.
113. ibid., p. 112.
114. ibid., p. 88.
115. ibid., p. 100.
116. ibid., p. 101.
117. ibid., p. 104.
118. ibid.
119. ibid., p.105.
120. This is apparent from the CCYP organisational chart; see the NSW Government website, <www.kids.nsw.gov.au/kids/about/workingwithus.cfm> accessed 15 April 2009.
121. ACSAT, *Breaking the Silence*, 2006, p. 17.
122. ibid., p. 168.
123. ibid., p. 191.
124. ibid., p. 192.
125. ibid., p. 198.
126. ibid., p. 228.
127. ibid., p. 212.
128. ibid., p. 203.
129. New South Wales Government, *New South Wales Interagency Plan*, 2007.
130. ACSAT, *Breaking the Silence*, 2006, p. 292.
131. ABC News, 'NSW Aboriginal council to voice concerns', 2007.
132. Gibson, 'Too inept to save children', 2008.
133. Hope, *Record of Investigation Into Death of Susan Ann TAYLOR*, 2001, p. 28.
134. ibid., p. 16.
135. ibid., p. 23.
136. Gordon, Hallahan and Henry, *Putting the Picture Together*, 2002.
137. ibid., p. xx.
138. Gallop, 'Launch', 2003.
139. Government of Western Australia, *Putting People First*, 2002.
140. ibid., p. v.
141. ibid.
142. ibid.
143. ibid., p. 72.
144. Gallop, 'Launch', 2003, p. 4.
145. Gordon, Hallahan and Henry, *Putting the Picture Together*, 2002, p. 100.
146. ibid., pp. 254–7.

147. ibid., p. 205.
148. ibid., p. 277.
149. ibid., p. 301.
150. ibid., p. 449.
151. ibid., p. 449.
152. ibid., p. 454.
153. ibid., p. 458.
154. Hope, *Record of Investigation Into Death of Susan Ann TAYLOR*, 2001, p. 25.
155. Gordon, Hallahan and Henry, *Putting the Picture Together*, 2002, p. 457.
156. Le Grand, 'New call for action', 2004, p. 1.
157. Murray, 'WA out of step', 2004, p. 19.
158. Gibson, 'Abused children spur call to overhaul department', 2005, p. 6.
159. ibid.
160. ibid.
161. Penn, 'Gordon Inquiry plan has big faults', 2005, p. 13.
162. ibid.
163. Western Australia Legislative Assembly, *Community Development and Justice Standing Committee Inquiry*, 2008, p. 139.
164. Pickering, 'Aboriginal children "need own advocate"', 2007, p. 42.
165. Gordon, Hallahan and Henry, *Putting the Picture Together*, 2002, p. 438.
166. ibid., p. 433.
167. ibid., p. 428.
168. ibid., pp. 445–6.
169. ibid., p. 168.
170. ibid., p. 386.
171. ibid., p. 428.
172. ibid., p. 422.
173. McGlade, 'Susan Taylor Foundation', 2009.
174. Aboriginal and Torres Strait Islander Women's Task Force on Violence, *The Aboriginal and Torres Strait Islander Women's Task Force on Violence Report*, 1999, pp. vi–vii.
175. ibid., p. xiii.
176. ibid., p. xi.
177. ibid., p. 100.
178. ibid.
179. ibid., p. 101.
180. ibid., p. 101.
181. ibid.
182. ibid., p. 239.
183. ibid., p. 101.
184. ibid., p. 240.
185. ibid.
186. ibid., p. 56.
187. ibid., p. 178.
188. ibid., p. 118.
189. ibid., p. 224.
190. ibid., p. 233.

191. ibid., p. 120.
192. ibid., pp. 212–13.
193. ibid.
194. ibid., p. 243.
195. ibid., p. 255.
196. Cossins, *Alternative Models*, 2010, pp. 356–8.

Chapter 5 — The criminal justice response to child sexual assault

1. Davies, *Asking the Law Question*, 2002, p. 168.
2. Breckenridge, 'An exotic phenomenon?', 1992, pp. 18–37.
3. Goddard, *Child Abuse and Child Protection*, 1996, p. 145.
4. ibid.
5. ibid.
6. ibid.
7. ibid., p. 146.
8. Western Australia Legislative Assembly, *Community Development and Justice Standing Committee Inquiry*, 2008.
9. ibid., pp. 50–1.
10. ibid., p. 53.
11. ibid., p. 54.
12. ibid., p. 102.
13. ibid.
14. ibid., p. 62.
15. ibid., p. 123.
16. Eastwood, *The Experiences of Child Complainants*, 2003.
17. ibid., p. 1.
18. ibid.
19. ibid., p. 6.
20. ibid., p. 2.
21. ibid.
22. ibid.
23. ibid.
24. ibid., p. 3.
25. ibid.
26. ibid., p. 4.
27. ibid.
28. ibid.
29. ibid., p. 5.
30. ibid.
31. ibid.
32. ibid.
33. ibid., p. 6.
34. ibid., p. 2.
35. ibid., p. 6.
36. Richards, *Child complainants and the court process*, 2009.
37. ibid., p. 2.
38. ibid., pp. 2–4.

39. ibid., p. 4.
40. ibid., p. 5.
41. ibid., p. 6.
42. ibid.
43. Veldhuis and Freyd, 'Groomed for silence', 1999, p. 276.
44. ibid.
45. AIC, *Child Sexual Abuse*, 2003.
46. ibid., p. 3.
47. ibid., p. 4.
48. ibid., p. 8.
49. ibid., p. 2.
50. ibid., p. 3.
51. ibid., p. 5.
52. ibid., p. 8.
53. ibid., pp. 4–14.
54. ibid., p. 15.
55. ibid., p. 16.
56. ibid.
57. Taylor, *Court Licensed Abuse*, 2004.
58. ibid., p. 47.
59. ibid., p. 20.
60. ibid., p. 1.
61. Bavin-Mizzi, 'Aboriginal women and rape', 1993.
62. ibid., p. 183.
63. ibid., p. 199.
64. ibid., pp. 187–8.
65. Bligh, 'A study of the needs of Aboriginal women', 1983.
66. ibid, p. 101.
67. ibid.
68. Lievore, *No Longer Silent*, 2005.
69. ibid., p. 111.
70. ibid.
71. ibid., p. 112.
72. ibid., p. 113.
73. ibid., p. 112.
74. ibid., p. 111.
75. Morrison, 'What is the outcome of reporting rape to the police?', 2008, p. 9.
76. Department for Women, *Heroines of Fortitude*, 1996.
77. ibid., p. 97.
78. ibid., p. 119.
79. ibid., p. 4.
80. ibid., p. 100.
81. ibid.
82. ibid., p. 105.
83. ibid.
84. ibid., pp. 101–2.
85. ibid., p. 109.

86. ibid., p. 102.
87. ibid.
88. ibid., p. 4.
89. ibid., p. 108.
90. ibid.
91. ibid., p. 108.
92. ibid., p. 108.
93. Cited in McRae, Nettheim and Beacroft, *Indigenous Legal Issues, Commentary and Materials*, 1997, p. 380.
94. Bolger, *Aboriginal Women and Violence*, 1991, p. 50.
95. ibid., p. 50.
96. ibid., p. 85.
97. ibid., pp. 80–1.
98. Bell and Nelson, 'Speaking about rape is everybody's business', 1989, p. 409.
99. Payne, 'Aboriginal women and the law', 1992, p. 37.
100. ibid., p. 37.
101. Shaw, '(Post) colonial encounters', 2003.
102. ibid., p. 324.
103. ibid.
104. ibid.
105. ibid.
106. ibid.
107. ibid.
108. Toohey, 'Black, white and blurred', 2002.
109. ibid.
110. Bryant, 'Promised marriages', 2002.
111. Toohey, 'Black, white and blurred', 2002.
112. ibid.
113. Bryant, 'Promised marriages', 2002, p. 20.
114. ibid.
115. ibid., p. 21.
116. Toohey, 'Black, white and blurred', 2002.
117. United Nations Economic and Social Council, *Forced Marriage of the Girl Child*, 2007, p. 9.
118. *Hales v Jamilmira* [2003] NTCA 9.
119. ibid. at 6.
120. ibid. at 3.
121. ibid. at 3.
122. ibid. at 8.
123. ibid. at 5.
124. Toohey, 'Black, white and blurred', 2002.
125. *Hales v Jamilmira* [2003] NTCA 9 at 7
126. Bryant, G., 'Promised marriages', 2002, p. 21.
127. Kimm, *A Fatal Conjunction*, 2004, p. 69.
128. ABC Radio, 'Customary law and sentencing', 2002. Reproduced by permission of the Australian Broadcasting Corporation and ABC Online, © 2010 ABC, all rights reserved.
129. Toohey, 'The age of contempt', 2005.

130. ibid.
131. Michelmore, 'Traditional role queried', 2005.
132. ibid.
133. Toohey, 'The age of contempt', 2005.
134. ibid.
135. ABC Television, 'Sentence sparks outrage across Australia', 2005.
136. *The Queen v GJ* [2005] NTCCA 20, 40.
137. *R v Wurramara* (1999) 105 A Crim R 512 at 26.
138. ibid. at 22.
139. ibid. at 29.
140. ibid.
141. ABC Radio, 'NT rape case sparks demand for legal change', 2005. Reproduced by permission of the Australian Broadcasting Corporation and ABC Online, © 2010 ABC, all rights reserved.
142. Cited by McGlade, 'Aboriginal women, girls and sexual assault', p. 10.
143. ibid.
144. Meade and Elks, 'Girl endured six weeks of sex attacks', 2007.
145. See Koch, 'Child safety failed rape girl', 2007.
146. ibid.
147. ibid.
148. Meade, 'Call for inquiry into court's findings', 2007, p. 2.
149. ibid.
150. Langton, 'Stop the abuse of children', 2007.
151. ibid.
152. ibid.
153. Calma, 'Aurukun Story a clarion call for change', 2007.
154. Cripps and McGlade, 'Safety of kids is priority', 2007.
155. *R v KU & Ors; ex parte (Qld)* [2008] QCA 154.
156. ibid. at 38.
157. ibid.
158. ibid. at 2–5.
159. ibid. at 39.
160. ibid. at 35.
161. ibid. at 40.
162. ibid. at 41.
163. ibid. at 68.
164. ibid. at 62.
165. Meade and Elks, 'Girl endured six weeks of sex attacks', 2007.
166. ibid. at 32.
167. ibid. at 28.
168. ibid. at 10.
169. ibid. at 27, 28.
170. ibid. at 83.
171. ibid. at 41.
172. ibid. at 43–4.
173. ibid. at 43.
174. ibid.
175. ibid. at 83.

176. ibid.
177. ibid. at 85.
178. *R v KU & Ors; ex parte (Qld)* [2008] QCA 154, at 38, 44.
179. ibid.
180. ibid. at 45, citing *R v Daniel* [1998] 1 Qd R 499 at 531.
181. ibid. at 50.
182. ibid. at 51.
183. Skelton, 'Rape judge "ignored our pleas"', 2007.
184. *R v KU & Ors; ex parte (Qld)* [2008] QCA 154, at 43.
185. Shaw, '(Post) colonial encounters', 2003, p. 324.
186. Discussed by Gotell, 'Rethinking affirmative consent', 2008, pp. 865–98, 889–94.
187. Native Women's Association of Canada, Factum of Intervenor, *R v Edmondson*, 2004, p. 4.
188. Gotell, 'Rethinking affirmative consent', 2008, p. 865.
189. Native Women's Association of Canada, Factum of Intervenor, *R v Edmondson*, 2004.
190. Gotell, 'Rethinking affirmative consent', 2008, p. 890.
191. ibid., p. 893.
192. ibid., p. 894.
193. ibid., p. 867.
194. ibid., p. 898.
195. Razack, *Looking White People In The Eye*, 1998.
196. ibid., p. 80.
197. ibid., p. 59.
198. ibid., p. 79.
199. ibid., p. 62.
200. ibid., p. 72.
201. Submission to the Senate Standing Committee on Legal and Constitutional Affairs in Relation to the Provisions of the Crimes Amendment (Bail and Sentencing) Bill 2006, 25 September 2006, at <www.alrc.gov.au/submissions/ALRCsubs/2006/2509_p2.htm#_Toc146706417>.
202. ibid., p. 48.
203. *The Queen v GJ* [2005] NTCCA 20, at 10 [47].
204. United Nations Division for the Advancement of Women, *Expert Group meeting*, 2008.
205. ibid.
206. Section 91 of the *Northern Territory National Emergency Response Act 2007* (Cth) provides that in determining a sentence to be passed on an offender, a court must not take into account customary law or cultural practice as a reason for excusing, justifying or authorising the criminal behaviour.
207. *The Queen v Wunungmurra* [2009] NTSC 24 at 3.
208. ibid. at 11.
209. Ravens, 'Laws result in unjust sentence', 2009.

Chapter 6 — Close to home

1. Wilson Clarke, 'Child abuse victims warned off courts', 2004.
2. ibid.

3. ibid.
4. ibid.
5. Donna Kickett, transcript of interview, Perth, 13 July 2005, transcript held by the author, p. 1.
6. ibid., p. 5.
7. ibid., pp. 9–10.
8. ibid., p. 4.
9. ibid., p. 4.
10. ibid., p. 6.
11. Taylor, C., *Court Licensed Abuse*, 2004.
12. ibid., p. 226.
13. Donna Kickett, transcript of interview, 13 July 2005, transcript held by the author, p. 7.
14. Taylor, C., *Court Licensed Abuse*, 2004, p. 259.
15. ibid., p. 77.
16. ibid., p. 262.
17. ibid., p. 269.
18. Donna Kickett, transcript of interview, 13 July 2005, transcript held by the author, p. 7.
19. Taylor, C., *Court Licensed Abuse*, 2004, p. 66.
20. Summit, 'The child sexual abuse accommodation syndrome', 2000, p. 160.
21. Goddard, *Child Abuse and Child Protection*, 1996, p. 60.
22. Finkelhor, 'Four preconditions', 2000, p. 179.
23. Donna Kickett, transcript of interview, 13 July 2005, transcript held by the author, p. 8.
24. Taylor, C., *Court Licensed Abuse*, 2004, p. 30.
25. See for example, *De Jesus v The Queen* (1986) 22 A. Crim. R 375.
26. Donna Kickett, transcript of interview, 13 July 2005, transcript held by the author, p. 3.
27. ibid., p. 2.
28. ibid., pp. 2–3.
29. ibid., p. 2.
30. ibid., p. 5.
31. ibid., p. 4.
32. Bessarab, 'A socio-political perspective', 2003, p. 97.
33. ibid.
34. Donna Kickett, transcript of interview, 13 July 2005, transcript held by the author p. 10.
35. Eades, 'Cross examination of Aboriginal children', 1995.
36. Aboriginal English has many variations, and can be spoken by many Aboriginal people. I use Aboriginal English during conversation with my family and other Noongar people but not usually with non-Aboriginal people.
37. Eades, 'Cross examination of Aboriginal children', 1995, p. 368.
38. Donna Kickett, transcript of interview, 13 July 2005, transcript held by the author.
39. Eades, 'Cross examination of Aboriginal children', 1995, p. 369.
40. ibid.

41. Donna Kickett, transcript of interview, 13 July 2005, transcript held by the author, p. 3.
42. ibid.
43. Eades, 'Cross examination of Aboriginal children', 1995, 369
44. Donna Kickett, transcript of interview, 13 July 2005, p. 4.
45. ibid., p. 6.
46. Keating, N., *Review of Services*, 2001.
47. Fryer-Smith, *Aboriginal Benchbook*, 2008.
48. Western Australia Legislative Assembly, *Community Development and Justice Standing Committee Inquiry*, 2008, p. 98.
49. ibid., p. 99.
50. Donna Kickett, transcript of interview, 13 July 2005, transcript held by the author p. 9.
51. ibid.
52. Keating, N., *Review of Services*, 2001, p. 113.
53. ibid.
54. Western Australia Legislative Assembly, *Community Development and Justice Standing Committee Inquiry*, 2008, pp. 129–30.
55. ibid., p. 132.
56. ibid.
57. Donna Kickett, transcript of interview, 13 July 2005, transcript held by the author p. 9.
58. ibid., p. 13.
59. ibid., p. 13.
60. ibid., p. 12.
61. Summit, 'The child sexual abuse accommodation syndrome', 2000, p. 169.
62. ibid., p. 166.
63. ibid., p. 169.
64. Laurie, 'Breaking The silence', 2006.
65. Ingrid Collard, transcript of interview, Perth, 7 June 2005, transcript held by the author, pp. 1–2.
66. ibid., p. 8.
67. Ingrid Collard, transcript of interview, 9 July 2006, transcript held by the author, p. 1.
68. ibid., p. 3.
69. ibid., p. 2.
70. ibid., p. 9.
71. ibid., p. 7.
72. ibid., p. 7.
73. ibid., pp. 3–4.
74. ibid., pp. 2–3.
75. ibid., p. 4.
76. ibid., p. 5.
77. Ingrid Collard, transcript of interview, 7 June 2005, transcript held by the author, pp. 8–9.
78. ibid.

79. Ingrid Collard, transcript of interview, 9 July 2006, transcript held by the author, p. 6.
80. ibid., p. 13.
81. ibid., p. 6.
82. ibid., p. 8.
83. ibid., p. 9.
84. ibid., pp. 6, 9.
85. ibid., p. 25.
86. Taylor, C., *Court Licensed Abuse*, 2004, p. 37.
87. Ingrid Collard, transcript of interview, 9 July 2006, transcript held by the author, p. 15.
88. ibid., p. 7.
89. ibid.
90. ibid., p. 17.
91. ibid.
92. ibid., p. 18.
93. ibid., p. 9.
94. ibid., p. 10.
95. ibid.
96. ibid., p. 10.
97. ibid., p. 11.
98. ibid., p. 14.
99. ibid.
100. ibid., p. 15
101. ibid., p. 12.
102. ibid.
103. ibid., p. 15.
104. ibid.
105. ABC News, 'Aboriginal elder jailed for abusing grand-daughter', 2006.
106. Lievore, *No Longer Silent*, 2005, p. 110.
107. *R v Bropho* [2004] WADC 182 at 3.
108. ibid. at 24.
109. ibid. at 34.
110. ibid. at 47.
111. ibid. at 45.
112. ABC Television, 'Indigenous DNA testing in doubt', 2004.
113. ibid.
114. Buckleton, Walsh and Mitchell, 'Case report: *R v Bropho*', 2005.
115. ibid.
116. Cunneen, M., 'Letter to the editor', 2005/2006.
117. ibid.
118. *R v Bropho* [2004] WADC 182 at 44.
119. This history, and the issue of corroboration warning today, was examined by the New South Wales Department for Women in a landmark inquiry; see Department for Women, *Heroines of Fortitude*, 1996, pp. 184–97.
120. *Christopher v The Queen* (2000) 23 WAR 106 at 117.
121. *R v Bropho* [2004] WADC 182 at 50.
122. ibid. at 51–52.

123. ibid. at 52.
124. ibid. at 13–14.
125. ibid. at 53.
126. ibid. at 55.
127 Boniface, 'The common sense of jurors', 2005.
128. ibid., p. 14.
129. ibid.
130. *R v Bropho* [2004] WADC 182 at 53.
131. ibid.
132. Department for Women, *Heroines of Fortitude*, 1996.
133. ibid., p. 8.
134. ibid.
135. ibid., p. 191.
136. ibid., p. 193.
137. ibid., p. 194.
138. *The State of Western Australia v Bropho* [2008] WADC 30.
139. ibid. at 19.
140. ibid.

Chapter 7 — Looking forward

1. ACSAT, *Breaking the Silence*, 2006, p. 281.
2. ibid., p. 292.
3. Northern Territory Government, *Little Children Are Sacred*, 2007, p. 131.
4. ibid.
5. ibid.
6. ibid., p. 132.
7. ibid., p. 134.
8. Cossins, *Alternative Models*, 2010, pp. 356–8.
9. Turpel-Lafond, 'Sentencing within a restorative justice paradigm', 2005, p. 281.
10. Monture-Angus, 'Thinking about change', 2005, p. 278.
11. Aboriginal Healing Foundation, *Final Report of the Aboriginal Healing Foundation*, 2006, pp. 1–2.
12. FaHCSIA, 'Healing Development Team'.
13. Ross, 'Aboriginal community healing in action', 2005.
14. Ross, 'The sentencing circle', 2005, p. 190.
15. Ross, 'Aboriginal community healing in action', 2005, p. 187.
16. Ross, 'The sentencing circle', 2005, pp. 190–1.
17. Bushie, 'Community Holistic Circle Healing', 2007.
18. ibid.
19. ibid.
20. ibid.
21. Ross, 'Aboriginal community healing in action', 2005, p. 185.
22. Native Counselling Services of Alberta, *A Cost-benefit Analysis*, 2001, p. 29.
23. ibid., p. 17.
24. Ross, *Returning to the Teachings*, 2006, p. 161.
25. ibid., p. 191.
26. ibid., p. 35.

27. ibid.
28. ibid., p. 175.
29. ibid., p. 195.
30. Bushie, 'Community Holistic Circle Healing', 2007.
31. ibid.
32. Ross, *Returning to the Teachings*, 2006, p. 189.
33. Aboriginal Corrections Policy Unit, *The Four Circles of Hollow Water*, 1997, p. 176.
34. ibid.
35. Ross, *Returning to the Teachings*, 2006, p. 191.
36. Dickson-Gilmore and LaPrairie, *Will the Circle Be Unbroken?*, 2005, p. 176.
37. ibid.
38. Native Counselling Services of Alberta, *A Cost-benefit Analysis*, 2001, pp. 51–65.
39. ibid. pp. 63–5.
40. ibid., p. 61.
41. Ross, *Returning to the Teachings*, 2006, p. 211.
42. ibid.
43. ibid.
44. ibid., p. 212.
45. ibid., p. 185.
46. ibid., p. 212.
47. ibid.
48. Crawford, Dudgeon and Briskman, *Developing Therapeutic Communities*, 2007.
49. ibid., p. 39.
50. ibid., p. 50.
51. ibid., p. 54.
52. ibid., p. 66.
53. ibid., p. 58.
54. Guest, 'Cops decry sex "slap on the wrist"', 2009.
55. Gooda, 'Imagining childhood, children, culture and community', 2005.
56. Blagg, 'Restorative justice and Aboriginal family violence', 2002, p. 198.
57. ibid.
58. ibid., p. 200.
59. ACSAT, *Breaking the Silence*, 2006, p. 282.
60. ibid., p. 211.
61. Save the Children, *Listen and Speak Out*, 2005.
62. ibid.
63. Burgess et al., *Sexual Assault of Children and Adolescents*, 1978, p. xx.
64. Giaretto, Giaretto and Sgroi, 'Coordinated community treatment of incest', 1978, p. 231.
65. ibid., p. 234.
66. ibid.
67. Turpel-Lafond, 'Sentencing within a restorative justice paradigm', 2005.
68. ibid., p. 281.
69. ibid., p. 282.
70. ibid., p. 286.
71. ibid., p. 292.
72. ibid.

73. LaRocque, 'Re-examining culturally appropriate models', 1997, p. 81.
74. ibid., p. 85.
75. Dickson-Gilmore and LaPrairie, *Will the Circle Be Unbroken?*, 2005, p. 196.
76. ibid., p. 197.
77. Stewart, Huntley and Blaney, *The Implications of Restorative Justice*, 2001.
78. ibid., p. 39.
79. ibid.
80. ibid., p. 45.
81. ibid., p. 53.
82. ibid., p. 56.
83. ibid., p. 41.
84. LaRocque, 'Re-examining culturally appropriate models', 1997, pp. 80–1.
85. Goel, 'No woman at the center', 2000, p. 324.
86. Daly, 'Seeking justice in the 21st century', 2008, p. 24.
87. ibid., p. 27.
88. Cunliffe and Cameron, 'Writing the circle', 2007.
89. ibid., p. 13.
90. ibid., p. 21.
91. ibid., pp. 21, 24.
92. ibid., p. 29.
93. ibid.
94. LaRocque, 'Re-examining culturally appropriate models', 1997, p. 89.
95. ibid.
96. ibid., p. 86.
97. ibid., p. 91.
98. Dodd, '"Rapist" strikes again', 2009.
99. ibid.
100. McGlade and Hovane, 'The Mangolamara case', 2007; Nielsen, 'Canadian Aboriginal Healing Lodges', 2003.
101. Chartrand and McKay, *A Review of Research*, 2006.
102. ibid., p. vi.
103. ibid., p. 49.
104. ibid., p. 54.
105. ibid.
106. ibid.
107. ibid., p. 52.
108. ibid., p. v.
109. ibid., p. 58.
110. ibid., p. v.
111. Deer, 'Decolonizing rape law: a native feminist synthesis', 2009.
112. ibid., p. 158.
113. ibid., p. 159.
114. ibid., p. 157.
115. Deer, 'Decolonizing rape law', 2010.
116. Deer, 'Decolonizing rape law: a native feminist synthesis', 2009, pp. 157–8.
117. LaRocque, 'Re-examining culturally appropriate models', 1997, p. 86.
118. ibid.
119. ibid.

120. Marchetti, 'Indigenous women and the RCIADC', 2007.
121. ibid., p. 6.
122. ibid.
123. ibid., p. 7.
124. ibid., p. 9.
125. Pearson, *Up from the Mission*, 2009, p. 193.
126. ibid.
127. ibid.
128. EchoHawk, 'Child sexual abuse in Indian country', 2001, pp. 109–10.
129. ibid., p. 85.
130. ibid., p. 84.
131. ibid., p. 95.
132. ibid., p. 87.
133. ibid., p. 95.
134. ibid., p. 96.
135. ibid., pp. 103–6.
136. ibid., p. 106.
137. ibid., p. 85.
138. ibid., pp. 108–9.
139. ibid.
140. ibid., p. 127.
141. Tribal Policy Clearinghouse, 'Children's Justice Act resources', no date.
142. ibid.
143. ibid.
144. EchoHawk, 'Child sexual abuse in Indian country', 2001, p. 90.
145. Harvard Project on American Indian Economic Development, *Honoring Nations*, 2000.
146. ibid., p. 8.
147. ibid., p. 9.
148. ibid.
149. ibid.
150. Warhaft, Palys and Boyce, 'This is How We Did It', 1999.
151. Calma, *Addressing Family Violence and Child Sexual Assault*, 2006.

Chapter 8 — Knowing from the heart

1. MacKinnon, *Women's Lives, Men's Laws*, 2007, p. 89.
2. ibid.
3. Hampson, 'Rape compo encourages lies, claims counsellor', 2007, p. 9.
4. Strutt, 'Pressure on police led to failed sex charges, says ALS chief', 2007, p. 7.
5. Strutt, 'Grasp the opportunity, says leader', 2007, p. 6.
6. ibid.
7. Indigenous Justice Taskforce, *A Review of the Indigenous Justice Taskforce*, 2009.
8. ibid., p. 7.
9. ibid., p. 14.
10. ibid., p. 10; it was reported that as at January 2009, 58 offenders were sentenced and 70 cases dismissed.
11. ibid., p. 13.

12. Indigenous Justice Taskforce, *A Review of the Indigenous Justice Taskforce*, 2009, p. 27.
13. Cameron, 'Sentencing circles and intimate violence', 2006, p. 511.
14. Deer, 'Decolonizing rape law: a native feminist synthesis', 2009, p. 164.
15. Australian Government, *Future Directions*, 2009, p. 25.
16. Nicholson et al., *Will They Be Heard?*, 2009.
17. Save the Children, *10 Essential Learning Points*, 2005, p. 8.
18. United Nations, *United Nations Declaration on the Rights of Indigenous Peoples*, 2008, p. 9.
19. Macklin, *Jenny Macklin, Fabian Society Annual Dinner*, 2009.
20. National Council to Reduce Violence Against Women and their Children, *Time for Action*, 2009.
21. ibid., p. 87.
22. ibid., p. 51.
23. Amnesty International Australia, *Setting the Standard*, 2008, p. 16.
24. Karvelas, 'Give Aboriginal women equal say', 2008.
25. Amnesty International Australia, *Setting the Standard*, 2008, p. 16.

Bibliography

ABC AM, 'Geoff Clark won't be charged with rape', transcript, reporter Michele Fonseca, 28 June 2002,<www.abc.net.au/am/stories/s593387.htm> accessed 5 May 2009.

ABC Lateline, 'Fallout continues after O'Shane comments', TV program transcript, reporter Sarah Clarke, 15 June 2001,<www.abc.net.au/lateline/stories/s313730.htm> accessed 25 June 2010.

—— 'Preventing violence in Aboriginal communities', TV program transcript, reporter Suzanne Smith, 1 December 2006, <www.abc.net.au/lateline/content/2006/s1802593.htm> accessed 16 March 2012.

ABC News, 'Aboriginal elder jailed for abusing granddaughter', 30 June 2006, <www.abc.net.au/news/stories/2006/06/30/1790620.htm> accessed 28 April 2012.

ABC News, 'NSW Aboriginal council to voice concerns over child abuse', 25 June 2007,<www.abc.net.au/news/stories/2007/06/25/1961190.htm> accessed 10 March 2010.

ABC Radio, 'Customary law and sentencing', *Law Report*, transcript, 22 October 2002, <www.abc.net.au/rn/talks/8.30/lawrpt/stories/s706299.htm> accessed 12 May 2010.

—— 'NT rape case sparks demand for legal change', reporter Anne Barker, *World Today*, 19 August 2005,<www.abc.net.au/worldtoday/content/2005/s1441538.htm> accessed on 12 May 2010.

ABC Television, 'Indigenous DNA testing in doubt', reporter Mick O'Donnell, *7.30 Report*, 26 August 2004,<www.abc.net.au/7.30/content/2004/s1186080.htm> accessed 2 June 2010.

—— 'Sentence sparks outrage across Australia', reporter Murray McLaughlin, *7.30 Report*, transcript, 12 October 2005,<www.abc.net.au/7.30/content/2005/s1480969.htm> accessed 12 May 2010.

Aboriginal and Torres Strait Islander Social Justice Commission, *Social Justice Report 2002*, HREOC, Sydney, 2002, <www.hreoc.gov.au/social_justice/sj_report/sjreport02/Social_Justice_Report02.pdf> accessed 16 March 2012.

Aboriginal and Torres Strait Islander Women's Task Force on Violence, *The Aboriginal and Torres Strait Islander Women's Task Force on Violence Report*, The State of Queensland, 1999.

Aboriginal Corrections Policy Unit, *The Four Circles of Hollow Water*, Ottawa, Ontario, 1997.

Aboriginal Healing Foundation, *Final Report of the Aboriginal Healing Foundation: A Healing Journey, Reclaiming Wellness*, Aboriginal Healing Foundation, Canada, 2006.

Absolon, Kathy and Cam Willett, 'Putting ourselves forward: location in Aboriginal research' in Leslie Brown and Susan Strega (eds), *Research as Resistance: Critical, Indigenous and anti-oppressive approaches*, Canada, 2005, pp. 97–126.

ACSAT (Aboriginal Child Sexual Assault Taskforce), *Breaking the Silence: Creating the future: Addressing child sexual assault in Aboriginal communities in NSW*, Attorney-General's Department NSW, Sydney, 2006.

AIC (Australian Institute of Criminology), *Child Sexual Abuse: Justice responses or alternative resolution*, Adelaide, 2003, <www.aic.gov.au/conferences/2003-abuse> accessed 11 May 2010.

AIDA (Australian Indigenous Doctors' Association), *Submission to the Northern Territory Emergency Response Review Board*, no date, <www.aida.org.au/pdf/submissions/Submission_8.pdf> accessed 3 February 2012, no page numbers.

Altman, Jon and Melinda Hinkson (eds), *Coercive Reconciliation: Stabilise, normalise, exit Aboriginal Australia*, Arena Publications, North Carlton, Vic, 2007.

Amnesty International Australia, *Setting the Standard: International good practice to inform an Australian National Plan of Action to eliminate violence against women*, NSW, 2008.

Andrews, Gavin, Bronwyn Gould and Justine Corry, 'Child sexual abuse revisited', *Medical Journal of Australia* 176 (10), 2002, pp. 458–9,<www.mja.com.au/public/issues/176_10_200502/and10179_fm.html> accessed 20 June 2010.

Anzaldúa, Gloria, 'Speaking in tongues, a letter to third world writers' in Cherríe Moraga and Gloria Anzaldúa (eds), *This Bridge Called My Back: Writings by radical women of color*, Persephone Press, USA, 1981, pp. 198–209.

—— 'La conciencia de la Mestiza: towards a new consciousness' in Kum-Kum Bhavnani (ed.), *Feminism & Race*, Oxford Readings in Feminism, Oxford University Press, UK, 2001, pp. 93–107.

Atkinson, Judy, 'Violence in Aboriginal Australia — colonisation and its impacts on gender', *Refractory Girl*, 36, 1990, pp. 21–4.

—— 'Stinkin' thinkin'' — alcohol, violence and government responses', *Aboriginal Law Bulletin*, 5–6, 1991, <www.austlii.edu.au/cgi-bin/sinodisp/au/journals/AboriginalLawB/1991/36.html?stem=0&synonyms=0&query=Judy%20Atkinson> accessed 14 March 2012.

—— *Trauma Trails, Recreating Songlines: The transgenerational effects of trauma in Indigenous Australia*, Spinifex Press, North Melbourne, 2002.

Attwood, Bain, *Telling the Truth about Aboriginal History*, Allen & Unwin, Crows Nest, 2005.

Australian Domestic and Family Violence Clearinghouse, *Australian Domestic & Family Violence Clearinghouse comment on the Federal Government's response to the issue of child sexual assault in Northern Territory Aboriginal communities*, undated, <www.austdvclearinghouse.unsw.edu.au/PDF%20files/response16072007.pdf> accessed 28 April 2010.

Australian Government, *Future Directions for the Northern Territory Emergency Response: Discussion paper*, Australian Government, Canberra, 2009.

Australian Government, *Stronger Futures in the Northern Territory*, 2012, <www.indigenous.gov.au/stronger-futures-in-the-northern-territory/> accessed 21 March 2012.

Baines, Pat, 'Seeking justice: traditions of social action among Indigenous women in the south west of Western Australia' in Peggy Brock (ed.), *Words and Silences: Aboriginal women, politics and land*, Allen & Unwin, Crows Nest, 2001, pp. 56–91.

Bargh, Maria, 'Hypocrisies', 2001, <www.aotearoa.wellington.net.nz/he/hyp. html> accessed 16 October 2004.

Bavin-Mizzi, Jillian, 'Aboriginal women and rape: the case of Lucy Morgan in 19th century Australia' in Penelope Hetherington and Philippa Maddern (eds), *Sexuality and Gender in History: Selected essays*, Centre for WA History, WA, 1993, pp. 182–201.

Behrendt, Larissa, 'Aboriginal women and the white lies of the feminist movement: implications for Aboriginal women in rights discourse', *Australian Feminist Law Journal* 1, 1993, pp. 27–44.

Bell, Diane, 'Intraracial rape revisited: on forging a feminist future beyond fractions and frightening politics', *Women's Studies International Forum*, 14, 1991, pp. 385–412.

—— 'Letters to the editor', *Women's Studies International Forum*, 14(5), 1991, pp. 507–13.

—— and Topsy Napurrula Nelson, 'Speaking about rape is everybody's business', *Women's Studies International Forum* 12(4), 1989, pp. 403–16.

Bessarab, Dawn, 'A socio-political perspective of sexual violence and its impact on Aboriginal women's health' in Delys Bird, Wendy Were and Terri-Ann White (eds), *Future Imaginings: Sexualities and genders in the new millennium*, UWA Press, Crawley, 2003, pp. 87–99.

Blagg, Harry, 'Restorative justice and Aboriginal family violence: opening a space for healing' in Heather Strang and John Braithwaite (eds), *Restorative justice and family violence*, Cambridge University Press, Cambridge, 2002, pp. 191–205.

—— 'Colonial critique and critical criminology: issues in Aboriginal law and Aboriginal violence' in Thalia Anthony and Chris Cunneen (eds), *The Critical Criminology Companion*, Federation Press, NSW, 2008, pp. 129–43.

Bligh, Vivian, 'A study of the needs of Aboriginal women who have been raped or sexually assaulted' in Fay Gale (ed.), *We Are Bosses Ourselves: The status and the role of Aboriginal women today*, Australian Institute of Aboriginal Studies, Canberra, 1983, pp. 100–3.

Bolger, Audrey, *Aboriginal Women and Violence*, North Australia Research Unit Australian National University, Darwin, 1991.

Boniface, Dorne, 'The common sense of jurors vs the wisdom of the law: judicial directions and warnings in sexual assault trials', *University of New South Wales Law Journal*, 11(1), 2005, pp. 11–16.

Boyd, Cameron (in collaboration with Leah Bromfield), 'Young people who sexually abuse: key issues', *ACSSA Wrap*, 3, 2006.

Brayboy, Bryan McKinley Jones, 'Toward a tribal critical race theory in education', *The Urban Review*, 37(5), 2005, pp. 425–46.

Breckenridge, Jan, 'An exotic phenomenon? Incest and child rape' in Jan Breckenridge and Moira Carmody (eds), *Crimes of Violence: Australian responses to rape and child sexual assault*, Allen & Unwin, North Sydney, 1992.

—— and Moira Carmody (eds), *Crimes of Violence: Australian responses to rape and child sexual assault*, Allen & Unwin, North Sydney, 1992.

Browne, Angela and David Finkelhor, 'Impact of child sexual abuse: a review of the research' in Anne Cohn Donnelly and Kim Oates (eds), *Classic Papers in Child Abuse*, Sage Publications, Thousand Oaks, California, 2000, pp. 217–39.

Bryant, Colleen and Matthew Willis, *Risk Factors in Indigenous Violent Victimisation*, Technical and Background Paper, 30, Australian Institute of Criminology, Canberra, 2008.

Bryant, Gerard, 'Promised marriages: the Jackie Pascoe case', *Indigenous Law Bulletin*, 5(17), 2002, pp. 20–1.

Buckleton, John, Simon Walsh and John Mitchell, 'Case report: *R v Bropho* — a challenge to the use of DNA statistics in cases involving Indigenous Australians', *Forensic Bulletin*, Summer, 2005, pp. 12–13.

Burgess, Ann, A. Nicolas Groth, Lynda Holmstrom and Suzanne Sgroi (eds), *Sexual Assault of Children and Adolescents*, Lexington Books, Toronto, 1978.

Bushie, Berma, 'Community Holistic Circle Healing: a community approach', International Institute for Restorative Practices, 2007,<www.iirp.org/article_detail.php?article_id=NDc0> accessed 10 June 2010.

Calma, Tom, *Addressing Family Violence and Child Sexual Assault in Indigenous Communities — A human rights perspective*, Address to the Aboriginal Child Sexual Assault Forum, NSW Parliament House, 5 December 2006.

—— 'Aurukun Story a clarion call for change', *ABC Opinion and Analysis*, 13 December 2007, <www.abc.net.au/news/stories/2007/ 12/13/2117575. htm> accessed 12 May 2010.

Cameron, Angela, 'Sentencing circles and intimate violence: a Canadian feminist perspective', *Canadian Journal of Women and the Law* 18(2), 2006, pp. 479–512.

Candy, Phillip C., 'Alternative paradigms in educational research', *American Education Research*, 16(3), 1989, pp. 1–11.

Centre for Domestic and Family Violence Research, *The Big Picture — Putting the pieces together*, Centre for Domestic and Family Violence Research, Mackay, Qld, 2009.

Charlesworth, Hilary and Christine Chinkin, *The Boundaries of International Law: A feminist analysis*, Manchester University Press, UK, 2000.

Chartrand, Larry and Celeste McKay, *A Review of Research on Criminal Victimization and First Nations, Métis and Inuit Peoples 1990 to 2001*, Policy Centre for Victim Issues, Department of Justice, Ottawa, Ontario, 2006.

Chesterman, John and Brian Galligan, *Citizens without Rights: Aborigines and Australian citizenship*, Cambridge University Press, Cambridge, Melbourne, 1997.

Child Wise, 'What is child sex trafficking?', no date, <http://www.childwise.net/ Stop-Sex-Trafficking-of-Children-Young-People/what-is-child-sex-trafficking.html> accessed 15 March 2012.

Children's Commissioner Northern Territory, *Annual Report 2008–2009*, Office of the Children's Commissioner Northern Territory, Darwin, 2009.

Cho, Sumi and Robert Wesley, 'Historicizing critical race theory's cutting edge' in Francisco Valdes, Jerome McCristal Culp and Angela P Harris (eds), *Crossroads, Directions and a New Critical Race Theory*, Temple University Press, USA, 2002, pp. 32–70.

Choo, Christine, 'Sister Kate's Home for "nearly white" children' in Doreen Mellor and Anna Haebich (eds), *Many Voices: Reflections on experiences of Indigenous child separation*, National Library of Australia, Canberra, 2002.

Committee on the Rights of the Child, *Indigenous Children and Their Rights under the Convention*, General Comment No. 11, 2009.

Cossins, Annie, *Alternative Models for Prosecuting Child Sex Offences in Australia*, National Child Sexual Assault Reform Committee, University of New South Wales, Sydney, 2010.

Crawford, Frances, Pat Dudgeon and Linda Briskman, *Developing Therapeutic Communities for Abused Aboriginal Children and Their Families: An Indigenous practitioner's cooperative inquiry*, Curtin University of Technology, Perth, 2007.

Crenshaw, Kimberle Williams, 'Mapping the margins: intersectionality, identity politics, and violence against women of color' in Kimberle Crenshaw, Neil Gotanda, Gary Peller and Kendall Thomas (eds), *Critical Race Theory: The key writings that formed the movement*, New Press, USA, 1995, pp. 357–83.

Cripps, Kylie and Hannah McGlade, 'Safety of kids is priority', *Australian*, 14 December 2007, <http://blogs.theaustralian.news.com.au/yoursay/index.php/theaustralian/comments/safety_of_kids_is_priority/> accessed 12 May 2010.

—— and Hannah McGlade, 'Indigenous family violence and sexual abuse: considering pathways forward', *Journal of Family Studies*, 14(2–3), 2008, pp. 240–54.

Cunliffe, Emma and Angela Cameron, 'Writing the circle: judicially convened sentencing circles and the textual organization of criminal justice', *Canadian Journal of Women and the Law*, 19(1), 2007, pp. 1–35.

Cunneen, Chris, 'Racism, discrimination and the over-representation of Indigenous peoples in the criminal justice system: some conceptual and explanatory issues', *Current Issues in Criminal Justice*, 17(3), 2006, pp. 229–346.

Cunneen, Margaret, 'Letter to the editor', *Bar News*, Summer, 2005/2006, p. 4.

Daly, Kathleen, 'Seeking justice in the 21st century: towards an intersectional politics of justice', *Sociology of Crime Law and Deviance*, 11, 2008, pp. 3–30.

Darlington, Yvonne and Dorothy Scott, *Qualitative Research in Practice: Stories from the field*, Allen & Unwin, Crows Nest, 2002.

Davies, Margaret, *Asking the Law Question*, Law Book Company, Sydney, 1994.

—— *Asking the Law Question* (2nd edn), Law Book Company, Sydney, 2002.

Davis, Megan, 'A woman's place…', *Griffith Review* 24, 2009, pp. 156–62.

—— and Hannah McGlade, 'International human rights law and the recognition of Aboriginal customary law' in Law Reform Commission of WA, *Aboriginal Customary Laws: Background papers*, State Solicitor's Office, Perth, 2006, pp. 381–429.

Daylight, Phyllis and Mary Johnstone, *Women's Business: Report of the Aboriginal Women's Taskforce*, AGPS, Canberra, 1986.

Deer, Sarah, 'Decolonizing rape law: a native feminist synthesis of safety and sovereignty', *Wicazo Sa Review*, 24(2), 2009, pp. 149–67.

—— 'Decolonizing rape law', *Radical Profeminist*, 26 April 2010, <http://radicalprofeminist.blogspot.com/2010/04/decolonising-rape-law-by-sarah-deer.html> accessed 14 June 2010.

Delgado, Richard and Jean Stefancic, *Critical Race Theory*, New York University Press, USA, 2001.

Denzin, Norman K. and Yvonna S. Lincoln, 'The discipline and practice of quali-
tative research' in Norman K. Denzin and Yvonna S. Lincoln (eds), *The Sage
Handbook of Qualitative Research* (3rd edn), Sage Publications, Thousand Oaks,
CA, USA, 2001, pp. 1–32.

Department for Women, *Heroines of Fortitude. The experiences of women in court as
victims of sexual assault,* Department for Women, NSW, 1996.

Dickson-Gilmore, Jane and Carol LaPrairie, *Will the Circle Be Unbroken? Aboriginal
communities, restorative justice and the challenges of conflict and change,* University of
Toronto Press, Canada, 2005.

Dodd, Mark, '"Rapist" strikes again while on bail in Broome', *Australian*,
13 October 2009, <www.theaustralian.com.au/news/nation/rapist- strikes-
again-while-on-bail/story-e6frg6pf-1225786083115> accessed 12 June 2010.

Dodson, Mick, 'Healing body, mind and spirit — it's time we took a stand', edited
version of a speech to the National Indigenous Men's Issues Conference at
Coolangatta on 25 October 2002, *On Line Opinion*, <www.onlineopinion.com.
au/view.asp?article=1042> accessed 8 February 2012.

—— 'Violence dysfunction Aboriginality', Speaking Notes, National Press Club,
11 June 2003, <law.anu.edu.au/anuiia/dodson.pdf> accessed 25 April 2010.

Dudgeon, Pat, 'Mothers of Sin: Indigenous women's perceptions of their identity
and gender' in Rosalie Thackrah and Kim Scott (eds), *Indigenous Australian
Health and Cultures: An introduction for health professionals*, Pearson, Frenchs
Forest, 2011.

Eades, Diane, 'Cross examination of Aboriginal children: the Pinkenba case',
Aboriginal Law Bulletin 75(10), 1995, reproduced in Heather McRae, Garth
Nettheim and Laura Beacroft (eds), *Indigenous Legal Issues: Commentary and
Materials* (2nd edn), Law Book Company, Pyrmont, NSW, 1997, pp. 367–9.

Eastwood, Christine, *The Experiences of Child Complainants of Sexual Abuse in the
Criminal Justice System*, Trends and Issues in Crime and Criminal Justice No.
250, Australian Institute of Criminology, Canberra, 2003.

EchoHawk, Larry, 'Child sexual abuse in Indian country: is the guardian keeping
in mind the seventh generation?', *NYU Journal of Legislation and Public Policy* 5,
2001, pp. 83–127.

Egan, Colleen, 'Black jail terms "low"', *Australian*, 19 March 2002, p. 6.

FaHCSIA (Department of Families, Housing, Community Services and Indigenous
Affairs), 'Healing Development Team', <www.fahcsia.gov.au/sa/indigenous/
progserv/engagement/HealingFoundationDevelopmentTeam/Pages/default.
aspx> accessed 3 December 2009.

—— *Overview of Monitoring Data*, Australian Government, 2009.

Finkelhor, David, *Childhood Victimization: Violence, crime, and abuse in the lives of
young people*, Oxford University Press, Oxford, 2008.

—— 'Four preconditions: a model' in Anne Cohn Donnelly and Kim Oates (eds),
Classic Papers in Child Abuse, Sage Publications, Thousand Oaks, California,
2000, pp. 173–85.

Fryer-Smith, Stephanie, *Aboriginal Benchbook for Western Australian Courts,* Australian
Institute of Judicial Administration, Carlton, Victoria, 2008.

Gale, Fay, *We Are Bosses Ourselves: The status and role of Aboriginal women today*, Australian Institute of Aboriginal Studies, Canberra, 1983.

Gallop, Hon. Dr Geoff MLA Premier of Western Australia, 'Launch of the Rio Tinto Child Health Partnership Telethon Institute for Child health Research', 25 September 2003, <www.premier.wa.gov.au/docs/speeches/RioTintoChildHealth_250903_FINAL.pdf>.

Giaretto, Henry, Anna Giaretto and Suzanne M. Sgroi, 'Coordinated community treatment of incest' in Ann Burgess, A. Nicolas Groth, Lynda Holmstrom and Suzanne Sgroi (eds), *Sexual Assault of Children and Adolescents*, Lexington Books, Toronto, 1978, pp. 231–40.

Gibson, Dawn, 'How probe into child sex abuse went awry', *West Australian*, 19 October 2005, p. 40.

—— 'Abused children spur call to overhaul department', *West Australian*, 5 December 2005, p. 6.

Gibson, Joel, 'Too inept to save children', *Sydney Morning Herald*, 19 June 2008, <www.smh.com.au/news/national/too-inept-to-save-children/2008/06/18/1213770732783.html> accessed 12 March 2010.

Goddard, Chris, *Child Abuse and Child Protection: A guide for health, education and welfare workers*, Churchill Livingstone, South Melbourne, 1996.

Goel, Rashmi 'No woman at the center: the use of the Canadian sentencing circle in domestic violence cases', *Wisconsin Women's Law Journal*, 15, 2000, pp. 293–334.

Gooda, Mick, 'Imagining childhood, children, culture and community', speech, Alice Springs, 20 September 2005, <www.crcah.org.au/communication/.../20905Mick-Imagining-Childhood.pdf> accessed 12 June 2010.

Goodall, Heather and Jackie Huggins, 'Aboriginal women are everywhere: contemporary struggles' in Kay Saunders and Raymond Evans (eds), *Gender Relations in Australia: Domination and negotiation*, Harcourt Brace Jovanovich, Sydney, 1992, pp. 398–424.

Gordon, Sue, Kay Hallahan and Darrell Henry, *Putting the Picture Together: Inquiry into response by government agencies to complaints of family violence and child abuse in Aboriginal communities*, Department of Premier and Cabinet, Western Australia, 2002.

Gotell, Lise, 'Rethinking affirmative consent in Canadian sexual assault law: neoliberal sexual subjects and risky women', *Akron Law Review*, 41, 2008.

Government of Western Australia, *Putting People First*, Government of Western Australia, 2002.

Green, Joyce (ed.), *Making Space for Indigenous Feminisms*, Zed Books, Canada, 2007.

Greens WA, 'Ease ordeal of rape survivors says MLC', press release, 25 June 2004.

—— 'Reinstate community — Greens MLC', press release, 18 November 2004.

Greer, Germaine, *On Rage*, Melbourne University Press, 2008.

Gubrium, Jaber F. and James A. Holstein, *The New Language of Qualitative Method*, Oxford University Press, USA, 1997.

Guest, Debbie, 'Cops decry sex "slap on the wrist"', *Weekend Australian*, 29–30 August 2009, p. 3, <www.theaustralian.com.au/news/ nation/police-decry-slap-on-wrist-for-illegal-sex/story-e6frg6pf-1225767255980> accessed 12 June 2010.

Haebich, Anna, *For Their Own Good: Aborigines and government in the southwest of Western Australia, 1900–1940*, UWA Press, Perth, 1992.

Hampson, Katie, 'Rape compo encourages lies, claims counsellor', *West Australian*, 15 December 2007, p. 9.

Harris, Angela P., 'Race and essentialism in feminist legal theory' in Richard Delgado and Jean Stefancic (eds), *Critical Race Theory: The Cutting Edge*, Temple University Press, Philadelphia, 2000, pp. 261–74.

Harrison, Dan, 'Call for NT intervention policy to face human rights test', *Sydney Morning Herald*, 13 March 2012, <www.smh.com.au/national/call-for-nt-intervention-policy-to-face-human-rights-test-20120312-1uwjd.html> accessed 20 March 2012.

Harvard Project on American Indian Economic Development, *Honoring Nations: Tribal Governance Success Stories, 2000,* Harvard Project on American Indian Economic Development, Harvard University, 2000.

Hassell, Ethel, *My Dusky Friends*, C.W & W.A. Hassell, Perth, 1975.

Herman, Judith, *Trauma and Recovery: The aftermath of violence — from domestic abuse to political terror*, Basic Books, USA, 1997.

Hill Collins, Patricia, *Black Feminist Thought, Knowledge, Consciousness and the Politics of Empowerment*, Routledge, USA, 1990.

hooks, bell, 'Theory as liberatory practice', *Yale Journal of Law and Feminism* 4(1), 1991.

Hope, Alastair, *Record of Investigation Into Death of Susan Ann TAYLOR*, Ref. No: 31/01, 2001.

House of Representatives, *Apology to Australia's Indigenous Peoples: Speech*, Commonwealth of Australia, Canberra, 2008, <http://parlinfo.aph.gov.au/parlInfo/genpdf/chamber/hansardr/2008-02-13/0003/hansard_frag.pdf;fileType=application%2Fpdf> accessed 15 March 2012.

Howe, Adrian, *Sex, Violence and Crime: Foucault and the 'man' question*, Routledge-Cavendish, Abingdon, UK and New York, 2008.

—— 'Addressing child sexual assault in Australian Aboriginal communities — the politics of white voice', *Australian Feminist Law Journal*, 30, 2009, pp. 41–61.

HREOC (Human Rights and Equal Opportunity Commission), *Bringing Them Home: Report of the National Inquiry into the Separation of Aboriginal and Torres Strait Islander Children from Their Families*, Commonwealth of Australia, Sydney, 1997.

—— *Bringing them Home: A guide to the findings and recommendations of the National Inquiry into the Separation of Aboriginal and Torres Strait Islander Children from their Families*, Commonwealth of Australia, Sydney, 1997.

Huggins, Jackie et al., 'Letters to the editor', *Women's Studies International Forum*, 14(5), 1991 pp. 505–7.

Human Rights Committee, Ninety-fifth session, Geneva, 2 April 2009, CCPR/C/ AUS/CO/5, <www2.ohchr.org/english/bodies/hrc/hrcs95.htm> accessed 14 March 2012.

Hunter, Ernest, 'Little children and big sticks' in Jon Altman and Melinda Hinkson (eds), *Coercive Reconciliation: Stabilise, normalise, exit Aboriginal Australia*, Arena Publications, North Carlton, Vic, 2007, pp. 126–9.

Indigenous Justice Taskforce, *A Review of the Indigenous Justice Taskforce*, WA Department of Attorney General, 2009.

Itzin, Catherine (ed.), *Home Truths about Child Sexual Abuse: Influencing policy and practice — a reader*, Routledge, London, 2000.

Jarrett, Stephanie, *Violence: An inseparable part of traditional Aboriginal culture*, Occasional Paper 3, Bennelong Society, 2009, <www.bennelong.com.au/ occasional/stephFinal3.pdf> accessed 25 June 2010.

Johnston, Elliott, Martin Hinton and Daryle Rigney (eds), *Indigenous Australians and the Law* (2nd edn), Routledge-Cavendish, Oxon, London, 2008.

Karvelas, Patricia, 'Give Aboriginal women equal say, says Hannah McGlade', *Australian*, 22 August 2008, <www.theaustralian.com.au/in-depth/aboriginal-australia/give-aboriginal-women-equal-say/story-e6frgd9f-1111117266419> accessed 21 June 2010.

Kearney, Simon and Ashleigh Wilson, 'Raping children part of "men's business"', *Australian*, 16 May 2006, p. 1.

Keating, Nuala, *Review of Services to Victims of Crime and Crown Witnesses*, Office of the Director of Public Prosecutions, WA, 2001, pp. 112–21.

Keating, Paul, 'The Redfern Park speech' in Michelle Grattan (ed.), *Essays on Australian Reconciliation*, Black Inc., Melbourne, 2000, pp. 60–5.

Kelly, Kerrie, Pat Dudgeon, Graham Gee and Belle Glaskin (on behalf of the Australian Indigenous Psychologists Association), *Living on the Edge: Social and emotional wellbeing and risk protection factor for serious psychological distress amongst Aboriginal and Torres Strait Islander people*, Co-operative Research Centre for Aboriginal Health, Darwin, 2009.

Kelly, Liz, Linda Regan and Sheila Burton, 'Sexual exploitation: A new discovery or one part of the continuum of sexual abuse in childhood' in Catherine Itzin (ed.), *Home Truths about Child Sexual Abuse: Influencing policy and practice — a reader*, Routledge, London, 2000, pp. 70–86.

Kimm, Joan, *A Fatal Conjunction: Two laws two cultures*, Federation Press, Annandale, NSW, 2004.

Kingston, Margo, 'Rape and racism', *Sydney Morning Herald*, 18 June 2001, <www.smh.com.au/articles/2003/11/24/1069522516783.html> accessed 15 March 2012.

—— 'The sound of values clashing', *Sydney Morning Herald*, 20 June 2001, <www.smh.com.au/articles/2003/11/24/1069522518528.html> accessed 15 March 2012.

—— 'Ray and Terry', *Sydney Morning Herald*, 26 June 2001, <www.smh.com.au/ articles/2003/11/24/1069522519571.html> accessed 16 March 2012.

—— 'Ending the cover-up', *Sydney Morning Herald*, 27 June 2001, <www.smh.com.au/articles/2003/11/24/1069522519673.html> accessed 25 June 2010.

Kissane, Karen, Jamie Berry and Ben Doherty, 'Vindication at last: jury says Clark was a rapist', *Sydney Morning Herald*, 1 February 2007, <www.smh.com.au/news/national/vindication-at-last-jury-says-clark-was-a-rapist/2007/01/31/1169919402606.html> accessed 5 May 2010.

Koch, Tony, 'Child safety failed rape girl', *Australian*, 11 December 2007, p. 1.

Kwast, Elizabeth and Sophie Laws, *United Nation's Secretary-General's Study on Violence against Children Adapted for Children and Young People*, Office of the United Nations High Commissioner for Human Rights, Switzerland, International Save the Children Alliance, London, and Child Rights Information Network, London, no date, <www.unicef.org/violencestudy/pdf/Study%20on%20Violence_Child-friendly.pdf> accessed 21 March 2012.

Langton, Marcia, 'Stop the abuse of children', *Australian*, 12 December 2007, < http://blogs.theaustralian.news.com.au/yoursay/index.php/theaustralian/comments/stop_the_abuse_of_children/> accessed 12 May 2010.

—— 'The end of "big men" politics', *Griffith Review*, 22, 2008, p. 13.

LaRocque, Emma, 'Re-examining culturally appropriate models in criminal justice applications' in Michael Asch (ed.), *Aboriginal and Treaty Rights in Canada: Essays on law, equality and respect for difference*, UBC Press, Vancouver, BC, 1997, pp. 75–96.

Laurie, Victoria, 'Breaking The silence', *Australian*, 17 August 2006.

Lawrence, Charles, 'Foreword' in Francisco Valdes, Jerome McCristal Culp and Angela P. Harris (eds), *Crossroads, Directions and a New Critical Race Theory*, Temple University Press, Philadelphia, 2002.

—— 'Who are we? And why are we here? Doing critical race theory in hard times' in Francisco Valdes, Jerome McCristal Culp and Angela P. Harris (eds), *Crossroads, Directions and a New Critical Race Theory*, Temple University Press, Philadelphia, 2002.

Le Grand, Danielle, 'New call for action of child abuse', *West Australian*, 25 June 2004, p. 1.

Leiboff, Marett and Mark Thomas, *Legal Theories: In principle*, Law Book Company, Sydney, 2004.

Libesman, Terri, 'Indigenous children and contemporary child welfare' in Geoff Monahan and Lisa Young (eds), *Children and the Law in Australia*, Butterworths, Chatswood, NSW, 2008, pp. 329–51.

Lievore, Denise, *No Longer Silent: A study of women's help-seeking decisions and service responses to sexual assault*, a report prepared by the Australian Institute of Criminology for the Australian Government's Office for Women, Commonwealth of Australia, Canberra, 2005.

Lucashenko, Melissa, 'Violence against Indigenous women: public and private dimensions' in Sandy Cook and Judith Bessant (eds), *Women's Encounters with Violence: Australian experiences*, Sage Publications, Thousand Oaks, California, 1997, pp. 147–58.

McGlade, Hannah, 'Aboriginal women and the Commonwealth Government's response to Mabo – An international human rights perspective' in Peggy Brock (ed.), *Words and Silences: Aboriginal women, politics and lands*, Allen & Unwin, Crows Nest, NSW, 2001, pp. 139–57.

—— (ed.) *Treaty: Let's get it right!*, Aboriginal Studies Press, Canberra, 2003.

—— 'Native Title, "tides of history" and our continuing claims for justice — sovereignty, self-determination and treaty' in Hannah McGlade (ed.), *Treaty: Let's get it right*, Aboriginal Studies Press, Canberra, 2003.

—— 'Race discrimination in Australia: A challenge for treaty settlement?' in Marcia Langton, Maureen Tehan, Lisa Palmer and Kathryn Shain (eds), *Honour Among Nations: Treaties and Agreements With Indigenous Peoples*, Melbourne University Press, 2004, pp. 273–87.

—— 'Aboriginal women, girls and sexual assault: the long road to equality', *ACCSA Aware*, 12, 2006, pp. 6–13.

—— 'Justice as healing: developing Aboriginal models to address child sexual assault', *Indigenous Law Bulletin* 7, 2006, pp. 10–14.

—— 'The 'fair skinned' children of Sister Kate's: negotiating for the past and future', *Australian Feminist Law Journal* 26, 2007, pp. 31–46.

—— 'The Sister Kate's Home Kids Healing Centre: early beginnings', *Australian Indigenous Law Review* 12 (special edition), 2008, pp. 32–8.

—— *Indigenous violent victimisation: What place has consent?*, ABC Indigenous Online, 24 February 2009, <www.abc.net.au/indigenous/stories/s2500123. htm> accessed 26 June 2010.

—— 'Susan Taylor Foundation', draft notes, 2009.

—— 'Sacred yet unprotected', *ABC Drum Unleashed*, 16 February 2010, <www.abc. net.au/unleashed/stories/s2822577.htm> accessed 3 February 2012.

—— 'Aboriginal Child Sexual Assault (CSA) and the criminal justice system: The last frontier', doctoral thesis, Centre for Aboriginal Studies, Curtin University, Perth, 2010.

—— and Victoria Hovane, 'The Mangolamara case: improving Aboriginal community safety and healing', *Indigenous Law Bulletin*, 6(27), 2007, pp. 18–21.

MacKinnon, Catharine, 'Keeping it real: On anti-essentialism' in Francisco Valdes, Jerome McCristal Culp and Angela P. Harris (eds), *Crossroads, Directions and a New Critical Race Theory*, Temple University Press, Philadelphia, 2002, pp. 71–83.

—— *Women's Lives, Men's Laws*, Belknap Harvard Press, USA, 2007.

Macklin, Jenny, *Jenny Macklin, Fabian Society Annual Dinner, 4 September 2009*, address, Australian Fabians, 4 September 2009, <www.fabian.org.au/1128. asp> accessed 21 June 2010.

McRae, Heather, Garth Nettheim and Laura Beacroft, *Indigenous Legal Issues: Commentary and materials* (2nd edn), Law Book Company, Pyrmont, NSW, 1997.

Marchetti, Elena, 'Indigenous women and the RCIADC — Part I', *Indigenous Law Bulletin*, 7(1), 2007, pp. 6–9.

Martin, Karen Booran Mirraboopa, 'Ways of knowing, ways of being and ways of doing: a theoretical framework and methods for Indigenous and indigenist research', *Journal of Australian Studies*, 76, 2003, pp. 203–04.

Matsuda, Marie, 'Beyond, and not beyond, black and white' in Francisco Valdes, Jerome McCristal Culp and Angela P. Harris (eds), *Crossroads, Directions and a New Critical Race Theory*, Temple University Press, Philadelphia, 2002, pp. 393–8.

Meade, Kevin, 'Call for inquiry into court's findings,' *Australian*, 11 December 2007, p. 2.

—— and Sarah Elks, 'Girl endured six weeks of sex attacks', *Australian*, 4 December 2007, p. 4.

Memmott, Paul, Rachael Stacy, Catherine Chambers and Catherine Keys, *Violence in Indigenous Communities*, Report prepared for Commonwealth Attorney-General's Department, Commonwealth Government, Canberra, 2001.

Merlan, Francesca, 'Child sexual abuse: the intervention trigger' in Jon Altman and Melinda Hickson (eds), *Culture Crisis: Anthropology and Politics in Aboriginal Australia*, UNSW Press, Sydney, 2010, pp. 116–35.

Meuleners, Lynn, Delia Hendrie and Andy H. Lee, *Measuring the Burden of Interpersonal Violence in Western Australia*, Trends and Issues in Crime and Criminal Justice No. 352, AIC, Canberra, 2008.

Michelmore, Karen, 'Traditional role queried', *Northern Territory News*, 17 August 2005, <www.ntnews.news.com.au/printpage/ 0,5942,16292520,00.html> accessed 30 August 2005.

Montoya, Margaret, 'Celebrating racialised legal narratives' in Francisco Valdes, Jerome McCristal Culp and Angela P. Harris (eds), *Crossroads, Directions and a New Critical Race Theory*, Temple University Press, Philadelphia, 2002, pp. 243–50.

Monture-Angus, Patricia, 'Thinking about change' in Wanda D. McCaslin (ed.), *Justice as Healing Indigenous Ways: Writings on Community Peacemaking and Restorative Justice from the Native Law Centre*, Living Justice Press, St Paul, Minnesota, 2005, pp. 275–9.

Moreton-Robinson, Aileen, 'Tiddas talking up to white women: when Huggins et al took on Bell' in Michele Grossman (ed.), *Blacklines: Contemporary critical writings by Indigenous Australians*, Melbourne University Press, Carlton 2003, pp. 66–77.

Morrison, Zoe, 'What is the outcome of reporting rape to the police? Study of reported rapes in Victoria 2000–2003: Summary research report', *ACCSA Aware Newsletter* 17, 2008, pp. 4–11.

Mullighan QC, Hon. E.P., *Children on Anangu Pitjantjatjara Yankunytjatjara (APY) Lands Commission of Inquiry: A report into sexual abuse*, Government Publishing, SA, 2008.

Murray, Paul, 'WA out of step on child abuse', *West Australian*, 24 July 2004, p. 19.

Nancarrow, Heather, 'In search of justice for domestic and family violence: Indigenous and no-Indigenous Australian women's perspectives', *Theoretical Criminology*, 10(1), 2006, pp. 87–106.

National Council to Reduce Violence Against Women and their Children, *Time for Action: The National Council's Plan for Australia to reduce violence against women and their children, 2009–2021*, Commonwealth of Australia, Canberra, 2009.

Native Counselling Services of Alberta, *A Cost-benefit Analysis of Hollow Water's Community Holistic Circle Healing Process*, Aboriginal Corrections Policy Unit, Canada, 2001.

Native Women's Association of Canada, Factum of Intervenor, *R v Edmondson*, unpublished, 2004.

New South Wales Government, *New South Wales Interagency Plan to Tackle Child Sexual Assault in Aboriginal Communities 2006–2011*, New South Wales Government, 2007, <www.daa.nsw.gov.au/data/files//NSW%20Govt%20 Plan%20to%20Tackle%20Aboriginal%20Child%20Sexual%20Assault.pdf> accessed 8 February 2012.

Nicholson, Alastair, Larissa Behrendt, Alison Vivian, Nicole Watson and Michele Harris, *Will They Be Heard? — A response to the NTER consultations, June to August 2009,* Jumbunna Indigenous House of Learning, Sydney, 2009.

Nielsen, Marianne O., 'Canadian Aboriginal Healing Lodges: a model for the United States?', *Prison Journal* 8(1), 2003, pp. 67–89.

NIITF (National Indigenous Intelligence Task Force), Indigenous Violence or Child Abuse No. 2 (NIITF), Special Intelligence Operation, <www.crimecommis sion.gov.au/our_work/determinations/niitf.htm> accessed 10 December 2009.

Northern Territory Government, *Ampe Akelyernemane Meke Mekarle 'Little Children are Sacred'*, Report of the Northern Territory Board of Inquiry into the Protection of Aboriginal Children from Sexual Abuse, Darwin, 2007.

Nowra, Louis, *Bad Dreaming: Aboriginal men's violence against women and children*, Pluto Press, North Melbourne, 2007.

O'Neill, Rosemary, 'Our leader is listening to the cry of the mothers', *Weekend Australian*, 30 June–1 July 2007, pp. 1, 6.

O'Shane, Pat, 'Is there any relevance in the women's movement for Aboriginal women?', *Refractory Girl*, 12, 1976, pp. 31–4.

Olafson, Erna, 'When paradigms collide: Roland Summit and the rediscovery of child sexual abuse' in Jon Conte (ed.), *Critical Issues in Child Sexual Abuse: Historical, legal and psychological perspectives*, Sage Publications, Thousand Oaks, California, 2002, pp. 71–106.

Overington, Caroline, 'Sex abuse part of culture, boys told', *Australian*, 8 September 2006, p. 7.

Paisley, Fiona, *Loving Protection? Australian feminism and Aboriginal women's rights 1919–1939*, Melbourne University Press, Carlton, 2000.

Payne, Sharon, 'Aboriginal women and the law' in Chris Cunneen (ed.), *Aboriginal Perspectives on Criminal Justice*, Institute of Criminology, Sydney, 1992, pp. 31–40.

Pearson, Noel, *Up from the Mission: Selected writings*, Black Inc., Melbourne, 2009.

Penn, Simon, 'Gordon Inquiry plan has big faults: auditor', *West Australian*, 24 November 2005, p. 13.

Pickering, Helen, 'Aboriginal children "need own advocate"', *West Australian*, 15 August 2007, p. 42.

Powell, Renee and Bernadette Kennedy, *Renee Baker File #28/E.D.P*, Fremantle Arts Press, Perth, 2005.

Price, Bess, 'Against change for the wrong reason', *Australian*, 27 August 2009, <www.theaustralian.com.au/news/opinion/against-change-for-the-wrong-reasons/story-e6frg6zo-1225766571739> accessed 10 March 2010.

—— 'I have seen violence towards women every day of my life', *Australian Feminist Law Journal* 30, 2009, pp. 149–51.

Ravens, Tara, 'Laws result in unjust sentence', *National Indigenous Times*, 25 June 2009, <http://nit.com.au/News/story.aspx?id=18089> accessed 18 June 2010.

Razack, Sherene H., *Looking White People in the Eye: Gender, race and culture in court-rooms and classrooms*, University of Toronto Press, Canada, 1998.

Reynolds, Henry, *With the White People*, Penguin, Ringwood, Vic, 1990.

——— *Why Weren't We Told? A personal search for the truth about our history*, Penguin, NSW, 1999.

Richards, Kelly, *Child Complainants and the Court Process in Australia*, Trends and Issues in Crime and Criminal Justice No. 380, Australian Institute of Criminology, Canberra, 2009.

Roberston, Boni, *The Aboriginal and Torres Strait Islander Women's Task Force on Violence*, Queensland Government, QLD, 1999.

———, Warren Mundine and Chris Cunneen, 'Three commentaries on Nowra, L, 2007, *Bad dreaming: Aboriginal men's violence against women and children*', *Australian Domestic and Family Violence Clearinghouse Newsletter* 30, 2007, pp. 8–10.

Robinson, Natasha, 'Dogmatic about outcomes', *Australian*, 26 December 2009, <www.theaustralian.com.au/news/opinion/dogmatic-about-outcomes/story-e6frg6zo-1225813625191> accessed 14 March 2012.

Ross, Rupert, 'Aboriginal community healing in action: the Hollow Water approach' in Wanda D. McCaslin (ed.), *Justice as Healing Indigenous Ways: Writings on Community Peacemaking and Restorative Justice from the Native Law Centre*, Living Justice Press, St Paul, MN, 2005, pp. 184–9.

——— 'The sentencing circle: seeds of a community healing process' in Wanda D. McCaslin (ed.), *Justice as Healing Indigenous Ways: Writings on Community Peacemaking and Restorative Justice from the Native Law Centre*, Living Justice Press, St Paul, MN, 2005, pp. 190–5.

——— *Returning to the Teachings: Exploring Aboriginal justice*, Penguin, Canada, 2006.

Rule, Andrew, 'Geoff Clark: power and rape', *Age*, 14 June 2001, p. 1.

Sanderson, Christiane, *Counselling Adult Survivors of Child Sexual Abuse* (3rd edn), Jessica Kingsley Publishers, London, 2006.

Save the Children, *10 Essential Learning Points: Listen and speak out against sexual abuse of boys and girls*, Save the Children, Norway, 2005.

——— *Listen and Speak Out against Sexual Abuse of Girls and Boys*, Save the Children, Norway, 2005.

SCRGSP (Steering Committee for the Review of Government Service Provision), *Overcoming Indigenous Disadvantage: Key Indicators 2011*, Productivity Commission, Canberra, 2011, p. 22.

Sculthorpe, Heather, 'Review of domestic violence resource materials', *Aboriginal Law Bulletin* 2(46), 1990, p. 19.

Scutt, Jocelynne, 'Invisible women? Projecting white cultural invisibility on black Australian women', *Indigenous Law Bulletin* 2(46), 1990, pp. 4–5.

Secretariat of the Permanent Forum on Indigenous Issues, *State of the World's Indigenous Peoples*, ST/ESA/328, United Nations, New York, 2009.

Shaw, Wendy, '(Post) colonial encounters: gendered racialisations in Australian courtrooms', *Gender Place and Culture*, 10(4), 2003, pp. 315–32.

Simon, Bill, Des Montgomerie and Jo Tuscano, *Back on The Block: Bill Simon's story*, Aboriginal Studies Press, Canberra, 2008.

Skelton, Russell 'Rape judge "ignored our pleas"', *Age*, 19 December 2007, <www.theage.com.au/news/national/rape-judge-ignored-our-pleas/2007/12/18/1197740272600.html> accessed 12 May 2010.

Smith, Andrea, *Conquest: Sexual violence and American Indian genocide*, South End Press, Cambridge, MA, 2005.

Smith, Linda Tuhiwai, *Decolonising Methodologies: Research and Indigenous peoples*, Zed Books, New Zealand, 1999.

Smith, Suzanne, 'Sexual abuse reported in Indigenous community', *Lateline*, 21 June 2006, <www.abc.net.au/lateline/content/2006/s1668773.htm> accessed 3 March 2010.

SNAICC (Secretariat of National Aboriginal and Islander Child Care), *Through Young Black Eyes: A handbook to protect children from the impact of family violence and child abuse*, SNAICC, Victoria, 2002.

Spatz Widom, Cathy, 'Does violence beget violence? A critical examination of the literature' in Anne Cohn Donnelly and Kim Oates (eds), *Classic Papers in Child Abuse*, Sage Publications, Thousand Oaks, CA, 2000, pp. 309–51.

Stanley, Janet, Adam M. Tomison and Julian Pocock, 'Child abuse and neglect in Indigenous Australian communities', *Child Abuse Prevention Issues*, 19(Spring), 2003, <www.aifs.gov.au/nch/pubs/issues/issues19/issues19.pdf> accessed 15 March 2012.

Statham, Larine, 'Sex abuse reports soar in Alice Springs', *Sydney Morning Herald*, 6 January 2010, <http://news.smh.com.au/breaking-news-national/sex-abuse-reports-soar-in-alice-sprigs-20100106-lu6m.html> accessed 3 February 2012.

Steele, Brandt F., 'Psychodynamic factors in child abuse' in Anne Cohn Donnelly and Kim Oates (eds), *Classic Papers in Child Abuse*, Sage Publications, Thousand Oaks, California, 2000, pp. 239–71.

Stephen, Sarah, 'What's behind the media campaign against Geoff Clark?', *Green Left Weekly*, 27 June 2001, <www.greenleft.org.au/back/2001/453/453p11.htm> accessed 8 February 2012.

Stewart, Wendy, Audrey Huntley and Fay Blaney, *The Implications of Restorative Justice for Aboriginal Women and Children Survivors of Violence: A comparative overview of five communities in British Columbia*, Law Commission of Canada, Canada, 2001.

Strutt, Jessica, 'Grasp the opportunity, says leader', *West Australian*, 14 December 2007, p. 6.

—— 'Pressure on police led to failed sex charges, says ALS chief', *West Australian*, 14 December 2007, p. 7.

Su, Julie and Eric Yamamoto, 'Critical coalitions: theory and praxis' in Francisco Valdes, Jerome McCristal Culp and Angela P. Harris (eds), *Crossroads, Directions and a New Critical Race Theory*, Temple University Press, Philadelphia, 2002, pp. 379–92

Summit, Roland, 'The child sexual abuse accommodation syndrome' in Anne Cohn Donnelly and Kim Oates (eds), *Classic Papers in Child Abuse*, Sage Publications, Thousand Oaks, California, 2000, pp. 155–71.

Sykes, Bobbi, 'Black women in Australia: A history' in Jan Mercer (ed.), *The Other Half: Women in Australian Society*, Penguin, Ringwood, Vic, 1975, pp. 313–21.

Taylor, Caroline, *Court Licensed Abuse: Patriarchal lore and the legal response to intra-familial sexual abuse of children*, Peter Lang, New York, 2004.

Taylor, Paige, 'Land campaign hid child sex abuse', *Australian*, 1 March 2008, <www.theaustralian.com.au/news/nation/land-campaign-hid-child-sex-abuse/story-e6frg6pf-1111115683716> accessed 3 February 2012.

—— and Debbie Guest, 'Aboriginal camp boss Robert Bropho dies at 81', *Australian*, 24 October 2011, <www.theaustralian.com.au/news/nation/aboriginal-camp-boss-robert-bropho-dies-at-81/story-e6frg6nf-1226175614316> accessed 15 March 2012.

Tickner, Robert, *Taking a Stand: Land rights to reconciliation*, Allen & Unwin, Crows Nest, NSW, 2001.

Toohey, Paul, 'Black, white and blurred', *Weekend Australian*, 12–13 October 2002, p. 21.

—— 'The age of contempt', *Australian*, 17 August 2005.

—— 'Last drinks: the impact of the Northern Territory intervention', *Quarterly Essay* 30, 2008, p. 47.

Tribal Policy Clearinghouse, 'Children's Justice Act resources', no date, <www.tribal-institute.org/lists/cja.htm> accessed 14 June 2010.

Turpel-Lafond, Mary Ellen, 'Sentencing within a restorative justice paradigm: procedural implications of *R v Gladue*' in Wanda D. McCaslin (ed.), *Justice as Healing Indigenous Ways: Writings on Community Peacemaking and Restorative Justice from the Native Law Centre*, Living Justice Press, St Paul, Minnesota, 2005, pp. 280–95.

UNICEF, *From Invisible to Indivisible: Promoting and protecting the right of the girl child to be free from violence*, in the follow up to the UN Secretary-General's Study on Violence against Children, no date.

United Nations, *United Nations Declaration on the Rights of Indigenous Peoples*, 2008, <www.un.org/esa/socdev/unpfii/documents/DRIPS_en.pdf> accessed 21 March 2012.

United Nations Division for the Advancement of Women, *Expert Group meeting on good practices in legislation on violence against women*, EGM/GPLVAW/2008/BP.017May008, May 2008, <www.un.org/womenwatch/daw/egm/vaw_legislation_2008/vaw_legislation_2008.htm> accessed 13 May 2010.

United Nations Economic and Social Council, *Forced Marriage of the Girl Child: Report of the Secretary-General*, 2007, <www.ungei.org/resources/files/Girlchildreport.pdf> accessed 21 March 2012.

United National General Assembly, Human Rights Council, *Rights of the child: the fight against sexual violence against children*, A/HRC/13/L.21, 2010, p. 3.

United National General Assembly, *The girl child*, Report of the Secretary-General, A/64/315, p. 5

United Nations Non-governmental Liaison Service, 'International Expert Group meeting on combating violence against indigenous women and girls: Article 22 of the United Nations Declaration on the Rights of Indigenous People', *NGLS e-Roundup*, March 2012, <www.un-ngls.org/IMG/pdf/ RU_Indigenous_Women.pdf> accessed 21 March 2012.

Veldhuis, Cindy B. and Jennifer J. Freyd, 'Groomed for silence, groomed for betrayal' in Margo Rivera (ed.), *Fragment by Fragment: Feminist perspectives on memory and child sexual abuse*, Gynergy Books, Canada, 1999, pp. 253–82.

Warhaft, E. Barry, Ted Palys and Wilma Boyce, '"This is How We Did It": one Canadian First Nation community's efforts to achieve Aboriginal justice', *Australian and New Zealand Journal of Criminology* 32(2), 1999, pp. 168–81.

Watson, Irene, 'Naked peoples: rules and regulations', *Law Text Culture*, 4(1), 1998, pp. 1–17.

—— 'Aboriginal women's laws and lives: how might we keep growing the laws?' in Elliott Johnston, Martin G. Hinton and Daryle Rigney (eds), *Indigenous Australians and the Law* (2nd edn), Routledge-Cavendish, Abingdon, UK, and New York, 2008, pp. 15–29.

Western Australia Legislative Assembly, *Community Development and Justice Standing Committee Inquiry into the Prosecution of Assaults and Sexual Offences*, Report No. 6 in the 37th Parliament, Western Australia, Perth, 2008.

Western Australia Legislative Council, *Report of the Select Committee on Reserves (Reserve 43131) Bill 2003 in Relation to the Reserves (Reserves 42121) Bill 2003*, November 2004.

White, Rob and Santina Perrone, *Crime, Criminality and Criminal Justice*, Oxford University Press, South Melbourne, 2010.

Williams Jnr, Robert A., 'Vampires anonymous and critical race practice' in Richard Delgado and Jean Stefancic (eds), *Critical Race Theory: The Cutting Edge*, Temple University Press, Philadelphia, 2000, pp. 614–21.

Wilson Clarke, Charlie, 'Child abuse victims warned off courts', *West Australian*, 3 April 2004, p. 64.

Windschuttle, Keith, *The Fabrication of Aboriginal History: Volume One Van Diemen's Land 1803–1847*, Macleay Press, Sydney, 2002.

—— 'Flawed history keeps myth alive', *Weekend Australian*, 30–31 January 2010.

Wing, Adrien Katherine, *Critical Race Feminism: A reader*, New York University Press, 2003.

Wundersitz, Joy, *Indigenous Perpetrators of Violence: Prevalence and risk factors for offending*, Research and Public Policy Series No. 105, Australian Institute of Criminology, Canberra, 2010.

Yamamoto, Eric K., 'Critical race praxis: race theory and political lawyering practice in post-civil rights America', *Michigan Law Review* 95, 1997, pp. 821–900.

Yeatman, Anna, 'Voice and representation in the politics of difference' in Sneja Gunew and Anna Yeatman (eds), *Feminism and the Politics of Difference*, Allen & Unwin, Crows Nest, 1993, pp. 228–45.

Yu, Peter, Marcia Ella Duncan and Bill Gray, 'Executive summary' in *Report of the NTER Review Board*, Commonwealth of Australia, Canberra, 2008, pp. 9–11.

Cases and coroner decisions

Bropho v The State of Western Australia [No 2] [2009] WASC 94

Christopher v The Queen (2000) 23 WAR 106

De Jesus v The Queen (1986) 22 A. Crim. R. 375

Hales v Jamilmira [2003] NTCA 9

Longman v The Queen (1989) 168 CLR 79

R v Bropho [2004] WADC 182

R v KU & Ors; ex parte (Qld) [2008] QCA 154.

R v Wurramara (1999) 105 A Crim R 512

The Queen v GJ [2005] NTCCA 20

The Queen v Wunungmurra [2009] NTSC 24

The State of Western Australia v Bropho [2008] WADC 30

Hope, Alastair, *Record of Investigation Into Death of Susan Ann TAYLOR*, Ref. No: 31/01, 2001.

Native Women's Association of Canada, Factum of Intervenor, *R v Edmondson*, unpublished, 2004.

Northern Territory Coroner, Inquest into the death of Kunmanara Forbes [2009] NTMC 024.

INDEX